THE FREE TRADE STORY

FAITH & FEAR

G. BRUCE DOERN & BRIAN W. TOMLIN

First published in 1991 by
Stoddart Publishing Co. Limited
34 Lesmill Road
Toronto, Canada
M3B 2T6

Canadian Cataloguing in Publication Data

Doern, G. Bruce, 1942-
Faith and fear: the free trade story

Includes index.
ISBN 0-7737-2534-2

1. Free trade — Canada. 2. Free trade — United States.
3. Canada — Commercial policy. 4. United States —
Commercial policy. 5. Canada — Commerce — United
States. 6. United States — Commerce — Canada.
I. Tomlin, Brian W., 1944-. II. Title.

HF1766.D64 1991   382′.971073   C91-094811-9

Cover Design: Leslie Styles
Typesetting: Tony Gordon Ltd.

Printed and bound in the United States of America

For Joan and Georgia

CONTENTS

PREFACE

Shortly after the Mulroney government's free trade initiative was announced in 1985, we began the research and planning for this book. Our purpose was to produce as independent an account of the free trade story as possible, one that would be of interest to a wide cross-section of Canadian readers. Though each of us has twenty years of academic experience to inform our work, and both of us have drawn on a careful reading of all or most of the relevant literature, we have not tried to write a traditional academic account. The free trade decision is important to Canadians as a whole, and we were determined to contribute to a wider understanding of the events in this fascinating story through a more generally available book.

The preparation for writing this book consisted of equal parts of research, detective work, and logical deduction. It is mainly about the political dynamics of the free trade decision, and information was derived from four basic sources: published literature, government documents, our own previous and concurrent research on related policy fields, and interviews.

The interviews involved discussions with more than 100 players in the free trade drama, on both sides of the 49th parallel. They were conducted on the undertaking that there would be no direct attribution or quotation. Our confidential interviews were conducted with ministers, government officials, and business and social coalition members over the 1986 to 1990 period. We are especially indebted to these many individuals who generously granted us time, many of them on more than one occasion. In a matter as important and complex as free trade, perceptions of exactly what happened often vary greatly. Even when only a few persons were present at the meetings or negotiations, they often saw them from very different perspectives and sometimes provided quite dissimilar descriptions of what had occurred. The truth of events can never be determined to all observers' complete satisfaction. That is why it was necessary to interview as many of the persons involved as possible. Because of this, we think our account comes far closer than any other published to date in providing an understanding of what actually happened in the story of free trade. We hope that some of the key players, not to mention future historians, will write of their understanding of events and subject it to the same public examination we have chosen for the events portrayed in this book.

But the free trade story goes beyond what can be derived from interviews alone. We have consulted other research and other published accounts to reinforce our interpretation of the events and their consequences. For specialized readers, we have indicated those published sources in notes and in the list of references that follows the final chapter, although we have provided less detail than is traditional in academic works. In areas where we have elaborated on our arguments in other published work, we have listed these publications in the endnotes.

While our account of free trade is comprehensive, we still cannot claim to have covered all aspects of the story in equal depth. We have focused on the political dynamics in certain areas and issues and omitted others entirely. Space and resources dictated most of these choices. Nonetheless, we have tried to deal with all of the key issues that emerged in the free trade debate. Future research by historians in years to come will undoubtedly add to our understanding of this historic decision.

Special thanks are owed to several persons who read earlier drafts of the book as a whole, or particular chapters, and offered constructive comment and criticism. These persons include Michael Hart, Maureen Molot, Michael Prince, Michael Dolan, Glen Williams, Richard Lipsey, Frances Abele, Allan Maslove, Robert Young, Gil Winham, Fred Bienefeld, and Sylvia Bashevkin. All have helped to strengthen the final product, but none bears any responsibility for remaining inadequacies in the book, and their views do not necessarily coincide with any of our overall conclusions.

Able research assistance was provided to us by Scott Bryce, Claire Turenne Sjolander, and Beverley McGee. We also gladly acknowledge the financial assistance received in the form of research grants from the Social Sciences and Humanities Research Council of Canada, the Max Bell Business-Government Research Program at York University, and Carleton University.

BRUCE DOERN AND BRIAN TOMLIN
Ottawa
April 1991

1

UNEXPECTED
BEGINNINGS

Gerald Regan, Canada's minister for international trade, gave last-minute instructions to his staff, then headed out the door of his office, accompanied by two of his aides. They walked quickly along the nearly empty corridors of the Confederation Building, a parliamentary edifice in the baronial French-chateau style of the Centre Block, located just to the west of Parliament Hill in Ottawa. An elevator took the group down to the building's ground floor. Stepping out into an unadorned lobby, Regan acknowledged the security guards lounging at the reception desk, and he and his aides made their way down a short set of marble steps and out through the heavy brass doors, emerging on the northwest corner of Wellington and Bank Streets. The three men entered the minister's car, which was idling just outside the doors, for the short ride to the National Press Building, a half block up Wellington Street on the south side, across from the West Block of Parliament Hill. The car edged out into the traffic, past indifferent tourists making their way to Parliament Hill on a typically clear and cool end-of-summer Ottawa day.

The date was August 31, 1983, and Regan was on his way to a press conference in the theatre of the Press Building, where he was scheduled to unveil a government paper on Canada's trade policy. The Liberal trade minister's planned presentation on an esoteric topic like trade policy would normally have had little news value, even in Ottawa's political and seasonal doldrums, but Regan was anxious to meet reporters, because this time he was sure he had a trade policy that would capture media attention. Nearly buried in the numbing prose reaffirming the multilateral approach to Canadian trade policy that had been dominant since the Second World War was a proposal that Canada pursue sectoral free trade with the United States.

Sectoral free trade with the Americans was Regan's hook for the assembled media. While his bureaucrats had laboured to reaffirm the virtues of multilateralism, their minister had picked up on the one unusual, albeit secondary, aspect of the review. Regan was not simply playing to the gallery. The minister from Nova Scotia shared the considerable sympathy for free trade that he believed prevailed in Atlantic Canada. And a policy proposal for free trade with the United States, even if only in certain industrial sectors, would almost certainly prove newsworthy. Emerging from the car at the Press Building, Gerald Regan moved into the bright sunlight of an Ottawa morning on a course that would help transform the shape of Canada's political landscape and alter the course of Canadian history.

THE FREE TRADE STORY

The Canadian-American free trade story is a demonstration of the power of economic forces to shape political outcomes, of chance occurrences that made the difference between change and the status quo, and of determined men and women who made events bend to their will. It is an important story because free trade was one of the most significant policy initiatives in the life of the Canadian nation, and Canadians had to look deeply into their national soul to decide where they would stand on the issue. The national debate over free trade evoked historic images of

Canada and exposed stark divisions in the political fabric of the nation, especially in the area of ideas and values touching on the the role of governments versus the role of markets in Canadian society. It forced a redefinition of traditional concepts of nationalism and continentalism, and challenged the characteristic Canadian tendency to define ourselves in relation to the pervasive influence of the United States of America. Above all, free trade is a story of both faith and fear for almost all Canadians who were involved in or touched by it.

The story has three distinct phases. It begins with the Canadian decision to seek a free trade arrangement with the United States. This agenda-setting phase lasted roughly from 1983 to the late summer of 1985, when Brian Mulroney announced his government's intention to seek negotiations. How the issue went from nowhere to the top of the national policy agenda in two short years is an intriguing tale of the power of entrenched interests to steer the ship of state, as well as their determined leadership and ability to turn fortuitous events to their advantage. This part of the story must locate free trade in the historical context of developments in trade policy, with a particular focus on the early 1980s, and describe its place in the Conservative agenda constructed by Brian Mulroney and his party. Finally, it is necessary to consider the contents of the Free Trade Agreement itself in order to relate its complex issues to the unfolding narrative. These tasks we undertake in Part I.

The second phase tells the story of the negotiations themselves, spanning the period from May 1986 to December 1987. The metaphor of a three-ring circus is appropriate here to describe the complex management task that faced the government as it attempted to deal simultaneously with Canadian business, the provinces, and the United States. The story culminates in the whirlwind final two days of negotiation in Washington on a weekend in October 1987. The bargain that was struck that weekend must be understood in relation to the strategies employed by the various players throughout the piece, their relative leverage and power, and the skill, personalities, and dispositions of the officials and politicians engaged in the negotiations. The story of the negotiations is presented in Part II.

The story does not end with the deal that was struck in Washington on that October weekend. It continues into a third phase with the political challenge that was mounted against free trade in Canada and the election in the fall of 1988 when Canadian voters returned Mulroney and his Conservatives to a second consecutive majority government. Whether or not the 1988 election hinged entirely on the single issue of free trade, as some have claimed, there is no doubt that it decided the free trade question in Canada. The account of events in this phase of the free trade saga must include a larger cast of Canadian institutions and interests — political parties and parliament, labour unions, the mass media, and opposing and supportive coalitions of interest groups, as well as the unprecedented extent of involvement by the business community in electoral politics in defence of the Mulroney Conservatives and the agreement. These events are recounted in Part III.

The story offers an account of the politics of free trade — how the issue got to the top of the agenda, why the negotiations produced the particular document that was finally signed by the American president and Canadian prime minister, and why the 1988 election resulted in the Conservative victory that ultimately decided the issue. This story would be incomplete, however, without an assessment of the consequences of free trade for Canada. The political wars over the issue were fought under the banners of heaven and hell, with supporters promising a nirvana of economic expansion and increased national self-assurance, and opponents warning of an inferno of socio-economic decay and continental absorption. Only time can test these competing visions of a world of free trade. Its more immediate effects will be reflected in the constraints and opportunities that free trade will present to policy-makers as they attempt to chart a course through the 1990s. These policy effects are assessed in Part IV.

THE PEOPLE

Although the origins of the free trade drama lie in the economic and political forces that shaped events during the 1980s, the playing out of the story was affected fundamentally by its central characters. The men and women who played the major roles in the story also exerted a powerful influence on events. At the centre of the stage stood Martin Brian Mulroney and Ronald Wilson Reagan, an unlikely pairing but one that turned out to be oddly approriate. The former head of the Canadian branch of an American multinational corporation and denizen of Conservative back rooms, Mulroney was generally viewed as being long on politics and short on policies when he took office. He was also viewed with suspicion by Canadian nationalists because of his pro-American tendencies. Mulroney had made improved relations with the United States a plank in his 1984 election campaign, although he had rejected free trade. He also made a point of travelling to Washington to meet with Reagan shortly after being sworn in as prime minister, and the two men declared their intention to put the Canada-U.S. relationship on a new footing. However, Mulroney's conversion to the free trade gospel was not a foregone conclusion in 1984.

Reagan, too, was judged to be more than a little thin on policy, although by 1984 his administration had demonstrated its resolve to pursue a neo-conservative agenda in both domestic and foreign policy. The Reagan administration had fought an aggressive campaign against Canada's National Energy Program and Foreign Investment Review Agency in 1980–81, and welcomed Mulroney's early initiatives to dismantle both. Reagan had earlier floated the concept of a North American accord to more closely integrate the economies of Canada, Mexico, and the United States, but there was little substance to the idea, and he quickly dropped it when it provoked heavy criticism. Even though Reagan was a hands-off president, the fact remained that issues on the presidential agenda received the lion's share of attention in Washington. As a result, Mulroney's personal relationship with Reagan turned out to be an important factor in the free trade story. Whereas Mulroney would be deeply involved in the issue throughout the process, however, Reagan left free trade, as he did virtually all other issues, to trusted lieutenants, in this case James Baker III.

Baker is a patrician Texan, heir to old money in Houston, who served as the White House chief of staff during Reagan's first term, and secretary of the treasury in the second. With a reputation as a remarkably skilled political tactician and a considerable record of success in the political jungles of Washington, he wielded substantial influence in the Reagan administration and was managing its international economic policies as chairman of the cabinet's Economic Policy Council during the negotiations. Baker had all the prerequisites when the time came to do a deal — an ability to master the complex issues in the free trade brief, a sure knowledge of the corridors of power in Washington, and the authority to speak for the president. The time to deploy these forces came in October 1987 when Baker turned in a virtuoso performance, almost singlehandedly conducting the U.S. side of the weekend negotiations. In the view of many of those present, were it not for Baker, no deal would have been done.

Baker's counterpart on the Canadian side was Derek Burney. If a leading character is to be identified in the free trade story, it must be Burney. A career diplomat with a decisive and forthright style, he oversaw the conception and gestation of the free trade initiative from senior positions within the Department of External Affairs, putting first the sectoral and then the comprehensive options before the government. Burney gained considerable credit with the prime minister for the job he did in organizing the first "Shamrock Summit" in March 1985. Two years later, he became Mulroney's chief of staff, and rapidly the most powerful man in Ottawa. When the free trade initiative seemed to have foundered, Burney took charge of the Canadian team in Washington and hammered out the deal with Baker.

Throughout the free trade negotiations, the public spotlight was focused not on the prime minister and the president, nor on their principal lieutenants, but on the chief negotiators for Canada and the United States. In Simon Reisman and Peter Murphy, free trade had its own odd couple. Reisman had a formidable reputation in Ottawa, where he had finished his long public service career at the pinnacle, as deputy minister of finance. He had extensive experience in multilateral trade negotiations, and had also been a key player in the negotiation of the Canada-U.S. Auto Pact in 1965. After retiring from the public service, Reisman headed a high-profile consulting firm until, in his mid-60s, he was chosen by Brian Mulroney to be Canada's chief free trade negotiator, at a fee of $1,000 a day. Reisman's reputation owed as much to his personal style as to his senior position in the Ottawa mandarinate. A short, bellicose man, Reisman was loquacious, blunt to the point of rudeness, and often profane. His outbursts of temper with subordinates and superiors alike were legendary. He was also extremely capable, and was hired by the prime minister precisely because it was difficult to imagine the Americans riding rough-shod over Simon Reisman.

Facing off against Reisman, and at least a foot taller, was Peter Murphy. Although only in his mid-30s, Murphy, too, had considerable negotiating experience. He had cut his teeth on international textile negotiations, where the need to be responsive to import-sensitive industries and congressional pressures taught him the importance of domestic constituencies in the politics of American trade policy. A favourite of Deputy U.S. Trade Representative Michael Smith, Murphy advanced quickly, becoming first the chief U.S. textile negotiator and then permanent representative to the General Agreement on Tariffs and Trade in Geneva, in rapid succession. Murphy and Reisman were opposites not only in age and physical appearance, but also in style. Where Reisman was voluble and direct, Murphy was taciturn and cryptic. Rather than making for good chemistry, however, these opposites did not attract, a fact that would plague, and nearly bring down, the negotiations.

In addition to these central characters in the free trade drama, there were several others who played important roles at the climax of the negotiations in October 1987. On the U.S. side was Clayton Yeutter, who took on the position of U.S. trade representative in mid-1985. Although he was deputy USTR in the Nixon administration, Yeutter's grip on trade policy during the period of the negotiations was not especially firm. Nominally Murphy's boss, Yeutter oversaw the negotiations but was not really a part of them until the October weekend when he sat with Baker as part of the American negotiating team.

Finance Minister Michael Wilson was an important supporting player on the Canadian side. Wilson was the most powerful member of Mulroney's cabinet, and his department was in firm control of the Conservative agenda being fashioned in Ottawa. The Finance minister had been an early and strong backer of the free trade initiative, and he was chosen by Mulroney to accompany Burney to Washington for the final effort to get an agreement in October 1987. Wilson's support for free trade grew out of his belief that the Canadian economy was in a state of profound malaise, for which there could be no easy cure. Wilson told senior Finance officials in the fall of 1984 that he did not believe Canada could tax or spend its way out of its economic troubles. Instead, the country would have to grow its way out of the problems that beset the economy, and the key to this growth was a significant increase in Canadian trade. When the trade negotiations eventually collapsed in the autumn of 1987, Wilson's rapport with his U.S. counterpart, Treasury Secretary James Baker, made him one of the key points of contact in the efforts to restart the talks.

Also at the table that weekend was Trade Minister Patricia Carney. As minister of Energy, Carney had made her reputation negotiating with Western Canada for a new energy regime. Chosen by Mulroney in July 1986 to raise the free trade profile, she had immediately demonstrated her inability to hang tough during the battle with the U.S. over exports of Canadian softwood lumber. Carney had also been forced to endure endless turf battles with Reisman, who refused to be answerable to anyone except the prime minister and cabinet on the negotiations. Finally, on the Canadian side, there was Canada's ambassador to Washington, Allan Gotlieb. A former under-secretary of state for External Affairs, Gotlieb had taken Washington by storm following his appointment as ambassador, holding power parties and mounting an active lobby on Capitol Hill in support of Canadian interests.

These were the principal characters in the free trade story. Together they would respond to, and shape, events to write the unfolding drama of the most significant public issue for Canada in the 1980s. In telling their story, however, we do not want to lose sight of the central public policy issues that gave rise to the interest in free trade with the United States.

THE ISSUES

To conclude the free trade story, it is important to arrive at answers to a number of key questions about the decision to create a Canadian-American free trade arrangement. First, we will want to know how the issue got on the Conservative agenda, despite Brian Mulroney's public rejection of free trade two years before coming to power. This was not a prime minister inclined to take large risks, and free trade carried a substantial potential risk. Dealing with a power like the United States, and on an issue where Canada was the *demandeur*, that is, the party seeking negotiations as a means to resolve a problem, could not be called ideal conditions for a favourable outcome, especially when any deal would be subject to microscopic scrutiny by suspicious nationalists. Mulroney knew he was not betting on a sure thing, therefore, and we want to know how he made the decision.

We will also want to carefully examine how the negotiations were managed politically, both in the extended period from mid-1986 to September 1987 when there was much talk but little actual progress, and in the final frantic weekend in Washington in October 1987. Free trade presented Mulroney and his officials with an issue of unprecedented magnitude and complexity. It required the government to manage relationships with diverse interests within the

Canadian business community as well as with the provinces, each of which had its own agenda on the issue. When the negotiating relationship with the United States — given the fragmented American system of policy-making — was added to this mix, it gave the government a potent brew to deal with. Considering this complexity and the high stakes involved, the metaphor of the three-ring circus, while it may be instructive, is probably too benign. The lions' cage may provide a more accurate metaphor for the task that faced the government. Given the degree of difficulty, it is natural to ask how well the government and the negotiators in the TNO (Trade Negotiations Office) performed this quintessential political task. While the difficulties that Canada faced in a negotiation where the U.S. held most of the cards must be acknowledged in attempting to answer this question, most will still want to know whether the Canadians succeeded in the negotiations, or were out-negotiated by a group of Yankee traders.

The FTA must also be judged by economic criteria. Many of those who championed free trade did so on the grounds that Canada was facing a major productivity crisis in the 1980s, a crisis that could only be remedied by exposing Canadian industry to increased competition and by enhancing its access to Canada's primary export market in the United States. This position was consistent with the general arguments about the benefits of trade liberalization that had been advanced by economists throughout the post-war period. In economic terms, the appropriate test of the FTA is not whether a different set of negotiators might have achieved a better deal, but whether the agreement made sense in the context of the economic conditions in the 1980s, and whether it positions Canada more favourably to face competitive pressures in the 1990s.

History provided a fitting climax to the free trade initiative in the Canadian general election of 1988. The election must figure as a central chapter in the free trade story because it offered a crucial, though perhaps not entirely valid, test of the bargain that was struck between Canada and the United States a year earlier. The election was unusual because the free trade issue so dominated the interest coalitions that were formed to do battle, pitting the Conservatives and a business-led coalition against the Liberals and New Democrats aligned with a people's coalition of uncommon breadth. While we will want to see how these alliances were formed, and how they operated to shape electoral choices, the coalitions do not tell the entire story of the election. Despite the dominance of the free trade issue, the election cannot be viewed simply as a referendum on free trade. While it was widely seen to legitimize the deal that Mulroney had made, individual votes were influenced by many factors that had little to do with the collective meaning ascribed to them. Our task in considering the election of 1988 is twofold: first, to analyse the electoral process and its outcome; and second, to assess the extent to which it legitimized the free trade agreement.

Finally, we must address the consequences of the agreement. What difference will free trade make to Canada? While it is too early to assess the economic effects of the continental rationalization that free trade is supposed to promote, we can investigate some of its effects on policy and political relationships. Specifically, we will want to describe how free trade will affect Canada's capacity to make policy in important areas — industrial, social, and trade policy, for example — in the 1990s and beyond. More speculatively, we should ask whether free trade might affect pressures toward regional decentralization within Canada, and how it might influence the balance between national and continental integration that has preoccupied Canadians since Confederation.

In search of answers to these questions, the free trade story begins in the following chapter with the severe recession that shook the economies of Canada and the United States to their foundations at the beginning of the 1980s, setting the stage for free trade.

PART I:
GETTING FREE TRADE
ON THE AGENDA

2

LIBERAL LEGACY FOR A CONSERVATIVE AGENDA

Free trade with the United States would have looked like a very long shot at the beginning of the 1980s. Few would have predicted that within four years Canada would propose sectoral free trade, and fewer still would have believed that two years later Canada would go the whole way and offer to negotiate a comprehensive free trade agreement with the Americans. But then, not many anticipated the economic debacle that was about to be visited upon Canada.

In the second half of 1980, the U.S. economy quietly entered a downward spiral into an economic collapse on a scale not experienced since the Great Depression of the 1930s. The collapse triggered events that would bring to an end the resurrection of the Liberal Party of Canada (which had occurred that same year) and dramatically alter federal politics in Canada. The economic crisis also unleashed forces that would transform Canada's relationship with the United States, leading to the free trade pact between the two countries.

The decision to negotiate free trade was a fundamental policy shift on the part of the government of Canada, and it was certainly not anticipated as the decade began, not even by those at the centre of the policy process. In early 1981, Canada's highest-ranking foreign policy official, Under-Secretary of State for External Affairs Allan Gotlieb, published an article heralding the rebirth in Canadian foreign policy of the Third Option. This was a short-lived effort in the 1970s, designed to promote restructuring of the Canadian economy and to diversify Canada's foreign economic relations away from the United States. Gotlieb, who was shortly to become Canada's ambassador to the U.S. and to play a role in the free trade negotiations, wrote:

> The nature of the Canadian economy and society has required government involvement to channel aspects of long-range development in beneficial ways. Similarly, it is axiomatic that the benefits of development have to be worked at by Canada. They will not fall out of a free trade, free investment, free-for-all continental economy. This is not an option for Canadian development.[1]

The story of Canada's movement from a revival of the Third Option to bilateral free trade in less than five years is a fascinating and instructive account of the ability of powerful and determined individuals to move institutions, and of the power of events to move both. The decision to negotiate free trade involved a basic redefinition of Canada's relationship with the United States.[2] It also represented a fundamental change in policy, not only because of the long-standing national debate on the issue but also because of the tremendous asymmetry in power between the two countries, which fuelled Canadian fears about U.S. domination. This fundamental policy shift originated in the unprecedented conditions of crisis and conflict that marked the early eighties.

CRISIS AND CONFLICT

The formal negotiations to conclude a free trade agreement that began between Canada and the United States in May of 1986 had their beginning in the acute bilateral conflict that erupted between the two countries in 1981 over Canadian energy and investment policies. The majority Liberal government elected in 1980 had adopted an ambitious national policy agenda designed to enhance the resources and visibility of the federal government. The Liberal aim was to redress what was viewed as a serious imbalance within Canadian federalism. Central to the Liberal strategy were initiatives such as patriation of the Constitution, a resources-first approach to economic development, renegotiation of social programs and equalization payments to the provinces, and the creation of a Western Development Fund.[3]

The National Energy Program (NEP) was also a central element in this overall strategy, but one that had negative consequences for foreign investors in the Canadian oil and gas industry. When the government also announced its intention to extend the mandate of the Foreign Investment Review Agency (FIRA) in the regulation of direct foreign investment, the howls of outrage from the American business establishment turned the guns of the Reagan administration on Canada. U.S. plans for retaliatory measures targeted the Canadian Achilles' heel of trade dependence on the United States.[4] The Liberal government, realizing it was in a vulnerable position, moved quickly to reassure the Americans that it had no plans to extend the Canadianization provisions of the NEP to other sectors of the economy. In addition, the government announced that it would not be introducing any changes to the FIRA mandate.

This acute conflict, and the fears it aroused in Canadians and their government, represented a turning point for Canada in its relations with the United States. The U.S. had openly threatened the security of Canadian access to a market on which Canada was overwhelmingly dependent. The implications for employment and investment in Canada were profound. Both business and government were forced to re-assess the value to Canada of secure and enhanced access to the U.S. market, especially in the context of the severe economic recession then developing. For the United States, the memory of the NEP and FIRA would linger, and the free trade initiative would be seized as an opportunity to ensure that American interests would never again be threatened by such policies.

The 1981 conflict was important because of the powerful influence it would exert subsequently on the way Canadians defined the problem in their relations with the United States. The channel for this influence was opened in a relatively innocuous fashion when the Priorities and Planning Committee of the federal cabinet initiated a wide-ranging review of government policies in September 1981. Coming at the peak of the conflict with the United States, the mandate included a trade policy review, as well as a separate assessment of Canadian-American relations.

A TRADE POLICY REVIEW

The trade policy review was started in the Department of Industry, Trade and Commerce (ITC). A concurrent review of the Canada-U.S. relationship was initiated by the Department of External Affairs (DEA). In January 1982, however, a major reorganization of ITC was undertaken in order to integrate the federal government's industrial and regional development policies. As a result, the trade elements of ITC were split off and integrated into a reorganized Department of External Affairs, as a new trade and economic wing reporting to its own minister for international trade. Consequently, in the spring of 1982, the trade policy review was shifted to an External Affairs task force. This shift was important, since the free trade option had less chance of emerging from ITC, with its mandate to protect and nurture Canadian industry. The new task force was under the management of Derek Burney, the assistant under-secretary for trade and economic relations in External Affairs. This was the first time — but certainly not the last — that Burney would be in a position to play a crucial role in the free trade saga.

By the time the trade policy issue had been handed to this task force, the "temporary slowdown" that had been anticipated in the U.S. economy for 1981 and part of 1982[5] had deepened, and the recession had followed its natural path to Canada. The two countries were on their way to experiencing their most severe recession since the 1930s, one that would hit the Canadian economy especially hard. As the task force conducted its review during 1982, the emerging economic crisis guaranteed that the threat to secure access to the American market for Canada's exports would be defined as the central problem for Canadian trade policy.

The decline in trade that accompanied the recession also made trade policy a central preoccupation for the Reagan administration. However, from Washington's perspective the problem was the unfair trading practices of its major trading partners, a problem made more serious, or at least more visible, by the severity of the recession. Protectionist pressures had increased during the 1970s as the U.S. lost its competitive edge in the world trading system. The recession added significantly to these pressures, prompting a greater willingness in the U.S. to move more aggressively to curb imports. Ironically, American disenchantment with the multilateral negotiations they were unsuccessfully promoting with their Japanese and European trading partners also produced greater interest in the prospect of bilateral trade agreements as an alternative to multilateralism.

The External Affairs task force began its trade policy review in the summer of 1982. The project director, Michael Hart, a departmental trade policy specialist, organized a series of consultations with representatives of the Canadian business community and the provincial governments. In these consultations, the task force was repeatedly told that the central goal of any trade policy should be to "get the Canada-U.S. relationship right." The U.S. market was fundamentally important to Canadian economic well-being, and preservation of that market required stability in the Canada-U.S. relationship. In particular, the government had to find a means to protect Canadian exporters from the application of the contingency protection provisions of the U.S. trade law.

Leading the Canadian business position were the Business Council on National Issues (BCNI), made up of major corporations operating within the Canadian market, and the Canadian

Manufacturers' Association (CMA). During 1982 and 1983, the president of BCNI, Thomas d'Aquino, was active in advocating negotiations for a comprehensive trade agreement as a means to guarantee access to the U.S. market. Equally important, however, was the reversal by the influential CMA of its long-standing opposition to free trade with the United States. It was the crisis in the economy that ensured that the task force examination of Canada's trade policy would centre on securing access to the U.S. market. And the Canadian business lobby saw to it that the negotiation of some form of trade liberalization was put forward as an option for consideration by the task force.

FREE TRADE REARS ITS HEAD

In its report,[6] the External Affairs task force played it absolutely safe and reaffirmed the centrality of the multilateral GATT (General Agreement on Tariffs and Trade) system for Canada. Secondarily, however, it also raised the prospect of pursuing *sectoral* free trade arrangements with the United States as an additional option for the government to consider. The sectoral option was not without precedent, since Canada already had three sectoral free trade arrangements with the U.S., covering automobiles, defence materials, and agricultural machinery. In fact, in 1981, Canadian Embassy officials in Washington, with Ottawa's knowledge, informally discussed broader sectoral free trade arrangements with officials in the Office of the U.S. Trade Representative (USTR). This initiative was part of the Canadian effort to resolve the conflict with the U.S. over the NEP and FIRA. It did not proceed, however, because of opposition from within ITC in Ottawa, which still carried the trade mandate at that time. Despite these precedents, free trade was a sensitive political issue in Canada. The pride of place given by the task force to the GATT undoubtedly eased the task of the new minister for international trade, Gerald Regan, who received the report and saw to its acceptance by cabinet.

Regan was a free trader from Nova Scotia, and it was the sectoral initiative that caught his attention in the report. Stressing the report's reaffirmation of the GATT, Regan persuaded his cautious cabinet colleagues to go along with its sectoral option as well, despite the suspicions of the "nationalist" group in the Liberal cabinet. With cabinet endorsement in hand, Regan turned the report upside down at his press conference in August 1983. Seizing on its most controversial element, the minister announced the demise of the Third Option and proclaimed the government's intention to pursue a limited free trade agreement with the United States. Regan's proclamation did not, by any means, reflect mainstream thinking in External Affairs. The concurrent review of the Canada-U.S. relationship that had been prepared for the deputy minister for foreign relations had reaffirmed the basic tenets of the Third Option. That report was overtaken by events, however. It was the trade policy review that provided the opening for fundamental change in Canadian-American relations, as sectoral free trade negotiations became the preferred option of the Liberal government of Pierre Trudeau.

This was no blind leap. During that summer of 1983, Derek Burney had provided a draft of the task force report to Deputy U.S. Trade Representative Michael Smith, in order to test American reaction. Although the Americans had strong general reservations about sectoral proposals, Smith was prepared to take up the Canadian proposal as one step toward more comprehensive arrangements. Accordingly, he told Burney that the Americans would react favourably to such an initiative. Immediately following Regan's announcement, U.S. Trade Representative William Brock endorsed the Canadian proposal.

The task of implementing the sectoral initiative from the Canadian side fell to Tony Halliday, an experienced trade official in External Affairs. In February 1984, he and his American counterparts in USTR were ready to bring Regan and Brock together in Washington, where they identified four sectors for officials from the two countries to focus on. By June, however, little progress had been made in these preliminary discussions, principally because USTR was unable to bring American industries on board. Although Regan and Brock agreed to explore alternative sectors, nothing further was decided on the question of whether and when to begin formal negotiations. It was apparent that initial American reservations about sectoral arrangements had been correct.[7]

BIGGER FISH TO FRY

The election of Brian Mulroney and the Conservatives in September 1984 offered the U.S. the prospect of bigger fish to fry. This was a government that American officials believed they could do business with, and the chances for a comprehensive trade agreement immediately looked brighter. However, the new Conservative government approached the Liberal free trade legacy in a gingerly fashion. Certainly, ministers were cautious at the outset. James Kelleher, the new minister for international trade, indicated in a September speech that Canada was prepared to continue discussions with the United States to identify potential areas for action on trade relations between the two countries, but not "to create fortress North America."[8] Similarly, External Affairs Minister Joe Clark, following his first meeting with U.S. Secretary of State George Shultz, would do no more than announce the need to study the implications of opening up more products for free trade across the border before entering into any agreements.

While the ministers temporized, External Affairs officials were taking a long, hard look at the sectoral proposal in preparation for an anticipated review by the new government. This External Affairs review was again headed by Derek Burney, now as assistant deputy minister for United States affairs in the department. The External Affairs group assessed the sectoral initiative, and found it wanting. The decision was made to have a task force undertake another review of trade policy options, this time including a comprehensive — meaning free trade — arrangement among the various alternatives to be presented for public discussion. Burney would direct the review.

As the task force proceeded, the United States continued down its own path toward the free trade option. During the autumn of 1984, the Senate and the House of Representatives passed a bill authorizing the administration to negotiate bilateral trade liberalization agreements. Although not specifically addressed to Canada, the legislation named only Canada and Israel as prospective parties to such bilateral agreements. In addition, the Reagan administration asked the U.S. International Trade Commission to study the likely effects of sectoral free trade with Canada, and the commission subsequently held hearings on the issue, as did the Office of the U.S. Trade Representative.

During the first few months in the term of their new government, Mulroney's Tories began to sketch the principal dimensions of what would become the Conservative policy agenda. In an economic and fiscal statement presented by Finance Minister Michael Wilson to the House of Commons in November 1984, the government identified its priorities as economic renewal and national reconciliation. Wilson also tabled a policy agenda, setting out a strategy for economic renewal. One element of the strategy was increased and secure access to markets for Canadian exports, especially in the U.S. Referring to sectoral free trade, the Finance agenda noted[9] that "this initiative has generated public interest in exploring broadly based bilateral arrangements with the U.S."

The Tories were still some distance from free trade at this early stage in their mandate. The Finance economic renewal statement had not been prepared especially for the Conservatives, but was begun in May 1984 while the Liberals still held power. Nor had the concept of "broadly based bilateral arrangements" been cleared through Trade Minister Kelleher, who was not consulted on the Finance statement. Nevertheless, the autumn of 1984 saw pressures mount for the government to pick up the free trade agenda. Canadian business organizations engaged in a vigorous lobbying effort to shore up support for a comprehensive free trade arrangement, and their position was given serious attention by a government committed to making Canada a better place to do business.[10]

LEAP OF FAITH

The negotiation option probably received its most substantial boost in November 1984 from Donald Macdonald, a former Liberal cabinet minister and chairman of the Royal Commission on the Economic Union and Development Prospects for Canada. Appointed by Pierre Trudeau in 1982, the Macdonald Commission was examining Canada-U.S. free trade as part of its study of the Canadian economy. Although the commission had neither completed its studies nor framed its conclusions, Macdonald nevertheless announced that he favoured free trade between Canada and the United States as the principal long-term solution to Canada's economic problems.

Acknowledging that Canadians might be nervous about maintaining their sovereignty in a free trade arrangement with the United States, Macdonald nonetheless argued that "if we do get down to a point where it's going to be a leap of faith, then I think at some point Canadians are going to have to be bold and say, yes, we will do that."[11]

Macdonald's call for a "leap of faith" was a big news item in Canada. And because the commission was bipartisan and seemingly authoritative, Macdonald's support provided important momentum to the free trade option at a critical juncture, as the new government was considering its options. This endorsement was followed by a series of government reports and consultations that moved the Mulroney cabinet ever closer to a final commitment to negotiation.

The first of the reports was the product of the review of trade policy options initiated by Derek Burney in the Department of External Affairs. That review generated sharp conflicts, both in External Affairs and with the Department of Regional Industrial Expansion (DRIE), the successor to ITC. The conflict resulted from opposition to Burney's determination to put the comprehensive free trade option before the government. From a DRIE perspective, trade liberalization would threaten Canadian industries supported by an average tariff that was roughly double that of their American competition. In External, the opposition centred on traditional concerns over political autonomy. In the end, Burney was forced to override opposition from the most senior administrative levels of his own department, which wanted to suppress the free trade discussion. His task force presented comprehensive free trade as one of the options for Canada in the report prepared for Trade Minister James Kelleher. Kelleher did not share the reluctance of his senior officials to consider all of the options available to Canada in its relations with the U.S., and he released the report in January 1985.[12]

This government discussion paper, while acknowledging the importance of multilateral trade liberalization, confirmed the need to seek enhanced and secure access to the U.S. market. To this end, the paper suggested that some form of bilateral trade arrangement should be considered, and set out the options available to Canada. These were the status quo, sectoral arrangements, a comprehensive trade agreement (the Conservative euphemism for free trade) to remove tariff and nontariff barriers on substantially all bilateral trade, and a bilateral framework to discuss means to improve and enhance trade relations (a BCNI proposal). Although the paper was careful to avoid identifying a preferred option, it rejected the status quo as inadequate, sectoral arrangements as unattainable, and the BCNI framework as unnecessary.[13] Clearly the government was edging down the path to comprehensive free trade negotiations.

Some urgency was lent to this movement by the mounting tide of U.S. protectionism in 1984–85. There was an increase in the number of investigations of Canadian export practices under the American countervailing duty process, as well as the introduction of specific legislation in Congress that would limit Canadian exports to the U.S.[14] Not surprisingly, problems related to trade were at the top of the agenda for discussion between Brian Mulroney and Ronald Reagan at their first summit meeting in March 1985 in Quebec City, the "Shamrock Summit."

EDGING TO THE PRECIPICE

The Shamrock Summit was orchestrated in exquisite detail by Fred Doucet, a PMO (Prime Minister's Office) staffer and Mulroney confidant. Working closely with Doucet was Derek Burney, who oversaw the drafting of the trade declaration to be issued by the prime minister and the president. Although the declaration contained no explicit statement of bilateral trade policy by either government, it did call for an examination of ways to reduce and eliminate existing barriers to trade. Mulroney and Reagan instructed Trade Minister Kelleher and U.S. Trade Representative Brock to report in six months on mechanisms to achieve this end.

To plumb Canadian attitudes on the issue of comprehensive free trade, Kelleher set off in March 1985 on a cross-Canada tour to sound out the views of individuals and groups on the trade options presented in the paper prepared by Burney's group and released in January. This focus ensured that the "comprehensive trade agreement" option presented in the discussion paper would receive a full public hearing. In a series of public forums, Kelleher and his people heard from a wide variety of business and labour groups. What they heard from business indicated substantial, though not unanimous, support for a comprehensive bilateral trade deal that would secure access to the American market for Canadian companies. Labour was not similarly disposed, however. Kelleher's public forums were followed in May 1985 by a series of private consultations with Canadian firms and business organizations conducted by Tom Burns, former president of the Canadian Exporters Association. Burns's mission also centred on the trade options discussion paper, and provided further evidence of widespread support for some kind of comprehensive approach to bilateral trade. The results of Burns's soundings were reported through Kelleher back to the External Affairs task force.

Also circulating in Ottawa during this period of consultation was a C.D. Howe Institute study of Canada's trade options, co-authored by Richard Lipsey, one of Canada's most respected economists.[15]

Following publication of the study, Lipsey and Wendy Dobson, then head of the Howe Institute and later associate deputy minister of Finance in the federal government, launched a personal lobby in Ottawa to ensure that key ministers, their aides, and senior members of the bureaucracy were aware of the study's advocacy of the free trade option. Their efforts, along with the trade policy studies prepared by the Macdonald Commission, helped to shatter many of the prevailing myths about free trade. In particular, they vigorously argued the case that rather than representing a complete break with the Canadian past, the free trade option was quite consistent with Canada's commitment to trade liberalization throughout the post-war era.

Following the joint declaration at the Shamrock Summit, Burney's External Affairs task force fleshed out the free trade option and prepared to present a recommendation for cabinet decision. It continued to encounter opposition to a comprehensive agreement both within DEA and from other departments. The Kelleher and Burns consultations had provided evidence that Canadian business would be behind the initiative, however, and this could make all the difference in cabinet, especially with support from Michael Wilson in Finance. With Canadian business on side, and with the backing of the ministers of External Affairs, Trade, and Finance, Burney was determined to press ahead, despite continued opposition from senior officials.

Another incremental step toward a commitment to negotiate was also taken in May 1985 in the release of the government's green paper on foreign policy.[16] The paper reaffirmed the goal of enhanced and secure access to the U.S. market, set out the same options that had been presented in the January discussion paper, and again made the case for a comprehensive agreement by raising doubts about the other options. Green papers are intended to stimulate discussion of new directions in policy, so the publication of this paper offered another opportunity to measure reaction to the free trade option. However, in this case the government got more reaction than it bargained for. External Affairs Minister Joe Clark chose to have the paper serve as the basis for a review of foreign policy by a special joint House of Commons–Senate committee. In so doing, he provided the opposition parties with a very public forum in which to mount their challenge to the emerging free trade policy.

Opposition members on the special joint committee began their campaign by forcing separate hearings on the trade issue, along with that of Canadian participation in the U.S. Strategic Defense Initiative (SDI). The government had originally insisted that policy decisions on these two issues would have to be taken before the committee was able to report. The opposition charged that this made a mockery of the review process, and threatened to boycott the committee. Given his public commitment to the virtues of parliamentary review, Clark was forced to accede to opposition demands and agree to separate hearings on trade and the SDI. As well, the government agreed to defer decisions on these issues until the committee had reported.[17]

In its interim report of August 1985,[18] the committee recommended a fairly cautious approach to the trade issue in a recommendation drafted with the concurrence of both Conservative and Liberal members of the committee, but not New Democratic Party members, who issued a dissent. The report proposed that the government begin preliminary trade discussions with the U.S., but not move immediately to formal bilateral negotiations. Instead, the committee urged the government to centre the discussions on the resolution of existing trade irritants and the exploration of issues involved in further trade liberalization. These exploratory talks would determine whether a basis for more comprehensive negotiations existed.

BITING THE BULLET

The committee's caution was overtaken by events, however, when the report of the Macdonald Royal Commission was released two weeks later with its recommendation of free trade with the United States. The royal commission report was in the hands of the prime minister earlier in the summer, even as the special joint committee was conducting its hearings. He saw immediately the opportunity it presented for a bold policy initiative with ready-made bipartisan support. And Mulroney relished the prospect of using a former Liberal cabinet minister to give bipartisan legitimacy to the initiative. The volumes of the report arranged on his desk, Mulroney spread his hands over them and told officials present in his office that summer day that he would use the report to beat John Turner in the next election.

At almost the same time, Canadian officials were meeting with their U.S. counterparts to determine whether there existed a basis for negotiation. These preliminary soundings suggested that an agenda could be shaped to satisfy the interests of both countries. At the end of July 1985, Derek Burney travelled to Washington, accompanied by Michael Hart and Bob Martin, the latter from the Department of Finance. As he had done in 1983, Burney met with Deputy USTR Michael Smith, who was accompanied by his assistant USTR for North American affairs, William Merkin. Smith took the group out on Chesapeake Bay in his sailboat, and throughout a long day on the water the small group of officials laid out the essential elements of a potential free trade agreement between the two countries. Smith emphasized that the Americans would want a big deal, one that would address the key U.S. issues of investment, services, and intellectual property. He urged that negotiations begin with as broad an agenda as possible, with no issues excluded at the outset. For his part, Burney indicated that Canada was now considering a comprehensive agreement. He made clear the overriding Canadian interest in achieving secure access to the U.S. market, and the threat to security posed by the anti-dumping and countervailing duty (CVD) provisions of U.S. trade remedy law. Smith concurred that only a comprehensive agreement could address CVD and anti-dump, and indicated that a potential solution might lie in the application of disciplines on the use of subsidies. This creative ambiguity allowed Smith and Burney to adroitly sidestep a conflict on which the negotiations would, ultimately, almost founder, and permitted Burney to inform the ministers that a basis for negotiation had been identified.

By August, Kelleher was concluding the report on trade relations that he had been directed to prepare following the Shamrock Summit, and he made a preliminary oral presentation to the Priorities and Planning Committee of cabinet at its meeting in Vancouver. Although there had been no serious comprehensive discussion of the free trade issue by cabinet up to this point in the decision process, and despite lingering uncertainties on the part of some ministers, the committee moved quickly to confirm the decision the prime minister had already taken to seek comprehensive trade negotiations with the U.S. Following the Vancouver meeting, attention shifted to Washington again as the government took soundings to reassure itself that the Reagan administration could bring Congress on side.

Shortly after the September 5, 1985, release of the royal commission report, to ensure that free trade would be tied to Macdonald, the prime minister indicated, in reply to a question in the House of Commons on September 9, that the government had decided to pursue "freer" trade with the United States. On September 26, Mulroney told the Commons that he had telephoned U.S. President Reagan to ask him to explore with Congress Canada's interest in pursuing negotiations to reduce tariffs and nontariff barriers between the two countries. This call, and the formal written proposal that followed on October 1, finally brought to an end four years of policy transformation in Canada. With little fanfare, the government had decided to pursue comprehensive free trade negotiations with the United States.

WHY FREE TRADE FOR CANADA?

In his analysis of the free trade initiative, William Watson argued that it "does not make sense as a rational act of policy, and that the government has simply stumbled into it, more or less unwittingly."[19] On the contrary, our reconstruction of events between the decision to undertake a trade policy review in September 1981 and the September 1985 request for negotiations makes it clear that while the free trade decision was not foreordained, neither was the policy process that resulted in the choice haphazard. Certainly, the timing of the failure of the sectoral initiative and the 1984 federal election was fortuitous, as was Mulroney's majority, but free trade was the Liberals' legacy to the Conservative government. That legacy was nurtured and developed by a small and relatively isolated group of External Affairs officials led by Derek Burney, and supported by key ministers in the Conservative cabinet.

It was also clear that free trade did not lead the Conservative policy agenda, although it was nicely congruent with the general thrust of the programs for economic renewal and national reconciliation that the Tories were developing during their first year in office. Critical of existing programs for regional economic development and industrial adjustment, Mulroney and Wilson were determined to create a more open market within which business could operate with greater efficiency. A climate had to be created that would encourage firms to adapt to market conditions and invest for expansion. An important symbol of this determination was the legislation tabled in December 1984 to transform FIRA into Investment Canada, with a mandate to encourage foreign investment. Access to American capital markets was essential to Tory plans for economic expansion in Canada, and excessive regulation simply distorted the operation of the market to Canada's disadvantage. The Tories were also determined to undo the NEP, and the March 1985 Western Accord accomplished this by introducing significant deregulation in Canada's oil and gas industry. (If the government had already taken the decision to go for free trade, it would certainly have delayed the FIRA and NEP changes until the negotiations, when a price could be exacted for them from the Americans — at least it is comforting to assume so.)

For trade policy, the problem centred on achieving enhanced and secure access to the U.S. market for Canadian producers. In the context of the general Conservative agenda for economic renewal, opening up the markets of the two countries through the removal of barriers to trade would have intrinsic appeal precisely because it was congruent with the central thrust of that agenda. Free trade also served the Conservative priority of national reconciliation. Canada's western provinces had been deeply disaffected over the Liberal National Energy Program, and Mulroney and his Energy minister, Patricia Carney, wasted little time in undoing the NEP through the Western Accord. There also existed substantial support for free trade in the West, especially Alberta, long a stronghold of Conservative support. Alberta's Conservative premier Peter Lougheed, a strong supporter of the free trade option, was the principal exponent of Western grievances, and he held close counsel with Mulroney on the trade issue throughout the period leading up to the decision of September 1985.

Lougheed's support was important in shoring up Mulroney's resolve as the time for decision approached. Also important was the surprising degree of support for free trade in Quebec. Quebec was home to a substantial share of inefficient Canadian industries least likely to survive the elimination of protective barriers. The province's long-standing opposition to trade liberalization had been an important element in Canadian trade policy. All that changed, however, with the willingness of the Quebec business establishment to support free trade. Quebec's support would reinforce Mulroney's strategy to consolidate the Conservative landslide he had achieved in the province in 1984, and thus turn the political tables on the Liberals.

Mulroney's path to the free trade decision was also smoothed by the presence of Tory governments in most of the remaining provinces, with the notable exception of Ontario. These premiers were ideologically sympathetic to the pro-market approach of the federal party, and deeply concerned about American protectionism. As a result, they were generally positive about negotiating a comprehensive trade agreement for enhanced and secure access to the U.S. market, assuming of course that an agreement left untouched such "non-trade" shibboleths as agricultural marketing boards and regional development grants.

In their view of free trade primarily as a vehicle for enhanced and secure market access, the premiers were not alone. The policy papers prepared for ministers by Burney and his External Affairs group focused on the *trade* policy problem of securing access to the U.S. market in the face of growing American protectionism. Canadian business support for free trade was also directed to the need to secure access to their largest market and escape U.S. trade remedy law applications against Canadian exports. This view of free trade as a trade policy designed to address the problem of secure access was reflected in Mulroney's statement to the House in September 1985:

> Economics, geography, common sense and the national interest dictate that *we try to secure and expand our trade* with our closest and largest trading partner — protectionist measures are always self-defeating. This impulse to protectionism is defensive and negative — yet entirely understandable in human terms. This is what we are up against.
>
> The answer to this problem lies in sound agreements, legally binding, between trading partners, to secure and remove barriers to their mutual trade. That is our approach to world trade. And it is obvious that we must find special and direct means of *securing and enhancing* the annual $155 billion of two-way trade with the United States.[20]

Free trade is more than trade policy, however. It can also serve as an industrial policy to bring about restructuring and adjustment in the economy.[21] And it was primarily as an industrial policy, loosely defined, that free trade was advocated as the principal long-term solution to Canada's economic problems by the Macdonald Royal Commission. According to the commission's analysis, the source of Canada's economic problems could be found in a manufacturing sector that produces at too high a cost for too small a market. Free trade would at once expand the market and remove the protective barriers that insulate inefficient firms from competition. These firms would either adjust, by becoming larger and more competitive, or die. The result would be an increase in total national production. This analysis of industrial policy and its free trade prescription may represent sound economics, but not politics. With fewer but larger firms producing more, there are still likely to be large numbers of disaffected individuals and groups who have been "adjusted" out of jobs and out of business. It is for this reason that protectionist measures, first tariffs and more recently non-tariff barriers, have enjoyed such popularity with politicians in all countries.

For ministers, the central problem facing Canada was security of access to the country's major market. A comprehensive trade agreement with the United States offered an appealing, if politically sensitive, trade policy solution to the problem. Had the problem been defined primarily in terms of an uncompetitive manufacturing sector, however, then it is likely that a proposal for an industrial policy to subject the economy to a sudden cold shower through free trade would have been viewed as a considerably more risky venture. But these hard economic facts were not laid out for the prime minister, because he never received a comprehensive briefing from his senior trade officials on the economics of bilateral free trade. The way the problem was framed for Mulroney helps explain why this otherwise cautious prime minister would take such a leap of faith. As a trade policy, free trade offered the prospect of secure access to the American market. Although it carried some domestic political risk, the prospect of reducing protectionist harassment in Canada's dominant trade market would make the risk worthwhile. As an industrial policy, however, the removal of barriers to trade offers the potential for market gains, but at the risk of potential industry losses. Since the free trade option was framed as a means to avoid the loss of secure market access, it offered a more palatable choice to policy-makers who are naturally averse to taking major risks.

The significant partisan advantages that free trade offered the Conservative government also made the option of comprehensive negotiations attractive. Mulroney was determined to offer a clear alternative to the centralizing, interventionist policies of the Trudeau Liberals and to build a lasting power base for his party. A policy that was market oriented and had broad appeal in Western Canada and Quebec served both ends. The summer of 1985 also saw Mulroney and his ministers under fire for a lack of clear direction and purpose. Free trade offered the prospect of immediate partisan advantage to a government in search of a major policy on which to set sail. For all of these reasons, free trade looked like a policy whose time had finally arrived. With the Canadian decision made, the ball was handed over to the United States.

AN AMERICAN FUMBLE

Despite the support for comprehensive free trade that Deputy USTR Michael Smith had conveyed to Derek Burney, the climate in Washington was not entirely hospitable to the Canadian initiative. Although the formal response to the prime minister's proposal that came from the U.S. president was favourable, some administration officials viewed the timing of the proposal as unfortunate. Treasury Secretary Baker, in particular, wanted to delay the request to Congress for negotiating authority in order to concentrate on the tax reforms he was then attempting to negotiate through the House and Senate. As well, the protectionist mood in the Congress was turning ugly, with unhappiness over the president's trade policies running deep. A new offensive against unfair trade practices had just been announced by the administration to demonstrate presidential resolve to get tough on trade, but the Congress remained sceptical. In short, the Mulroney initiative landed in the quagmire of Washington politics.

As a result of the ensuing internal debate over proper timing, U.S. action on the Canadian initiative was postponed. It was not until December 10, 1985, that Reagan formally notified Congress of his administration's intention to begin negotiations. Notification of the House of Representatives Ways and Means Committee and the Senate Finance Committee was required in order for the negotiations to be handled under the so-called "fast track" negotiating authority. The fast track was important because it required Congress to vote any deal up or down, within a fixed period of time and without amendments. For Canada, this meant that American commitments made in the negotiations could not be undone piecemeal by Congress. For the U.S. administration, fast-track authority required approval by the committees and consultation with them during the negotiation process. No objection was raised by the House Ways and Means Committee, where Chairman Dan Rostenkowski and Sam Gibbons, chair of the subcommittee on trade, were both strong supporters of a trade agreement. The Senate was another story, however, and Canada's free trade leap very nearly ended on the rocks of the Senate Finance Committee.

Just days before his fast-track notification to the committees in December, Reagan vetoed a Senate bill to provide aid to the textile industry. Congressional dissatisfaction with the administration's trade policies had been growing for some time, fuelled by a record trade deficit and the president's denial of a role for Congress in trade policy. The Senate bill was an assertion of that role, the veto another denial. In this conflict between executive and legislative branches, key members of the Senate Finance Committee, including Chairman Robert Packwood and John Danforth, chair of the subcommittee on international trade, both Republicans, were looking for a hammer to get the president's attention, and free trade with Canada provided it.

The senators were especially frustrated by Reagan's refusal to take action against what they viewed as unfair trading practices by U.S. trading partners, including Canada. The American lumber industry had for some time complained that exports of Canadian softwood lumber to the U.S. were subsidized. Unable to secure punitive counter-measures from the administration, the industry turned to Congress for a more sympathetic hearing. A number of the members of the Senate Finance Committee joined lumber's cause, including Chairman Packwood and Max Baucus, from Oregon and Montana respectively, two of the largest lumber-producing states. Packwood and Baucus had been the principals in an October letter from the committee to Clayton Yeutter, who had replaced William Brock as U.S. trade representative, that linked free trade to a resolution of the lumber issues. This early signal of trouble was not viewed as a serious problem by the administration, however.

Yeutter wrote back his intention to resolve the issue, and requested immediate negotiations with the Canadians. During the late fall and early winter, Canadian and American officials held talks on lumber, but to no avail as both sides hardened their positions. Despite this impasse, and the October letter from the Finance Committee, the president did nothing special to protect the free trade initiative against the potential for the Senate to return the favour and "veto" *his* trade policy. USTR officials proceeded with business as usual, unwilling to believe that free trade could be tripped up by the relatively minor lumber issue.[22] When the Senate Finance Committee hearings on the president's request for negotiating authority opened on April 11, 1986, however, the hammer dropped.

Yeutter's prepared briefing for the committee was interrupted by a bitter attack by members on the Reagan administration. While some, like Baucus, were upset by the lack of movement on lumber, others, like Danforth, were unhappy with trade policy in general. Most were deeply frustrated over their exclusion from trade policy matters by the White House. Throughout the day, a majority of the members of the committee announced their readiness to veto the start of the negotiations. This included Chairman Packwood, who was working closely with the administration on other elements of its trade policy but was under intense pressure from Oregon lumber interests.

The committee's outburst clearly took Yeutter by surprise. Although aware of congressional frustration with the administration, USTR had simply not believed it would go this far. Never before, throughout the entire post-war era of trade liberalization, had Congress turned down a presidential request for negotiating authority. But this Congress was operating under the 1974 Trade Act, which had shifted significant powers over trade from the president to the legislature. And the committee's authorization hearings were being held under a change to the fast-track procedure that was made expressly to allow members to knock a negotiation off the track if they chose to do so. Finally, even with the trade deficit at a record level, the president seemed determined to continue to deny Congress any role in policy.

The free trade initiative offered senators a golden opportunity to turn the tables on Reagan. Although the revolt began with lumber, the issue quickly became the conduct of trade policy. The revolt did not represent a coordinated attack on the president, however, much less on the free trade initiative. As a senior member of the staff of one senator commented:

> I think the opposition, which had previously not all talked to each other, was somewhat surprised at the depth and strength of the opposition. That didn't become obvious until that day. It took us all by surprise.
>
> This was a member-led and member-dominated thing. Most of the staff had prepared semi-routine memos as to what the issues were and questions to ask and hadn't recommended opposition. It was the members who concluded there was going to be a serious problem.[23]

In a system where senators rarely take positions without the advice of their staffs, this independence was an ominous sign of the seriousness of the committee's opposition. The administration quickly concluded that the senators meant business, and set about trying to turn the game around.

THE ADMINISTRATION RECOVERS

The Canadians were aghast at the fumble. The free trade initiative was a gamble for the Mulroney government, and one with considerable risks. To have it end haphazardly as an incidental victim of presidential-congressional conflict was simply unacceptable. In Ottawa, Derek Burney, now associate under-secretary of state in the Department of External Affairs, spearheaded Canadian efforts to press the U.S. administration to pull out all the stops to secure the committee's approval. In Washington, Canada's ambassador, Allan Gotlieb, lobbied intensely to alter votes.

With 10 votes needed to ensure that a motion to disapprove the negotiations would fail on a tie vote, Yeutter and his staff calculated that they needed to change two votes. Intense pressure from the administration, including direct intervention by Reagan, and Canadian insistence that the initiative could not be delayed or allowed to die, produced the desired effect. Two of the lumber votes, Packwood and Steven Symms of Idaho, were brought around with assurances from the president that the issue would be resolved satisfactorily. Their speedy conversion owed much to a Commerce Department decision, released on April 14, that bolstered the case of the lumber industry on the issue of Canadian subsidies. With lumber satisfied, and the two votes on side, the administration appeared to have recovered.

At a meeting of the Finance Committee on April 22, however, one of the members absent on April 11, William Armstrong of Colorado, whom Yeutter had placed in the president's camp, indicated that he would oppose the request. A vote that day would go against the president. Packwood adroitly called a recess, delaying a final vote until the following day and allowing additional time for presidential arm-twisting.[24] Reagan met with a number of committee members the following morning and distributed a letter sent to Packwood setting out specific goals for the negotiations. This was sufficient for Spark Matsunaga of Hawaii to change his vote.[25] On April 23 a motion requiring the resubmission at a later date of the request for authorization of the negotiations failed by a 10-10 vote. The president had his authority to begin negotiations.

OPENING MANOEUVRES

While the U.S. administration was fumbling and recovering the negotiation ball, Canada was busy trying to shape the negotiating agenda. In an interview on September 14, Brian Mulroney began the Canadian campaign to limit the scope of the negotiations, indicating that issues such as the Strategic Defense Initiative and Arctic sovereignty would not be on the table. Although the prime minister's primary audience was domestic, the statement marked the beginning of government efforts to exclude sensitive issues from the negotiations. At the end of September 1985, Joe Clark announced Canada's intention to exclude the Auto Pact from the negotiations. Clark also subsequently indicated that Canada would not negotiate its subsidies to cultural industries, a position that was repeated by Mulroney before an American audience in December.

In November 1985, Canada gave a clear signal of the importance it attached to the prospective negotiations when Simon Reisman was appointed as chief negotiator. Earlier, on October 15, the prime minister had telephoned Reisman to invite the former senior government official and experienced negotiator to submit his views on the government's free trade initiative. Reisman took the invitation as an opportunity to draft one of the most important memos of his career. His response was a 15-page document in which he set out the issues that would be central to Canada-U.S. free trade, a general approach to their negotiation, and the broad outlines of what a final deal would probably look like. Reisman proposed the negotiation of a big and bold deal to remove virtually all barriers to trade between the two countries. He also identified important areas where exceptions would have to be arranged, including culture, social programs, agricultural marketing arrangements, and the auto sector. Finally, and for good measure, the memo also accused those who opposed free trade of being both ignorant and chauvinistic. The memo obviously struck a responsive chord, and a couple of weeks later Mulroney phoned Reisman again and asked him to come by for a talk. The prime minister offered Reisman the job of chief negotiator, at $1,000 a day, and authorized him to take his staff for a new Trade Negotiations Office from other government departments. With a high-priced chief negotiator and a big, new bureaucracy that would ultimately grow to over one hundred persons to back him up, Ottawa's stake in the negotiations was apparent.

In contrast, the choice in February 1986 of Peter Murphy as chief U.S. negotiator seemed to reflect the relatively low priority Washington attached to the negotiations. As a former chief U.S. textile negotiator and ambassador to the GATT, Murphy was not an inexperienced negotiator. But his appointment came about because Clayton Yeutter, recently confirmed as U.S. trade representative, wanted to replace Murphy with his own man as ambassador at the GATT. That made Murphy available, and Yeutter and his deputy Michael Smith decided that he should take on the bilateral negotiation as his next job. In essence, then, this was just another routine USTR assignment. For personnel, Murphy would have to rely for the most part on regular USTR staff, most of whom would continue with their normal duties within the organization, plus those assigned to the negotiations from individual government departments. What was a big deal for Canada looked very much like small potatoes for the Americans.

Throughout this period, the Americans were engaged in their own efforts to shape the negotiating agenda, concentrating on denying the exclusions that Canada was seeking to establish. When Clayton Yeutter visited Ottawa in November 1985, the newly appointed Reisman declared that "my objective is that by the year 2000 we will have a barrier-free border in goods and services." If the goal were kept that simple, he said, all that would be left would be to negotiate the speed and timing for the removal of barriers. The sweep of the stated objective was classic Reisman bravado, intended to get the big, bold deal front and centre. The exceptions would come later. Yeutter joined the game for his own ends, however, affirming his support for the goal of a broad agreement and declaring that "there should be no exceptions." Elsewhere, Yeutter argued that everything should be subject to negotiation in the talks requested by the president, including the Auto Pact and cultural industries. To do otherwise, he claimed, would threaten the success of the negotiations. The same argument was presented subsequently by U.S. ambassador to Canada Thomas Niles, as well as by Peter Murphy, who added social programs to the list of items that had to be on the table.

Following congressional authorization of the negotiations in April 1986, both countries produced even more detailed statements of appropriate agendas. In his letter to the Senate Finance Committee, Reagan identified clearly the goals that the U.S. would pursue in the negotiations with Canada. Principal among these was the reduction by Canada of government subsidies and support to industry. In addition, Reagan indicated that the U.S. would "retain full access to multilaterally sanctioned United States trade remedies." By this Reagan meant the contingency protection provisions of U.S. trade law that threatened the security of Canadian access to the U.S. market.

International Trade Minister Kelleher, in announcing the date for the first round of negotiations, similarly set out Canadian priorities a few days later. These would include a reduction in American tariffs as well as greater access to government procurement markets in the U.S. In addition, Kelleher indicated that Canada would be seeking relief from trade penalties imposed under the contingency protection provisions of U.S. trade law. In return, he speculated that the Americans would be seeking concessions on trade in services and on protection for intellectual property.

Services and intellectual property had indeed been items on the U.S. agenda as early as the previous summer when Canadian officials took preliminary soundings in Washington to determine whether an agenda could be shaped to satisfy the interests of both countries. However, national treatment and right of establishment for investment were also identified as American priorities, although Kelleher chose not to include them in his speculations. The potential link between American movement on trade remedies and Canadian disciplines on subsidy practices that the Canadians had discerned during the summer meeting between Smith and Burney now seemed to be precluded by the Reagan letter. And as the U.S. backed away from trade remedy law as a negotiable issue, so Canada endeavoured to keep investment off the table.

The differences in Canadian and American views of what would constitute appropriate issues for the negotiations were not resolved prior to the start of the preliminary negotiating sessions in Ottawa on May 21, 1986. The important differences in the agendas of the two countries would subsequently emerge as a significant issue in the negotiation process itself. For the U.S., a central aim of the negotiations would be to secure an agreement that would preclude any more FIRAs or NEPs. In addition, their focus would be on specific trade irritants, especially those involving Canadian subsidy practices. For Canada, on the other hand, the negotiations centred on the need for a new regime on American contingency protection, one that would remove the threat to Canadian exports resulting from the application of U.S. trade remedy laws to Canada.

These differences in agendas were a natural result of quite different definitions of the central trade policy problem facing each country. For Canada, the central problem was the use of the contingency protection measures available to American companies under U.S. trade remedy law to harass Canadian exporters. For the U.S., the problems confronting American trade resulted from the unfair trading practices of other countries, including Canada. The U.S. problem could be addressed in a negotiation focusing on the elimination of unacceptable Canadian practices. The negotiations would also provide an opportunity to develop a regime that would prevent future discrimination against foreign investment. For Canada, however, subsidy practices were not so much trade related as they were aspects of cultural and regional development policy. The Canadian agenda focused instead on the elimination of the means of harassment through the amendment of U.S. contingency protection measures as these applied to Canadians.

The divergence in agendas resulted not only from the different ways in which the two countries defined the trade problem confronting them, but also from the way in which the decision to negotiate evolved for each. On the Canadian side, the decision to negotiate a comprehensive free trade agreement emerged incrementally as a trade policy response to U.S. protectionism. Given the political sensitivity of the free trade issue, this policy development had to be incremental and could only be sustained by emphasizing the goal of securing market access for Canadian exports. This emphasis on market access was directed to the domestic decision-making process, however. It was only following the decision to seek negotiations that the Canadians shifted their public statements to attempt to define the agenda. For their part, the Americans were careful to follow the Canadian lead, emphasizing only their general commitment to trade liberalization. Once Canada's request set in motion the procedures for fast-track authorization, however, congressional imperatives dictated that greater emphasis be given to Canadian trade and investment sins in the formulation of the American agenda.

By May 1986, the long process of getting to the negotiating table was at an end. Canada's historic decision had been made, and had almost fallen incidental victim to Washington politics. The champions had been selected and were ready to square off. For the next two and a half years, free trade would be the dominant issue in Canadian political life.

3

A LONG AND WINDING ROAD

The Canadian journey down the road to free trade started long before the decade of the eighties, in fact a full century before. The journey began with one Macdonald, Conservative Prime Minister Sir John A. and his 1879 National Policy, when tariffs became the chief instrument of economic policy. The end of the road was marked by another Macdonald, a might-have-been Liberal prime minister whose royal commission set the stage for the final dismantling of the National Policy. En route, we will see the embrace of free trade by Canada's two main business lobbies, the Business Council on National Issues, and the Canadian Manufacturers' Association. Between the two Macdonalds, a strategic political role is played by Peter Lougheed, Alberta's premier and the Tory whom Brian Mulroney most respected as the kingpin of Western Canadian politics.

The path from the National Policy to the FTA cannot, however, be traced entirely over Canadian terrain. We must also look at the transformation of U.S. trade policies and political coalitions. Seen only in the context of the past four decades of Canadian politics, the Mulroney initiative on free trade seems like an aberration, a high-risk bilateral exception to the multilateral norm of Canadian trade policy. But it all depends on where one starts the historical journey. When viewed over Canada's 140-year trade policy history, bilateralism is the norm, and multilateralism is the exception. Accordingly, a sense of the longer history of Canadian and American trade policy is a prerequisite to understanding the FTA and the politics that shaped it.

BUSINESS EMBRACES FREE TRADE

The pivotal domestic political event on the longer road to the FTA was the embrace of free trade by the Canadian business community. The manufacturing sector, in particular, abandoned its historic opposition to free trade. An account of this change involves two parallel stories, one about the Business Council on National Issues (BCNI) and the other concerning the Canadian Manufacturers' Association (CMA). Other business lobbies such as the Canadian Chamber of Commerce and the Canadian Federation of Independent Business were also eventually involved, but it was the BCNI and the CMA that led the political way within the business community.

BCNI was the new player in the Canadian business lobby. Since its formation in 1976 it had quickly established a privileged position among business interest groups, primarily because it was composed of the chief executive officers (CEOs) of Canada's biggest multinational and Canadian firms. It had also established an active style of policy advocacy among ministers and senior officials in Ottawa.[1] Its CEOs, who could speak and act quickly on behalf of their firms, also spanned most sectors of the economy. Combined with the personal energy and contacts of its president, Thomas d'Aquino, the BCNI's influence was unmistakable. In contrast, the CMA was a century-old interest group and the chief representative of the manufacturing sector based in central Canada. While not composed of CEOs, it certainly involved many senior business leaders. However, the CMA was a coalition that contained the numerous sub-elements of the manufacturing sector, and this structure dictated a more complex decision process than prevailed at BCNI.

We have already identified the major reasons why the two leading business interest groups changed their position regarding free trade. These included the severe recession of 1982, intense opposition to the interventionist Liberal policies of 1980 and 1981, and fear about growing U.S. protectionism. But an understanding of the business embrace of free trade requires a somewhat more precise account. The BCNI shift to free trade began with its initial establishment of a trade policy committee in 1981, headed by Alton Cartwright, the CEO of Canadian General Electric (CGE). One of the first persons invited to speak to the trade committee was Canadian Senator George Van Roggen. Van Roggen's Senate Committee on Finance had been, along with the Economic Council of Canada, one of the early, lonely advocates of free trade with the United States. Van Roggen himself was viewed very sceptically by the Liberal political machine. The BCNI committee's reaction to Van Roggen's pitch for free trade in 1981 was one of curiosity but caution. Cartwright himself, and his company, CGE, epitomized the 1960s and '70s way of thinking about trade matters. There was a branch-plant confidence in, and comfort with, the status quo. But as the 1982 recession took hold there was a growing sense that something was wrong with the Canadian economy, and with the core of the economic and political relationship with the U.S.

As the BCNI trade committee underwent its own trade policy education, it grew more attracted to the idea of supporting a comprehensive trade-enhancement agreement with the United States. The germ of an idea for a comprehensive agreement was then under discussion within the federal bureaucracy among senior officials such as Gordon Osbaldeston, the head of the Ministry of State for Economic Development. These tentative thoughts did not arise out of some grand plan for free trade, however. Instead, they emerged out of the early discussions over a sectoral approach. Osbaldeston and others simply noted that it would be difficult to have sectoral agreements without an overall framework agreement. A BCNI report advocating a comprehensive agreement was circulated and discussed with trade officials who were then engaged in the government's own trade policy review.

In January 1983, several BCNI members met with U.S. Trade Representative William Brock. Brock was enthusiastic about the prospects for a trade-enhancement deal. If Canadian businessmen could persuade Canada's Trade minister, Gerald Regan, to go for the idea, Brock told his Canadian visitors he was sure he could put together a favourable U.S. coalition and pass a deal within a year. This initial probe was followed by a further testing of the waters on March 23, 1983, when BCNI members met for 90 minutes with the U.S. vice-president, George Bush, during his visit to Toronto. Bush seemed almost stunned by the idea of a comprehensive agreement. He confided that he had not thought of such a possibility, nor of the fact that Canada provided a potential market "the size of another California," as one BCNI member put it. While Bush did not gush with Brock-like enthusiasm, BCNI members came away believing that he was certainly interested.

If U.S. politicians were enthusiastic about a comprehensive trade agreement, American business was not, as BCNI members discovered when they made their first direct test of U.S. business opinion. Shortly after the meeting with Bush, BCNI met with its U.S. counterpart, the American Business Roundtable. There they found the American CEOs to be distinctly uninterested in the prospects for a special trade deal. Nevertheless, BCNI continued to press for a comprehensive trade agreement and for reciprocal trade enhancement. In 1984, with an election in the offing, BCNI brought its idea directly to the Liberal prime minister, John Turner, and his Finance minister, Marc Lalonde, as well as to the opposition leader, Brian Mulroney, and the Conservative trade critic, Michael Wilson. The trade ideas were also a central feature of the BCNI blueprint agenda paper that they presented to the Conservatives as the Tories took power following the 1984 election. Throughout this period, BCNI spoke only of a comprehensive agreement and of enhanced trade, deliberately avoiding the term "free trade."

The embrace of free trade by the Canadian Manufacturers' Association was much more gradual. While Van Roggen's Senate committee was ruminating about free trade in the late 1970s, the CMA polled its own members about their views. The results showed that about one-third favoured free trade, one-third were opposed, and one-third were undecided. CMA strategists read the undecideds as leaning towards the "anti" position, and decided to maintain the association's traditional opposition to free trade. The 1982 recession changed all that, however. The manufacturing sector felt the recession more acutely than did the more varied BCNI membership. Many CMA members were absolutely bludgeoned by the recession as, over a 14-month period, more than 300,000 employees of CMA firms were laid off.

While the recession was the jolt that prompted a new look at the world, other conditions were also important in shifting the CMA stance on free trade. The lowering of tariffs after the Tokyo Round of multilateral trade negotiations and the changes in trade patterns that resulted had gradually increased the degree of involvement in trade of CMA members. In the decade since the early 1970s, the proportion of its member companies that exported had risen from 15 to 40 per cent. The figures were similar for those member firms engaged in importing activity. In short, Canadian manufacturers were more engaged in international trade, and would benefit from a removal of barriers to that trade.

As CMA company executives faced the recession, and experienced Japanese and European business and production technologies first hand, they realized much more concretely that they simply had to increase their own ability to compete. "Competitiveness" became the central theme of a series of CMA position papers, and papers submitted to the trade policy task force in 1982–83 spoke of "preferred access" to the U.S. market. The association also arranged with the Macdonald Commission to be the first group to present a brief to the commission in its public hearings. The CMA wanted to set the tone and to convey the message that it was ready to accept a new policy course. Canadian manufacturers had completed their historic switch to free trade.

THE LOUGHEED FACTOR

While business was shifting direction and key players in the bureaucracy like Derek Burney were moving the free trade option forward, Peter Lougheed was supplying the essential ingredient of political and partisan influence on Brian Mulroney. This influence was multi-faceted and had its roots in the political skills and experiences of Alberta's premier. Lougheed's legendary political will may stem from his days in the early 1960s as a diminutive punt returner for the Edmonton Eskimos in the Canadian Football League. In those days it required special courage to be a punt returner in the CFL, since the rest of the team could not block on the runback of the kick. With no protection against the onrushing tacklers, returning punts was not a prized role — there was the kick, the catch, and the crunch. When Lougheed became the leader of the Alberta Progressive Conservative Party, he faced similar odds against an entrenched rural-based Social Credit government. Lougheed delivered his own kick against the Socreds, however, and quickly took his party from no seats to the government benches.[2] By the early 1980s, Lougheed was in his third term in office, and the dominant politician in Western Canada.

Taking on the promotion of free trade in Tory circles was no more daunting to Lougheed than any of his previous battles. Moreover, the free trade issue offered him an opportunity to gain a satisfying victory over those Eastern Canadian interests, centred in the Trudeau Liberal regime and Ontario, that had imposed the draconian National Energy Program (NEP) on Alberta and on Western Canada. While the NEP was central to Lougheed's political psyche,[3] his political views on free trade were a product of more than just anger over the NEP and traditional Western Canadian alienation. He was one of the few Canadian political leaders who had developed good political contacts in the U.S. Congress, as opposed to the administration. These included friendships with senators such as the late Henry "Scoop" Jackson, a central player on U.S. energy matters. Each spring in the early 1980s, Lougheed had gone to Washington to cultivate his political contacts and test American political moods in the Congress.

Lougheed was also more informed about trade matters than most Canadian political leaders. He had long felt that Alberta had been unfairly treated in the Tokyo GATT round on issues such as petro-chemicals and agriculture. Like many others at that time — the early 1980s — he was worried about U.S. protectionism and he was determined to do something about it. In his 1983 and 1984 Washington visits, he began raising the possibility of using GATT Article 24, the clause that permitted the establishment of free trade areas, to address the problem. He also travelled to Geneva to discuss these issues with GATT leaders. Following one of his Washington sojourns in 1983, Lougheed met Brian Mulroney at a fund-raising event for St. Francis Xavier University, and he outlined his developing ideas on Canada-U.S. free trade. Then a candidate challenging Tory leader Joe Clark, Mulroney was a trade neophyte who had already expressed opposition to free trade. Lougheed saw Mulroney again in 1984 and again discussed his trade ideas with him. Lougheed had little respect for Joe Clark, his fellow Albertan and a former prime minister, but he was beginning to see in Mulroney both a far better politician and a potential friend of Western Canada. He continued to cultivate the relationship, and when the Mulroney Conservatives released their Prince Albert statement containing an array of policies for Western Canada, it included the dismantling of the NEP, an unmistakable imprint of the Mulroney-Lougheed alliance.

The final event in the new leadership chemistry occurred in February 1985 at the Mulroney government's inaugural first ministers' conference in Regina. Lougheed requested, and Mulroney agreed, that Alberta lead the discussion when the economic portion of the agenda came up. Once again Lougheed advocated free trade, with Mulroney listening attentively. By this time,

Lougheed knew that fellow Western Premiers Bill Bennett and Grant Devine, and even Manitoba's NDP Premier Howard Pawley, would support his initiative. There is little doubt that Lougheed's influence was important in persuading Mulroney to take on the political risks associated with the free trade initiative. It helped convince Mulroney that a deal would facilitate the healing process with Western Canada. In addition, Mulroney trusted and respected Lougheed's political judgement. If free trade made sense to the dean of Tory premiers, it was fine for Canada's newest Tory first minister too.

Peter Lougheed left office in November 1985, but he influenced later aspects of the free trade story as well. As we show in Chapter 9, he was an active player in the pro-free trade coalition, the Canadian Alliance for Trade and Job Opportunities. Lougheed was also a major factor in keeping the opposition of Ontario Premier David Peterson muted. Between the premiers' conference in August 1985 and the 1988 Calgary Olympics, Lougheed never lost an opportunity to remind Peterson that if free trade were lost because of Ontario's opposition there would be irrevocable damage to national unity. Western Canadian interests would have been twice thwarted by Eastern Canada in the same decade. In Lougheed's political thinking, the FTA and the NEP were firmly intertwined.

THE MACDONALD COMMISSION:
BIPARTISAN BLESSINGS

Donald Macdonald's role in the free trade story provides the irony that makes politics interesting and unpredictable. In the mid-1970s he was Peter Lougheed's nemesis as federal Energy minister, when he introduced many of Ottawa's first interventionist energy policies. But in the free trade election of 1988, Macdonald and Lougheed were joint chairmen of the pro-free trade coalition. Throughout his political career Macdonald was known as a strongly partisan Liberal and a member of the nationalist wing of his party. Yet he and the commission he headed provided non-partisan legitimacy for free trade and a reduction in the role of government as a policy for Canada's economic salvation.

The Royal Commission on the Economic Union and Development Prospects for Canada (the Macdonald Commission) was established by the Trudeau government in the midst of the constitutional battles and economic turmoil of the early 1980s. It was initially seen by Liberal strategists as a way of supplying greater intellectual justification for enhanced federal powers in relation to the provinces in an era of increasing global interdependence. The phrase "the economic union" in the commission's title and mandate referred to Canada's internal economic unity and the threat that was posed to it by balkanizing provincial policies and practices. The "development prospects" that were to be examined were Canada's long-term prospects for economic growth in the wake of the 1982 recession, a subject that also justified a wide-ranging look at the effectiveness of Canada's basic political institutions in the promotion of growth.

Thirteen commissioners were drawn from across Canada and included a considerable range of partisan and philosophical views. The commission began its work in 1983 and did not table its final report until September 1985. At the mid-point of the commission's work, one staffer deadpanned that the report would probably be long enough to include "one page for every Canadian"! The prospect was not entirely unlikely, since the commission held extensive hearings across Canada and produced more than 70 research studies and a final report of nearly 2,000 pages. After its first year of operation, Donald Macdonald was acutely aware of the fact that his unwieldy think-tank needed a unifying theme. That theme emerged in November 1984 when Macdonald went public with his now famous "leap of faith" statement advocating free trade. It occurred at a conference held in New York State and attended by several Canadians, including *Globe and Mail* reporter William Johnson. Macdonald's statement was originally made off the record, but Johnson asked if he would repeat it for the record, and Macdonald agreed. Johnson showed Macdonald the draft of the article he intended to write. Macdonald suggested a few changes, and the "leap of faith" statement became a part of Canadian history.

While at this stage Macdonald had not convinced his fellow commissioners of the value of free trade, his public use of the words made the concept more acceptable in polite company. The process of de-mythologizing free trade in Canada had received an important boost. The November 1984 statement was not inspired only by the immediate need for a unifying theme for his commission's report, however. The transformation in Macdonald's views had begun earlier that year. One pivotal event was a visit to Sweden in April 1984. Accompanying him on the trip was fellow commissioner Albert Breton, the distinguished economist from the University of Toronto. Macdonald was already trying out his free trade arguments on Breton, who seemed open to persuasion but was not convinced. It seems paradoxical that support for free trade would come out of a visit to Sweden, but in fact Macdonald was very impressed in his discussions with Swedish officials, businessmen, and bankers with the extent to which Sweden had already eliminated its tariffs and was trading competitively in the larger European market. If a country with half Canada's population could achieve this, then in Macdonald's view Canada could as well.[4] Macdonald also saw Sweden's social welfare and labour market policies as a key part of that country's economic success. Some of these policy links would show up in the final report of the commission, in the form of proposals for an extensive adjustment fund and a guaranteed annual income to accompany free trade. The proposals were largely ignored by the Mulroney government, however.[5]

A second influence on Macdonald's adoption of free trade came from the business community's own presentations, public and private, to him and his commission in 1983 and early 1984. Despite the recession, or perhaps because of it, business interests almost uniformly told Macdonald that they could compete with the Americans and with the world if given the chance. Macdonald was impressed by this expression of Canadian entrepreneurial nationalism. As he frequently said to his staff and fellow commissioners,

"If these people say they can compete in a free market, who am I to say that they cannot?"

The final factor shaping Macdonald's views was his early discussions with key commission advisers, such as University of Western Ontario economist John Whalley. Whalley had been brought in initially to look at the problem of interprovincial barriers to internal economic union, but he quickly concluded that this was not the central economic problem facing Canadians. Instead, the main problem confronting Canada, according to Whalley, was gaining access to a larger market in which it could achieve economies of scale, enhanced productivity, and a new competitiveness. This view was reinforced by Macdonald's meetings with other economists such as the Wonnacott brothers, Paul and Ron, who had long advocated free trade for Canada, and by the lobbying efforts of Richard Lipsey and Wendy Dobson of the C.D. Howe Institute. The influence of these Canadian economists during the agenda-setting phase of the free trade process should not be underestimated. They made the case that high gains and low adjustment costs could be expected from continued trade liberalization. This position was adopted in the work of the Macdonald Commission where it was reinforced by the commission's own researchers, academics such as Gil Winham, a political scientist from Dalhousie University, and David Laidler, another economist from the University of Western Ontario, as well as by Michael Hart, who had been seconded to the commission from External Affairs where he had worked for Derek Burney on the trade policy review. All of these were strong free trade advocates.

Despite his early public advocacy of free trade, it was not until the very end of the writing process that Macdonald brought most of his fellow commissioners on side. There were minority reports on this issue, but the commission as a whole, despite many reluctant pens, signed on to Macdonald's own choice of the words "free trade" in the report. On its release, the commission's product became instantly known as the free trade report. It argued that Canada needed expanded and more secure access to the large

American market, that vastly improved productivity for manufacturing could only come from free market competition, and that GATT multilateral negotiations, although preferable, were too slow and cumbersome for the problems at hand.[6] The commission also argued that a free trade agreement would enhance national unity because it would remove a major source of regional alienation, the tariff, and because all regions could gain economically from free trade.

The Macdonald Commission's vision of a future agreement was simultaneously bolder and more conservative than the final 1988 FTA, depending on the provisions at issue. It proposed a much more elaborate "court-like" dispute-settlement machinery that would, in principle, have involved a much larger surrender of sovereignty than that required by the FTA. On the other hand, it expressed caution about any open inclusion of services, agriculture, energy, or culture.[7] It was also ambiguous in its treatment of investment. The commission made no attempt at a strategic analysis of how to negotiate with the United States. However, it suggested the core trade-off would have to involve a reduction in Canadian subsidies and expanded U.S. opportunities for trade in services in exchange for guarantees of improved access for Canadian exports through the imposition of constraints on U.S. trade remedies, especially countervailing duties. Last, but certainly not least, the commission advocated major social and labour market policy changes as necessary accompaniments to its free trade and other market-oriented proposals. In the commission's view, free trade and broader competitive pressures required far better social and labour adjustment policies, or Canada would not survive economically or socially. The commission did not directly link free trade with the need for a large adjustment program. However, when combining free trade with a number of other major market-oriented policies, such as privatization and deregulation, the commission argued that the uncertainty created for Canadians required a new social contract where the working poor, in particular, could be given better opportunities. The commission's social and labour market proposals were frequently forgotten in the rhetoric of the free trade debate but, as we show in Chapter 11, they ought to be an essential part of the reality of a post-FTA world in the 1990s and beyond.

The Mulroney government was fully briefed on the content of the Macdonald Commission report well before the report's release in early September 1985. Alan Nymark, the commission's policy director and later a senior official in the TNO, was briefing both the Finance Department and the Privy Council Office in May and June of 1985. Mulroney was impressed by the commission's work and its line of argument. And the politician in him knew that the endorsement of free trade by a prominent Liberal and former Finance minister like Donald Macdonald was politically advantageous. As his government struggled in the summer of 1985 to put a new face on its frayed image, the Macdonald Commission supplied both intellectual and bipartisan legitimacy for its emerging free trade plans. The fact that business support, Lougheed's influence, and the report of the Macdonald Commission were all necessary to the making of the free trade decision raises an important question. What was it about free trade that made it so politically risky? The answer lies in even earlier historical stages on the road to the FTA, beginning with the other Macdonald, Sir John A., and with the evolution of trade policy and politics in the United States.

THE NATIONAL POLICY AS SECOND PRIZE

Prime Minister John A. Macdonald is rightly portrayed in Canadian history as both the chief architect of Confederation in 1867 and the author of the 1879 National Policy of high tariffs. Less celebrated in Canada's historical mythology is the fact that the second of these initiatives was Macdonald's second choice. To appreciate this fact, we must briefly retrace the Confederation story. Confederation established a new political community and an economic common market in Canada, but only after the failure to reinstitute the Reciprocity Treaty of 1854.[8] The 1854 treaty between Canada and the United States was a limited free trade agreement, mainly involving natural resource products, including minerals, forest products, fish, meat, dairy, and several agricultural products. Most manufactured goods were excluded, in part because tariffs on them were the key source of government revenues. The Reciprocity Treaty contributed to a long period of economic prosperity in Canada. But in 1866 it was abrogated by the United States, partly because of domestic economic pressure, and partly because of antagonism over Canada's actions during the American Civil War. Canada's interest in the 1854 Reciprocity Treaty originated in the ending of another special bilateral trade relationship — the one with Britain. When Britain repealed the Corn Laws in 1846, it brought to an end imperial preferences for its colonies' produce and forced the search in Canada for alternative markets. After Confederation there were immediate attempts, in 1869, 1871, and 1874, to negotiate a new trade arrangement with the United States. These failed primarily because of strong protectionist sentiment in the U.S. Congress.

It is in this sense that Macdonald's National Policy of 1879 was second prize for Canada, a reaction to the U.S. rejection of efforts to reinstitute reciprocity.[9] The National Policy imposed high tariffs to protect Canadian manufacturing, but Macdonald also viewed it as a device to persuade the United States to agree to another free trade pact. Throughout these bilateral beginnings, free trade was politically popular in Canada. The political risks associated with free trade grew only after business interests had grown accustomed to the protective cover of the National Policy. By the 1891 election, business support for protectionism was strong enough that Macdonald easily turned back the Liberals, who had campaigned on a policy of unrestricted reciprocity (free trade) with the United States. Second prize had become the electoral gold ring for Macdonald and his Conservatives.

POLITICAL GHOSTS OF 1911

Ultimately, however, it was the ghosts of the 1911 election that the Mulroney free trade initiative had to exorcise. The Liberal government of Wilfrid Laurier had negotiated a reciprocity treaty with the

U.S. following an American initiative for free trade. The pact was put to the electoral test, and the 1911 election became the last great free trade election prior to 1988. Although there were other issues involved, the election turned largely on the trade question. Financial and manufacturing interests united behind the Conservatives, headed by Robert Borden who mounted a strong nationalist campaign to defeat the Laurier Liberals. While the 1911 election rang the death knell for free trade, there were several further behind-the-scenes efforts to revive it. Ministerial initiatives by Canada were made in 1922 and 1923, but died in the face of a protectionist drift in U.S. policy. In 1935 and 1938, modest bilateral trade agreements were achieved under a new regime of U.S. trade legislation designed to untangle the disastrous effects of the super-protectionist 1930 Smoot-Hawley Act, American trade legislation that had greatly worsened the depression of the 1930s.

The last free trade effort prior to the 1986–87 negotiation was in 1947. Prime Minister Mackenzie King had seized on another U.S. initiative, but did so through secret negotiations. This venture failed because of King's own caution, fuelled by memories of the Laurier election, and because of considerable uncertainty about just how the deal would be approved in the U.S. There existed nothing like the present fast track, which forces Congress to accept or reject a whole package, rather than being able to amend it in classic congressional log-rolling fashion. A couple of lessons were drawn from these various attempts to pursue free trade.[10] While these were not cast in stone, they became part of the conventional wisdom for subsequent political leaders and trade negotiators. The first and most obvious was that the trade relationship with the United States is always vital, and largely beneficial. But at the same time, free trade discussions evoke intense nationalist feelings because they concern the very definition of Canada in relation to the giant to the south. As a result, they involve great political risk. Furthermore, a free trade initiative would be more likely to succeed if it was seen to come from Canada, rather than the U.S. At the same time, it is extremely difficult for Canada to attract sufficient political interest in the U.S. to overcome the classic American indifference to Canada. These lessons would be applied in the 1980s as well.

MULTILATERAL IDEALS AND BILATERAL REALITIES

From 1947 until the FTA, Canada's trade policy was built on the proposition that Canadian trading interests were best advanced through multilateral negotiations under the General Agreement on Tariffs and Trade (GATT). GATT was itself one of the trio of international institutions devised after the war to help ensure that economic reconstruction would occur and that a repetition of the depression of the 1930s would be forever avoided. This institution-building era was led by the United States, but Canada, as a significant power in the post-war world, played a major role in the design of the institutions. The GATT joined the International Monetary Fund and the World Bank to provide the international institutional foundation for Western economies.

GATT was in fact an institution that evolved out of a more ambitious plan to create an International Trade Organization (ITO).[11] GATT was established initially as a temporary agreement until the ITO was in place. The ITO never did materialize, however, largely because the United States Congress failed to ratify it. GATT is therefore more an agreement and a set of processes than it is an organization with any substantive policing powers. As it has evolved, a number of aspects of its institutional role have become important. Successive rounds of negotiations (the Dillon, Kennedy, Tokyo, and the current Uruguay Rounds) have brought tariffs down and reduced other barriers to trade, contributing greatly to liberalized trade and post-war economic prosperity. Consultation, investigation, and settlement procedures for trade disputes have evolved through the GATT as well. Though these are often slow and cumbersome, given the diverse interests of the approximately one hundred members of GATT, they are nonetheless still superior to trade wars. Finally, GATT has entrenched two major principles essential to the long-term achievement of liberalized trade. The two are the principles of most favoured nation (MFN) and national treatment (NT).[12] Underlying both is the concept of non-discrimination, which ensures security of market access. This security is necessary to underpin investment decisions designed to exploit comparative advantage among countries. MFN is the principle that addresses the issue of external discrimination among foreigners. It ensures that goods produced by country A will be treated at the border no less favourably than those of country B. It is a principle extended unconditionally in that its benefits are available to any member of GATT.

National treatment is the principle that addresses the issue of internal discrimination between foreigners and domestic interests once the border has been crossed. It ensures that once goods have entered, they will be treated no less favourably than goods of domestic origin with respect to the application of domestic laws, taxes, regulations, and other measures. It is important to stress that national treatment does not imply that one must treat incoming goods the same way they are treated in the *exporting* country. It is domestic laws that cannot discriminate. For example, Canada may have more stringent environmental laws governing products than the United States, as long as they are applied equally to both foreign and Canadian producers of those goods. Of the two GATT principles, MFN is by far the more entrenched. National treatment is far more controversial. Indeed, existing GATT agreements formally permit two exceptions to the principle, in the areas of procurement decisions by government and domestic production subsidies.

The achievements of the GATT regime are considerable, but its history and that of Western post-war trading relationships must be seen in the context of other imperatives of Western political and economic systems. Western governments, Canada among them, have certainly leaned strongly in a pro-market policy direction by supporting successive tariff reductions. But because free markets also produce economic casualties, Western governments, driven by strong domestic regional and interest group pressure, have simultaneously erected new forms of protection, called nontariff barriers.

Although they are not tariffs, they are barriers nonetheless. De-signed to take the rough edges off the market, they are viewed by domestic interests threatened by competition as policies to promote fairness, regional equity, or to stabilize things until a smoother adjustment to market forces can occur. The day of adjustment is frequently postponed indefinitely, however.

These new barriers escalated in volume and political ingenuity in the 1970s. But by the end of the Tokyo Round, knowledgeable voices in the Canadian trade policy community were expressing alarm at what was happening. One of these, Rodney Grey, sug-gested that these barriers, which he called devices for contingency protection, were undermining the benefits of GATT's earlier rounds of liberalization.[13] He was also among the first to publicly draw attention to the growing threat of U.S. protectionism, especially countervail practices. The failure in wider Canadian political circles to recognize the threat of emerging patterns in trade policy was undoubtedly a product of the overall success of the GATT in the 1950s and 1960s in promoting trade liberalization and economic prosperity. This success produced a new conventional wisdom in Canada about the durability of the liberal multilateral trade regime. The first formal test of its strength came in 1971 when the U.S. acted unilaterally to cut imports by imposing a surcharge on imported goods, and refused to grant Canada an exemption. Canada replied with its so-called "Third Option," which formally rejected closer integration with the United States in favour of diversified multilat-eral ties. The option took the explicit form of attempting to build a contractual link with Western Europe.[14]

Reinforced by both the successes and the mythology of Pearson-ian international diplomacy, the multilateral consensus took hold. But a more accurate description of actual Canadian policy over the entire period from 1947 to the early 1980s would show how the practice of multilateralism was often bilateralism under a different name. During the various rounds of multilateral GATT negotiations, Canada of necessity concentrated on bilateral Canada-U.S. trade. This bilateral focus permitted Canada "to pursue multilateralism without losing the margin of protection inherent in the National Policy of 1879."[15] After the Kennedy and Tokyo multilateral rounds, Canada's tariffs were still higher than those of the U.S., even though both were coming down. When the FTA negotiations began in 1986, the average Canadian tariff on dutiable imports was about 9 to 10 per cent compared to an average American tariff of 4 to 5 per cent.

Canada also saw fit to do a couple of special bilateral deals with the U.S. in the midst of its multilateral pursuits. First was the Defence Production Sharing Arrangement of 1959. This defence production pact between Canada and the United States was a direct result of the Diefenbaker government's decision in 1958 to cancel the production of the all-Canadian Avro Arrow jet fighter aircraft, partly under pressure from the U.S. To fill this manufacturing gap, the Conservatives negotiated the defence production pact, which provided Canada with guaranteed industrial access to a major part of the U.S. defence procurement market. Even more significant was the Automobile Products Trade Agreement of 1965. The Auto Pact resulted from an effort by Canada to head off a countervail suit launched in the U.S. by auto parts manufacturers against a Canadian duty remission program. The program was a Canadian response to the productivity crisis of the Canadian auto industry. The Canadian industry had built up behind high tariff walls, and suffered from the classic problems of high cost production due to short production runs forced by the small Canadian market. The Auto Pact provided for tariff-free trade in autos and original parts. It also contained investment safeguards for the Canadian industry, giving Canada the right to limit duty-free access to those firms that produced roughly as many cars in Canada as they sold in the country. Simon Reisman was a key member of the Canadian negotiating team.

This multilateral phase of Canada's trade policy history clearly was different in focus from the previous 90 years of largely bilateral trade policy. But there was still far more bilateral content than is often granted in the exaggerated accounts of the golden age of Canadian multilateralism. It is true, however, that the economic success of the GATT regime had largely de-politicized trade policy, shunting it off the main political agenda for discussion among members of a private club of trade professionals.

THE AMERICAN MERCANTILISTS' REVENGE

For the period from 1945 to the early 1970s, the United States was indisputably the world's dominant economy. Its technology led the industrialized world, and its trade policy was very much an adjunct of its foreign policy. The liberalized system of trade represented by the GATT was largely an American creation. Along with the IMF, the World Bank, and NATO, it was seen by the Americans as a support for a healthy world economy and also as an important weapon in the fight against Communism. Liberalism was a policy that Americans could afford since, unlike Canada, the U.S. was not heavily dependent on trade. Merchandise trade accounted for only about 5 per cent of its GNP (gross national product). At the same time, trade issues were manageable in the American political system because of the existence of a dominant, and fairly stable, congressional coalition in support of trade liberalization. The coalition reflected regional cleavages over trade, with the export-oriented South being inclined to favour free trade (much like Western Canada) and the industrial Northeast and Midwest supporting the tariff. The congressional seniority system for allocating committee chairmanships reinforced the stability of these underlying coalitions. There was less room than there would be in the late 1970s and early 1980s for congressional mavericks to play their own trade games.

The liberal orientation of trade policy in U.S. politics was not just a product of American domination of the international economy and general post-war prosperity. It was also a reaction to the excesses brought on by the Smoot-Hawley Tariff Act of 1930.[16] This statute represented U.S. protectionism at its most extreme, and it was indelibly associated in American minds with the Great Depression. Virtually every change in U.S. trade policy since its passage was directed against this unpleasant historical memory. Smoot-Hawley also reflected the pernicious effects of trade policy made directly by log-rolling politics in the U.S. congressional system. Under the U.S. Constitution, Congress is given several express powers over taxation, duties, imports and excises, and the regulation of commerce with foreign countries. As world commerce expanded, with the U.S. at its centre, congressional control over trade law made it increasingly difficult for other countries to try to make trade agreements with the United States. Deals made with the U.S. administration could not be relied on, since Congress could gut them during the approval process. As a result, soon after Smoot-Hawley there began a process of delegating trade policy to the president, but always with the retained right of congressional oversight.

Under the Reciprocal Trade Agreements Act of 1934, Congress delegated to the president the authority to negotiate agreements with other countries to reduce tariffs. With each subsequent renewal of this central trade law there were inevitable rounds of horsetrading between the president and Congress. As a result, each addition of delegated authority was accompanied by new provisions for congressional oversight. For example, in 1974 the legislation extended presidential authority to cover non-tariff areas and included provisions for the fast-track procedure eventually used for the FTA negotiations. But it simultaneously limited presidential discretion concerning where trade remedy law must apply. In the early 1970s, there began a gradual breakdown in the established trade policy coalitions of U.S. politics, and renewed support for protectionism led to increased use of trade remedy laws against foreign producers. Without doubt the most important cause was the challenge to U.S. economic dominance from Japan, West Germany, and, in specific sectors, the newly industrializing countries. The decline in the American position was evident in growing trade deficits. The U.S. was accustomed to being on top, and its people could not easily acknowledge that other countries might be producing superior goods, even though they were buying them in increasing quantities. The temptation to lash out against "unfair traders" in response was powerful. And it was given momentum by the breakdown in the regional stability of the pro- and anti-free-trade coalitions in the U.S. Congress. The transformation of the world economy, the growing importance of the service sector, and the decline of the U.S. industries that now make up the so-called "rust belt" meant that free-traders were increasingly pitted against anti-freetraders *within* regions. This greater dispersion of opposing forces made congressional log-rolling on trade matters not only more likely, but also more unpredictable in its effects.

The intensity of log-rolling was also aided by conditions within Congress.[17] The seniority system for committees broke down and individual legislators became more independent. The positions of the Republican and Democratic parties also changed. The Republicans had been the traditional protectionist party while the Democrats were the trade liberalizers. By the 1980s these positions had reversed. Trade policy also became a more intense focus for partisan differences on economic policy because a consensus existed among the parties on macroeconomic policy. The Reagan years were marked by growing budgetary deficits, financed by foreigners who bid up the value of the American dollar. The overvalued dollar made American goods more expensive in foreign markets and worsened an already serious trade deficit. The budget deficit could not be dealt with effectively because the Reagan administration had succeeded in its efforts to put tax increases beyond the political pale. Democratic presidential candidate Walter Mondale's tax plan in the 1984 election led to his political annihilation. From that point, Democrats were forced to demonstrate their differences from Republicans by emphasizing their protectionist hues on trade policy. While the Reagan administration ideologically believed in free trade, its rhetoric could not always be matched by reality. By 1985, with a variety of protectionist trade bills circulating in Congress, Reagan's trade policy was increasingly driven by the need to deal with short-term political pressures at home.

The U.S. was also losing faith in GATT, and was more willing to consider bilateral trade deals. As we pointed out previously, U.S. Trade Representative William Brock had indicated as early as 1983 that the U.S. would be prepared to look at a reciprocal arrangement with Canada, if Canadians initiated the process. While this bilateral aspect of U.S. trade policy was no doubt quite genuine, it was also a tactical effort to gain some leverage against the European Community and Japan, which were developing their own trading blocs. Finally, it was evident that the U.S. administration wanted to ensure that three newly important areas of trade were elevated to the top of the international agenda. These were investment, services, and intellectual property. The removal of barriers to investment had been a long-standing goal of U.S. policy. In the Canadian case, the U.S. wanted an end to all such controls. The services sector was also a key element in the American view of its international comparative advantage. The new pro-free trade coalition was in many ways being led in the U.S. by the service sector. And intellectual property issues were seen as an important beachhead for American high technology firms. Concern here was primarily with certain Third World countries that U.S. firms alleged were pirating electronic products. But there were also concerns with Canada's treatment of drug patents.

While these were important issues on the U.S. trade agenda, they were not the core Canadian-American trade issues. Instead, the two countries were in conflict over the increasing use of trade remedy law by U.S. firms and industries. There are four main types of action that American interests can launch under their trade remedy laws, all sanctioned by GATT. These are escape-clause actions, anti-dumping and countervailing duties, and general restrictions on imports where countries are engaged in unfair trade practices. Escape-clause or *safeguard* actions do not require proof of foreign misbehaviour. Trade may well be occurring fairly, even though American industries are suffering "serious" injury. The American action on imports of cedar shakes and shingles from Canada, announced the day after the start of the free trade negotiations, was taken under this safeguard provision. *Anti-dumping* measures, on the other hand, may be taken when firms "dump" their products in the U.S. at prices which are below average costs. *Countervail* actions result from unfair trade practices caused by foreign government actions, especially subsidies.

A study of the use of U.S. trade remedies against Canada between 1980 and 1986 shows that 51 actions were taken, split fairly evenly among escape-clause, anti-dumping, and countervailing duties. Similar actions had occurred in the 1970s, but their incidence escalated sharply after 1980.[18] And more than 75 per cent of preliminary rulings by the U.S. International Trade Commission (ITC) went against Canada. While the number of final rulings against Canada was not as high, Canadian concerns centred on the ominous trend, especially the increasing political influence evident in the decisions of the ITC. The inherent harassment potential of these actions was also worrisome, since they increased export, and therefore investment, uncertainty for Canadian firms selling into the American market.

American arguments about other countries' trade practices, including Canada's, were not entirely without merit. But the American view that other countries were subsidizers and unfair traders, and the U.S. was not, was becoming a dangerous obsession. And the separation of powers in the presidential-congressional system allowed the U.S. to play the harassment game very successfully. The U.S. administration was able to lay the blame for trade remedy law on Congress, arguing that the legislature was beyond the president's control. Nor was the government responsible for the decisions of its citizens to litigate against foreign producers under these trade remedy laws. This was their right as citizens. Finally, the administration could warn other countries that they had better not complain about the trade remedy laws too bitterly, because they provided a safety valve, affording protection against the even more blatant forms of protectionism that would occur if the full-scale congressional log-rolling that prevailed in the 1930s was ever unleashed again.

Like the Keynesian economic strategies that held sway in the aftermath of the Second World War, the pro-free trade, pro-market economic orthodoxy of the mid-1980s was driven in equal parts by a fear of the past economic depression, by economic and political evidence, and by ideology. The long and winding road to the FTA returned Canada to its bilateral beginnings. The route proceeded via the transformation of U.S. trade coalitions and the American politics of trade. It also required the political leadership of Peter Lougheed and the conversion of Donald Macdonald, who must stand as one of the oddest couples of Canadian politics in the 1980s. And most important, the road was marked by a change in the historical posture of the leadership of the Canadian business community toward free trade, a change that accelerated Canada down the road to free trade.

4

ADDING UP THE DEAL

One of the more graphic images of the great Canadian free trade battle was the television clip of Simon Reisman, the FTA in hand and tongue in cheek, wishing John Turner luck with Turner's promise to "tear up the agreement." The Canada-United States Free Trade Agreement that took effect on January 1, 1989, is a daunting read. The size of a telephone book, it is a volume that once put down is truly hard to pick up. Despite its massive size and legal jargon, we need to look at the structure and key provisions of the FTA. Only in this way can we assess the political nature of the bargain struck and come to grips with the political controversies that accompany the fine art of adding up the FTA. In later chapters, we deal more directly with the main economic criteria for assessing the negotiations.

The FTA consists of eight parts, 21 chapters, 153 articles, three agreed letters and numerous annexes.[1] The best initial way to appreciate its content is through a simple listing of the titles of its 21 chapters. The first table included here supplies this view of the FTA at a glance. Fourteen of the 21 chapters deal with issues or rules that are horizontal in nature, meaning that they cut across the entire economy. Six chapters deal more directly with vertical sectors of the economy such as autos, energy, and agriculture, and one chapter deals with an *ad hoc* list of trade irritants. This simple listing helps

THE FTA AT A GLANCE:
CHAPTERS OF THE AGREEMENT

1. Objectives and Scope
2. General Definitions
3. Rules of Origin for Goods
4. Border Measures
5. National Treatment
6. Technical Standards
7. Agriculture
8. Wine and Distilled Spirits
9. Energy
10. Trade in Automotive Goods
11. Emergency Action
12. Exceptions for Trade in Goods
13. Government Procurement
14. Services
15. Temporary Entry for Business Persons
16. Investment
17. Financial Services
18. Institutional Provisions
19. Binational Dispute Settlement in Antidumping and Countervailing Duty Cases
20. Other Provisions
21. Final Provisions
    Agreed Letters

explain why the agreement is viewed as a big, broad deal, and why many had difficulty assessing its overall, and sectoral, consequences. There was no precedent in the Canadian experience for a single negotiation of this magnitude. Also important, there are no separate chapters on the most contentious aspects of the free trade debate, items on the Canadian agenda such as cultural, social, or regional development policies, or on American concerns like intellectual property. Yet all of these were central to the free trade negotiations, and the debate that followed.

Many of the key sections of the FTA consolidate or elaborate Canada's GATT obligations. Thanks to general illiteracy in trade policy, however, most of these were unknown to Canadians, even though they had been obligations for decades. While the FTA was seen politically as an alternative to GATT, in fact it contains numerous GATT features, and had to adhere to GATT rules about the establishment of free trade areas. Finally, the FTA contains many features that are truly path-breaking in relation to existing world trade law and policy. These include provisions on investment, services, agriculture, and rules of origin. The FTA also truly institutionalizes the Canada-U.S. bilateral relationship. This occurs mainly through the dispute-settlement provisions in Chapters 18 and 19, but it is also reflected in numerous other sections where provisions for consultation and joint study are identified, including the contentious issue of subsidies.

Assessing the FTA Bargain

Most people interested in the FTA want to assess the bargain that was struck, and to do so we must deal with the problems inherent in evaluating the agreement.[2] At the broadest level, Canadians are interested in the actual short- and long-term economic and political consequences of the FTA. Although an assessment of many of these effects must await the test of time, the probable impact of free trade on Canada's capacity to make trade, industrial, and social policies is the focus of Chapter 11, and the politics and economics of the FTA are dealt with in Chapter 12. But in the 1987–88 period, Canadians were making judgements about whether the internal political trade-offs *within* the deal as a whole were good for Canada. Were Canadian negotiators successful in getting a reasonable deal, or were they out-negotiated? Others were concerned primarily about judging the deal within sectors. Were the gains and losses in financial services balanced? Did Canada lose or gain in the auto provisions?

An effort to assess the bargain struck in the FTA must bear in mind that in a deal of this scope, gains and losses occur across the agreement as a whole. Indeed, this is why a sectoral approach to free trade with the U.S. was unsuccessful in 1983–84. There is no law of negotiation that says a party must win in each sector or the deal is not a good one. In fact, such a requirement would likely make a negotiated agreement impossible to achieve, because the other party would be unlikely to accept such a bargain. Looking at the FTA as a whole also raises issues regarding the kind of scoring or grading system that might be used. For example, suppose the United States had 10 specific medium-sized items on its negotiating agenda, its so-called "irritants list," and succeeded in achieving gains on six. Suppose further that Canada had three large issues and succeeded in achieving gains on two. How is the score kept in this instance? Is this a six to two whipping at the hands of the Yankee trader, or is it a 600-plus batting average for both sides? Or should diving and swimming rules be applied and a "degree of difficulty" factor be added to the calculus? If so, perhaps the Canadian achievement of binational panel reviews of U.S. trade remedy decisions deserves an especially high weighting. And finally, how does one score items successfully kept off the agenda? None of these are easy questions, and the complexity of assessment helps account for the political bias that often accompanies FTA scorekeeping.

A further problem in adding up the FTA lies in how to deal with the different ways of expressing claims concerning gains and losses. Evidence can be cited in terms of provisions involving new rules or the elimination of existing rules, having current policies and practices grandfathered (recognized), protection against potential future actions by the other side, and the promise of policy gains when the other country makes good on promises of future action. Last, but hardly least, as one surveys the agreement there is the practical task of assessing it against the stated objectives of both Canada and the United States. Canada stated its goals first in terms of "enhanc-ing and securing markets," but as political rhetoric escalated in 1986-87, the security goal was expressed as a demand for a new trade remedy regime. For its part, the United States brandished a list of trade irritants against Canada and proclaimed a desire for progress in areas such as services and intellectual property, while unpleasant memories of the National Energy Program and Foreign Investment Review Agency remained sharp in American minds. All of these problems with scorecard logic have to be kept in mind for the assessment of the FTA that follows. In Chapter 12 we offer an overall judgement on the politics of the negotiation by relating the agreement to criteria such as process, agenda, and goals. As a first step, however, a summary of the provisions, controversies, and gains and losses associated with the various elements of the agree-ment is provided in the tables that follow as a guide to the assess-ment.

THE HEART OF FREE TRADE

The first six chapters of the FTA deal with the core ingredients of traditional trade policy — tariffs, related border measures and principles such as national treatment, items that lie at the heart of any free trade agreement. Most important, they provide for the elimination of tariffs either immediately or over agreed five- or 10-year reduction schedules in various industrial sectors. While tariffs come down, they are replaced by a complex new system of rules of origin, designed to ensure that only goods made in Canada or the United States are admitted. This means that most goods must incur 50 per cent of manufacturing costs in either or both countries. While the establishment and extension of the principle of national treatment was simply a reassertion of existing GATT principles, it was significant, and controversial, because it was extended to new areas such as services and investment. For free trade advocates, this principle was the essence of liberal economics. For anti-free trade

TARIFFS AND BORDER MEASURES
(CHAPTERS 2 TO 6)

KEY PROVISIONS	ISSUES, CONTROVERSIES, GAINS, AND LOSSES
• Tariffs reduced to zero immediately or over 5 or 10 year schedule.	• Little public attention but area of most significant gains for both countries.
• Rules of origin established to determine if goods are 50% Canadian or U.S. made.	• Extension of principle of national treatment highly controversial.
• Principles of national treatment established and extended.	• Technical barriers may become the source of a second generation of non-tariff barriers to trade.
• Technical barriers re labelling, packaging, certification of product standards reduced, simplified. Standards framed as performance rather than design characteristics.	

forces, it was at the heart of the sovereignty issue and constituted far too hasty a concession of the powers of the state.

The chapter on technical barriers concerns labelling, packaging, and certification of product standards, provisions that reduce and simplify many social and health and safety rules affecting commerce. In future, standards are to be framed in terms of general performance characteristics rather than in precise design specifications. This means that technical standards are to be devised and implemented so as not to constitute a barrier to trade. However, the FTA ensures Canada's capacity to practise desired health, safety, and environmental policy. Nonetheless, free trade opponents argued that this would yield irresistible pressure on Canada to harmonize its health, safety, and environmental regulations with those of the United States. While there is little doubt that some standardizing of these rules can help facilitate trade, these provisions also offer interests in both countries a possible new vehicle for erecting a second generation of non-tariff barriers. As existing barriers come down, markets will produce losers who will seek out new policy instruments to protect themselves. They will form a natural coalition with the political constituency for expanded environmental and health regulation that seems to be gaining strength, and will add to the pressure to use technical standards. While there are, to be sure, constraints against too blatant a use of this avenue for protection, it is likely to be tested once the FTA is in full operation.

THE FARMERS' REVENGE

Agricultural trade has not been a part of the GATT trade regime. The inclusion of an agriculture component in the FTA is therefore no small achievement, especially since the negotiating climate for agriculture in 1986–87 was not auspicious. During this period, the United States and the European Community were engaged in a particularly bitter conflict over subsidies.[3] Caught in the middle of this battle, Canada also had to deal with severe drought conditions in the Canadian prairies and with falling prices and farm incomes. Next to the cost of servicing the national debt, the Department of Agriculture's budget was the fastest-growing expense in Ottawa's budget in the 1985–88 period. The FTA eliminates agricultural tariffs between the two countries over a 10-year period. However, Canada can reimpose a temporary "snap-back" tariff on fresh fruits and vegetables under certain conditions. This power will exist for 20 years. While the FTA prohibits the use of export subsidies in bilateral

---

AGRICULTURE
(CHAPTER 7)

KEY PROVISIONS	ISSUES, CONTROVERSIES, GAINS, AND LOSSES
• Eliminate tariffs over 10 years.	• First trade agreements to begin GATT-like rules. Deal structured amidst larger U.S.-E.C. subsidy war.
• Canada can reimpose temporary "snap-back" tariff for 20 years on fresh fruits and vegetables.	• Varied gains and losses depending on specific product.
• Prohibits export subsidies on bilateral trade.	• Intense dispute in Canada between agricultural producers and food product manufacturers over marketing boards.
• Marketing Boards and systems retained.	

---

trade, it preserves the Canadian system of supply management and marketing boards. These have proliferated in the past two decades as a device to protect and stabilize farm incomes.

It is difficult to speak concretely of agriculture as a separate sector because it contains numerous types of products. Its geographical spread through every province, with varying product mixes, complicates the politics of agriculture policy, as does the overlapping or concurrent jurisdictional power of the federal government and the provinces. In the light of this complexity, it is not surprising that there was a mix of gains and losses affecting interests differently, ranging from red meat to potatoes to dairy products, to name only three. The most intense dispute centred on the issue of supply management, pitting primary agriculture producers against food product manufacturers. The producer groups defended marketing boards and other supply management devices as a necessary kind of social, and not just economic, policy. Critics of marketing boards argued that they imposed a hidden tax on consumers and disproportionately increased the income of very wealthy producers, especially in the dairy sector. Food product manufacturers opposed the supply management regimes on these standard grounds, and also because they knew that they would soon face intense competition from U.S. imports, whose input costs were much lower. This was partly because American product manufacturers paid market rather than administered prices for their agricultural inputs. In the final FTA provisions, the food product manufacturers lost this political battle.

LIFE'S TOO SHORT FOR BAD WINE

During the free trade debate, author Mordecai Richler deadpanned that he would only drink so much bad wine for his country. The FTA probably ensures that Richler and other Canadian wine drinkers will be free to demonstrate their patriotism in other ways. Richler's gain has to be counted as Canada's loss, however, since in pure negotiating terms this is an undisputed win for the U.S. The FTA reduces barriers arising from measures related to the internal sale and distribution of imported wines. These barriers resided mainly in provincial liquor board rules regarding the listing, pricing, distribution, and blending of products. Pricing differentials that exceed the liquor boards' cost of selling the imported product will be reduced over seven years. A key element of the wine and distillery business, the beer industry, succeeded in having measures that currently protect it grandfathered under the FTA. It is still extremely vulnerable, however, under normal GATT rules. The industry, because of provincial barriers to trade within Canada, had its production system hopelessly fragmented in numerous un-

---

WINE AND DISTILLED SPIRITS
(CHAPTER 8)

KEY PROVISIONS	ISSUES, CONTROVERSIES, GAINS, AND LOSSES
• Reduces barriers arising from measures related to their internal sale and distribution (e.g. listing, pricing, distributing and blending).	• U.S. gains
	• Key issue for Ontario even though it is a small-employment heavily protected industry.
• Pricing differentials that exceed the Liquor Board's cost of selling the imported product reduced over 7 years.	• Involved provincial jurisdiction.
	• Beer industry grandfathered after it threatened to go public against Free
• Beer is grandfathered.	Trade.

---

competitive plants across the country. It convinced the Canadian government that it could not compete successfully with big U.S. breweries. The pressure for Canada to grandfather beer-industry trade barriers was also backed by the industry's threat to go public against the entire FTA, a threat that Ottawa took seriously.

The fact that wine and distilled spirits have their own chapter in the FTA is, on the face of it, absurd. It is akin to having a separate chapter for the seat belt industry rather than including it in the automobile sector. Wine and distilled spirits are really no more than a sub-set of either the agricultural or food products sectors. The fact that they have their own pride of place in the FTA bears elegant testimony to the significance of symbolism in the whole free trade experience, especially in the relationship between Ottawa and the

Ontario government of David Peterson. Ontario, and to a lesser extent British Columbia and Quebec, used the wine issue not just out of concern for a local industry but also for tactical purposes during the negotiations. Peterson's government, which officially opposed the FTA, used wine and spirits to test just how far federal trade negotiators could go in dealing with matters that lay within the province's constitutional jurisdiction.

No More neps

For Alberta and other producer provinces in Western Canada, the FTA's energy provisions were seen as an insurance policy, not only against future U.S. protectionist actions, but even more against any more federal interference in provincial energy affairs. The National Energy Program (NEP), introduced by the Trudeau Liberals in 1980, was seen in Western Canada as unwarranted federal intervention, which Western interests were determined would never happen again. To them, the FTA offered an opportunity to forge an energy producers' charter of rights. The energy provisions were also a continuation of Mulroney's strategy of building a political base in Western Canada and Quebec. The FTA entrenched the free-market energy policies that had already been adopted by the Tories in 1985–86 in response to Western demands. It also cemented the Quebec relationship, since electricity exports were central to Premier Robert Bourassa's economic strategy for Quebec.

The energy provisions of the FTA build on existing GATT rights and obligations, although many of the GATT provisions were ignored by both countries in the previous two decades. The FTA prohibits the use of minimum export or import price measures. Both countries agree not to impose export taxes or charges on exports unless the same tax is applied to energy consumed domestically. There is a provision to restrict exports for reasons of conservation, but these restrictions may not reduce the proportion exported over the previous three years. This means that domestic consumption must be reduced as well. The FTA reduces, but does

ENERGY
(CHAPTER 9)

KEY PROVISIONS

ISSUES, CONTROVERSIES, GAINS, AND LOSSES

- Builds on existing GATT rights and obligations.

- Prohibits minimum export or import price measures.

- Agreement not to impose export taxes or charges on exports unless the same tax is applied to energy consumed domestically.

- Export restrictions may not reduce the *proportion* exported prior to the imposition of the restrictions.

- Existing and future incentives for oil and gas exploration and development recognized.

- Significant gain in terms of Canadian market access; viewed as extra insurance policy by industry against both U.S. protection and any future programs like the NEP.

- Proportionality clause viewed as confirming GATT-like practice of treating contracted customers/neighbours fairly.

- U.S. gains through enhanced energy security.

- Key part of Mulroney strategy vis-à-vis Western Canada (oil and gas) and Quebec (electricity).

- Loss to Canada of future policy flexibility, and hence is the ultimate legacy of the excesses of the NEP.

not surrender Canadian control over the energy sector. The agreement recognizes the use of existing and future incentives for oil and gas exploration and development, as well as Canadian ownership provisions.

The preference of the Canadian negotiators was not to have a separate energy chapter. In their view, it would have been better to treat energy as just another tradable commodity. The Americans insisted on a separate chapter, partly to sell the deal domestically as a U.S. gain in energy security. For Canada, the energy provisions offer security of market access for a trade area where Canada already enjoyed a $10 billion balance in trade. While the proportionality clause of the FTA created considerable controversy among anti-free trade forces, in fact it largely confirmed GATT practices in stating that contracted customers or neighbours should be treated fairly, and not be subject to arbitrary cutoffs from accustomed *contracted* supplies. There is no doubt, however, that the FTA energy provisions reduce the ability of future Canadian governments to intervene in the energy sector.

THE ONTARIO EQUATION

The auto sector, mainly through the auspices of the 1965 Auto Pact, is Canada's most important value-added area of manufacturing trade. Automotive trade balances were positive for Canada for most of the 1980s. Not surprisingly, a key element of the free trade debate centred on the Auto Pact and whether it would be the subject of negotiations. Both the pro- and anti-free trade forces cited the Auto Pact to bolster their case regarding the FTA as a whole. The Auto Pact was promoted as evidence of the need for "managed" sectoral trade by the free trade opponents, and as an example of the benefits to be gained from free trade by supporters. Free trade advocates portrayed labour leader Bob White, the head of the Canadian Auto Workers union, as a fat cat, living off the fruits of free trade in automobiles, while trying to deny the privilege to others. The Ontario government viewed the Auto Pact as man-

---

AUTOMOTIVE GOODS
(CHAPTER 10)

KEY PROVISIONS

- Each party to administer Auto Pact in the best interests of employment and production in both countries.

- 50% rule of origin on direct production costs to qualify under FTA.

- Canadian auto duty remissions ended or phased out.

- Elimination of Canadian used car embargo by 1993.

ISSUES, CONTROVERSIES, GAINS, AND LOSSES

- Balance of gains and losses for both countries.

- Canada gains from greater defacto entrenchment of the Auto Pact within the FTA.

- U.S. gains from elimination of duty remission.

- Key part of the Ontario political equation.

- Auto parts manufacturers on both sides of the border sought 60% rule of origin.

---

aged, rather than free, trade because it contained investment guarantees agreed to by the big three auto manufacturers. During the negotiations, Canadian negotiators insisted that the Auto Pact was not on the bargaining table. If not on, the pact was certainly under the table throughout the negotiations. In the final agreement, there were four main provisions regarding the auto sector. Each party is obliged by the FTA to administer the Auto Pact in the best interests of employment and production in both countries. The agreement applies a 50 per cent rule of origin on direct production costs, strengthening the conditions governing what trade will qualify under the pact. Canadian auto duty remission schemes, used by

Canada to attract mainly Japanese investment, are also ended or phased out. These remission schemes were probably doomed in any case, since they had been targeted for an intense U.S. attack in the event that there was no FTA. Finally, Canada agreed to eliminate by 1993 its embargo against American used cars.

These provisions contain a fairly evenly balanced set of gains and losses for both countries. Such balance was essential for Canada, not only on economic grounds, but also because Canadian negotiators knew that the auto sector was the key to managing the political relationship with David Peterson. Although Ontario eventually opposed the FTA, Ottawa wanted Peterson to restrain his opposition and allow the deal to be sold politically. For that reason, the Auto Pact had to be, and be seen to be, protected. While the agreement does not refer to investment guarantees, it does bring the Auto Pact within the ambit of the FTA and in this sense entrenches it. Many American interests wanted to end the Auto Pact altogether. To avoid this, Canada gave up the freedom to use duty remission programs. Auto-parts manufacturers and unions on both sides of the border were unhappy because they had sought a 60 rather than 50 per cent rule of origin.

A SMALL STEP FORWARD

The FTA provisions on government procurement are modest compared with what might have been achieved. They lower the threshold set out in the GATT code from about $171,000 U.S. to $25,000 for purchases by code-covered entities of covered goods. Purchases above this threshold are open for competition unless reserved for small business or excluded for reasons of national security. The FTA also improves the transparency of rules and establishes bid-challenge procedures. Canada was the *demandeur* on the procurement issue. The prospect of free Canadian access to the $750 billion American federal and state government procurement market must have delighted TNO negotiators. Although the Americans talked during the middle phases of the negotiations as though a fairly

GOVERNMENT PROCUREMENT
(CHAPTER 13)

KEY PROVISIONS	ISSUES, CONTROVERSIES, GAINS, AND LOSSES
• Lowers the threshold in the GATT code from about U.S. $171,000 to U.S. $25,000 for purchases by code-covered entities of covered goods. Purchases above this threshold are open for competition unless reserved for small business or excluded for reasons of national security.	• Canada was the *demandeur* on this issue. Sought big procurement deal.
	• Large deal thought possible at middle part of negotiations but U.S. pulled back.
	• Major provincial/state government jurisdictional obstacles as well as important to political patronage.
• Improves transparency and establishes bid-challenge procedures.	• Final gains important but modest.

large deal were possible, in the end they pulled back from a big procurement package.

Their lack of enthusiasm was due to American recognition that procurement, especially at the state level, provided some of the most effective U.S. instruments of protection. Furthermore, procurement issues would have involved potentially difficult matters of federal versus state jurisdiction. Beyond this, procurement is heavily tied to the not-so-subtle world of congressional patronage. These are areas in which U.S. negotiators would have to tread at their own risk, and they declined. In general, the procurement provisions represent only a very modest gain in freeing up markets.

Had the Americans wished to go further, the Canadians would have faced their own problems with provincial jurisdiction and regional development policy.

TRIAL BALLOON OR TROJAN HORSE?

The FTA was the first trade agreement to tackle the service sector in any significant way. The principle of national treatment was extended to the providers of a list of commercial services. At the same time, existing laws and practices were grandfathered, although they may not be made any more discriminatory. The FTA also reduced the obstacles to the temporary entry of business persons. American immigration law was especially troublesome in this regard. Two types of service provision were exempt from the FTA, one of special concern to Canada and the other to the United States. Health, education, and social services are exempt. Canadian concerns here were directly tied to the government's promise not to harm Canadian social programs. Transportation services were also excluded from the FTA, primarily because of a fierce lobbying campaign by U.S. maritime transport unions and firms, which feared competition from more efficient Canadian firms, especially in Great Lakes transport.

In the service sector, the United States was the *demandeur*. Pressure came from key service sector firms such as American Express that were spearheading the new American free trade coalition. Despite this apparent commitment, it must be said that both sides' knowledge of and preparedness for negotiations on the service sector were extremely limited. While both paid lip service to the conventional wisdom that "the service sector is where all the jobs are being created," in fact there was little research available on such key issues as productivity in the service sector.[4] This sector is incredibly embedded, service by service, in a host of regulatory regimes regarding qualifications and standards. As a result, it is a far more complex problem than the one that accompanied the unravelling of tariffs on goods over the past four decades of traditional trade policy. Anti-free trade

SERVICES
(CHAPTERS 14 & 15)

KEY PROVISIONS	ISSUES, CONTROVERSIES, GAINS, AND LOSS
• National treatment principle extended to the providers of a list of commercial services.	• Key U.S. demand and central part of U.S. pro-free trade coalition interests.
• Existing laws and practices are grandfathered but cannot be made any more discriminatory than they are.	• Both sides' knowledge and preparedness on the service sector was limited. Great complexity involved.
• Health, education and social services exempt but not management services.	• Anti-free trade coalition's concern that even if health and social services exempt, the inclusion of management services is the Trojan horse for the future erosion of public services.
• Transportation services excluded.	
• Temporary entry of business persons enhanced.	• Transport exclusion due to lobby by U.S. marine industry and unions.

forces were not satisfied with the exclusion of health, education, and social services. Pointing to the fact that *management* services were included in the list of services eligible for national treatment, they argued that their inclusion was like a Trojan horse, permitting a more gradual attack against the public provision of health, education, and social services in Canada. It was this line of argument, along with the more general concern about downward social policy harmonization, that ultimately struck the most responsive chord among Canadian voters. The more extreme claims about the demise of medicare were fairly easily rebutted by pro-free trade supporters. However, the larger case implied in the fears over national treatment in the social service sector could not be so easily dismissed in the free trade debate, although the likelihood of these fears being realized was quite remote, for reasons we discuss in Chapters 9 and 10.

CANADA FOR SALE?

Although investment was a key item on the U.S. agenda from the outset of the negotiations, the Canadian negotiators would not agree to even discuss the issue until 1987. But the Mulroney government revealed its approach to foreign investment in 1984 when it changed the mandate and title of the Foreign Investment Review Agency (FIRA). From the ashes of FIRA rose Investment Canada, with a mandate to promote foreign investment. One of Mulroney's most widely quoted speeches was made within weeks of taking office when he announced to New York investors that Canada was "open for business." By the time the free trade negotiations got under way, the changes to FIRA had already significantly reduced the screening powers and thresholds that the new Investment Canada would retain. This helps account for Canada's reluctance to bargain away more of these powers in the bilateral negotiations. The FTA extends the principle of national treatment to the establishment of new foreign-owned businesses. It provides for the gradual raising, in four steps, of the Canadian threshold for the review of takeovers to $150 million by 1992. This means that major foreign takeovers (more than $150 million) may continue to be reviewed, but smaller ones will escape scrutiny. The review of indirect acquisitions will be phased out entirely by 1992. The FTA also eliminated, partly because of previous GATT rulings, investment-related performance

INVESTMENT
(CHAPTER 16)

KEY PROVISIONS

ISSUES, CONTROVERSIES, GAINS, AND LOSSES

- National treatment extended on the establishment of new business.

- Canadian review threshold for direct acquisitions raised in 4 steps to $150 million by 1992.

- Review of indirect acquisitions to be phased out by 1992.

- Oil, gas, and uranium sectors exempt.

- Investment-related performance requirements that significantly distort trade are prohibited (e.g. local content, import substitution).

- Other existing laws, policies are grandfathered.

- Key U.S. demand. Canada did not agree to discuss it until later stages of negotiations.

- Canadian screening powers reduced re threshold but Canadian foreign investment rules recognized by U.S. for the first time.

- Mulroney policy had already weakened FIRA and converted it to Investment Canada with a "Canada is open for business" mandate.

- Liberals and NDP opposed this part of FTA but toned down their oppositional rhetoric.

requirements that significantly distort trade. These included local content, import substitution, and hiring practices, all requirements that the old FIRA had included in its reviews. The FTA also specifically exempted the oil, gas, and uranium sectors from this relaxation in provisions governing reviews. As well, it grandfathered other existing foreign investment laws and policies.

The investment provisions of the FTA are clearly ones that raise problems of scorecard logic. Canada conceded some powers that the opponents of free trade regard as essential. Reduced powers therefore equal a Canadian loss. But they were not powers that the government wished to retain. In addition, Canadian foreign investment review powers have received their first official recognition by the United States. Before the FTA, the U.S. refused to acknowledge the legitimacy of Canadian policies. The FTA grants this legitimacy. Free trade supporters also argued that the agreement was valuable to Canadian investors in the United States, because the Americans decided to forgo a counterpart right to review Canadian investment in the U.S. This may prove valuable in the event that the U.S. comes under increased domestic pressure in the 1990s to institute its own investment review laws, which would not now apply to Canada.

FUTURE CONSIDERATIONS

Whether treated separately or as a part of the service sector, the FTA provisions on financial services turn on several underlying conditions that were present at the time of the negotiations. Canada's banking system was acknowledged by both sides to be more protected. The U.S. had been much more hospitable to foreign banking. This meant it was the U.S. that was the *demandeur* on the issue. In addition, there were growing international economic and technological pressures to deregulate banking and break down the barriers between banking and securities. Canadian and U.S. banking systems were also quite different in their basic structures and regulations. Canada had a centralized system of big branch banks governed primarily by federal legislation. The U.S. system was decentralized, with a state government-led unit bank system stitched together by the federal Glass-Steagall Act. Framed in the depression of the 1930s, Glass-Steagall preserved a strong separation of the pillars of the financial system, especially between banking and security firms. Finally, and of considerable significance in the negotiations, there were jurisdictional imperatives regarding financial services within both governments. This meant that central finance authorities, the Department of Finance in Canada and the Treasury Department in the U.S., were not about to let mere trade negotiators handle these complex and sensitive issues. In the final stages of the negotiations, it was Michael Wilson and James Baker who directly handled financial services.

The FTA provisions reflect the finely crafted set of trade-offs required by these conditions. The agreement exempts U.S. firms and investors from key aspects of the federal "10/25" rule. This rule prevents any single non-resident from acquiring more than 10 per cent of the shares of a federally regulated financial institution and all non-residents together from holding more than 25 per cent of shares. U.S. bank subsidiaries are also exempt from the 16 per cent ceiling on the size of the foreign bank sector in Canada. These were the concessions made by Canada in recognition of the fact that Canadian rules had been more protectionist. In return, Canada gained in two areas. First, Canadian banks in the United States can now underwrite and deal in Canadian government securities. And second, Canadian firms will be accorded the same national treatment as U.S. firms with respect to future amendments to the Glass-Steagall Act. While the first gain is immediate, the second must be placed in the futures column of the FTA scorecard. Its value in terms of access to the American market could be considerable, however. Banking experts are convinced that the U.S. has little choice but to change Glass-Steagall in order to ensure that its own banks and securities firms can combine into one pillar and compete with the powerful and

FINANCIAL SERVICES
(CHAPTER 17)

KEY PROVISIONS

ISSUES, CONTROVERSIES, GAINS, AND LOSSES

- Exempts U.S. firms and investors from aspects of federal "10/25" rule — the rule that prevents any single non-resident from acquiring more than 10% of the shares and all non-residents from acquiring more than 25% of shares of federally regulated financial institutions.

- U.S. bank subsidiaries exempt from 16% ceiling on the size of the foreign bank sector.

- Canadian banks in U.S. can underwrite and deal in Canadian government securities.

- Canadian institutions will be accorded same treatment as U.S. with respect to amendments to U.S. Glass-Steagall Act.

- Important U.S. demand. Canadian laws more protectionist than U.S.

- Negotiated ultimately by Canadian Finance and U.S. Treasury departments.

- U.S. gains but Canadian gains could be substantial depending on future U.S. Glass-Steagall amendments.

- Canadian banks divided over FTA. Some support it on macro-economic grounds rather than on its banking provisions.

- Strong Canadian-owned sector should be able to compete.

- Dispute over whether Ontario deregulation in 1986 weakened bargining position.

far more integrated Japanese and German banks. When this occurs, Canadian banks will secure the same opportunities in the U.S. market.

THE DEAL MAKER

Two chapters of the FTA deal with institutional mechanisms for managing the agreement and for settling disputes. Chapter 18 covers the general institutional provisions for everything except financial services, which the Finance and Treasury departments of the two countries will continue to manage, and anti-dumping, and countervailing duties. The latter two areas are dealt with in FTA Chapter 19. The great majority of the FTA provisions are governed by Chapter 18, which builds extensively on the dispute-resolution procedures used in the GATT. It provides for a process of notification, information provision, consultation, referral if necessary to the newly established Canada-U.S. Trade Commission, and the subsequent use of three possible dispute settlement procedures. The commission is composed of the two ministers responsible for trade. Initially, the commission will not have an elaborate secretariat. If dispute settlement involves arbitration, then panels are selected composed of two Canadians, two Americans, and one other member chosen jointly.

The dispute-settlement provisions regarding countervail and anti-dump are spelled out in FTA Chapter 19. They arose from the failure of the negotiators to achieve agreement on rules regarding subsidies, dumping, and the use of countervail. The development of a subsidies code and some form of restraint on the use of American trade remedies was a key Canadian objective in the negotiations. However, the deal finally came together only when the two agreed to carry over the subsidies/trade remedies issue for further negotiation. Accordingly, Chapter 19 of the FTA provides for a further set of negotiations, over a five-to-seven-year period, to try to develop an agreement in this area. Until an agreement is concluded, Chapter 19 provides a system to replace each country's

---

INSTITUTIONAL PROVISIONS
(CHAPTER 18)

KEY PROVISIONS	ISSUES, CONTROVERSIES, GAINS, AND LOSSES
• Applies to general administration of FTA and to dispute settlement except for financial services, antidumping and countervail.	• Institutionalize the Canadian-U.S. relationship to an unprecedented extent.
• Sets out process built on GATT for notification of any measure, information provisions, consultation, referral if necessary to Canada-U.S. Trade Commission and 3 possible dispute settlement procedures.	• In the long run the Chapter 18 provisions may be more important than Chapter 19 but received little public debate. • Greater U.S. "pressure" in Canadian decision process on a regular basis.
• Commission established composed of the ministers reaponsible for trade.	
• Arbitration panels provided for (2 U.S., 2 Canadian and 1 member chosen jointly).	• But some Canadian gains in having equal representation on arbitration panels.

---

judicial review process for countervail and anti-dumping cases with binational review procedures. Instead of final anti-dumping and countervail orders being reviewed by the regular courts in each country, either country can request that they be reviewed by a

BINATIONAL DISPUTE SETTLEMENT
IN ANTI-DUMPING AND COUNTERVAIL
(CHAPTER 19)

KEY PROVISIONS

ISSUES, CONTROVERSIES, GAINS, AND LOSSES

- Development over 5 to 7 years of rules governing government subsidies and private dumping.

- Bilateral review of any changes in existing countervail or anti-dumping laws and regulations with the amendments actually specifying either Canada or the U.S. in the amending statute.

- The replacement of judicial review by domestic courts of countervailing and anti-dumping final orders by a binational panel.

- Key Canadian demand to institutionalize secure access.

- Rhetoric versus reality of what is meant by "binding."

- Failure to agree on definition or political attitudes towards subsidies.

- Important Canadian gain but disputed by FTA opponents since only judicial review achieved.

- Fear of have-not provinces that subsidies code would kill regional policy.

binational panel composed of two Canadians, two Americans, and one person chosen jointly. The panel would determine on a binding basis whether existing trade laws had been applied correctly and fairly. From the Canadian point of view, this provision was essential to help make countervail decisions less political, and reduce their value to American interests as a means to harass Canadian producers. This was one of the key provisions to ensure more secure access to the American market. Chapter 19 also contains a corollary provision that requires that Canada must be explicitly named in any amendment to existing countervail or anti-dumping laws in order for such changes to apply to Canada. In addition, any amendments that name Canada are subject to binational review to assess their consistency with the FTA and the GATT, and whether their effect is to overturn a previous decision of a binational panel.

In general, the provisions of FTA Chapters 18 and 19 institutionalize the Canada-U.S. relationship to an unprecedented extent. They profoundly change the nature of decision-making in Canada and, to a lesser extent, in the U.S. For Canada, there will be a greater U.S. presence in all areas of Canadian decision-making, required by the notification and consultation provisions. In the long run, the Chapter 18 provisions may be more important than those in Chapter 19, even though the latter received the bulk of attention in the free trade debate. The Chapter 19 provisions were at the centre of Canadian demands, and they became bound up in the inflated rhetoric over whether Canada achieved its free trade objectives. They are critical to the application of scorecard logic, however, since anti-free trade forces claimed the judicial review provisions represented only a modest gain when compared to what was given up in other areas of the FTA. Chapter 19 was also at the core of a fundamental paradox that marked Canada's position in the negotiation process. Getting the U.S. to agree to a subsidies code was central to the Mulroney-Reisman bargaining strategy. Had the strategy succeeded, however, it would probably have undermined the government's ability to sell the agreement in Canada, because the advantages of a code limiting Canadian subsidy practices would have been very difficult to explain in the politically charged atmosphere of the national debate over free trade. The unambiguous retention of subsidies for regional development and social policy purposes was essential for preserving a majority coalition in support of free trade in Canada.

SLEEPING DOGS LEFT LYING

Last but not by any means least among the FTA chapters is one misleadingly labelled "other provisions." In it there are at least three issues that figured prominently in the politics of free trade — intellectual property, cultural industries, and softwood lumber. The FTA contains only a general commitment by both countries to co-operate and work together toward better international intellectual property rules. A much more substantial chapter on this issue was within reach, but was withdrawn when the Americans decided they wanted a whole loaf rather than the half Canada was willing to offer. During the negotiations, the Conservative government was pushing through controversial changes in drug patent legislation.[5] The changes did not go nearly as far as the U.S. drug lobby wanted, however. In the later stages of the negotiations, the Americans tried to obtain still further intellectual property right protection for pharmaceuticals, but the Mulroney government refused.

The achievement of an exemption for Canadian cultural industries from the provisions of any agreement was a central promise of the Mulroney government. Cultural industries are specifically exempt from the FTA, except for specific provisions dealing with tariffs on inputs to, and products of, cultural industries; requirements to sell cultural firms that might be acquired as a result of indirect takeovers; cable television transmission rights; and magazine advertising. The last two provisions were long-standing items on the American trade irritants list against Canada. In addition, however, the chapter provides that the U.S. can retaliate, with measures of equivalent commercial effect, against actions by Canada in the cultural sphere that would have been prohibited by the FTA had cultural industries not been exempted. This means that the exemption the Americans granted in one article on culture, they tried to take back with another. Throughout the negotiations, because of the special access that U.S. cultural industries had to President Reagan, the Americans insisted on treating culture as just another name for the entertainment business, rather than as something central to Canadian identity.

OTHER PROVISIONS
(CHAPTER 20)

KEY PROVISIONS	**ISSUES CONTROVERSIES, GAINS, AND LOSSES**

INTELLECTUAL PROPERTY

• Commitment to cooperate and work toward better international intellectual property rules. • A more substantial chapter on intellectual property was dropped.	• U.S. issue. Could have had substantial deal but U.S. wanted to re-open Bill C-22 (patent) changes and were not satisfied with "half a loaf."

CULTURAL INDUSTRIES

• Are exempt from FTA except for 4 specific provisions dealing with tariffs on inputs to and products of cultural industries, requirements to sell after indirect take-overs, re-transmission rights, and magazine advertising.	• Key Canadian issue. U.S. reluctant to accept. Attitude was that culture was just the "entertainment" business.

SOFTWOOD LUMBER

• Grandfathers the Softwood Lumber Agreement of 1986.	• 1986 dispute became litmus test for both sides of why FTA was needed, or why it was a flawed initiative.

Finally, there was one marvellously short reference i[]
stipulating that the Softwood Lumber Agreement of 1986 ....
grandfathered. The softwood lumber dispute had become a *cause
célèbre* for both pro- and anti-free trade forces in Canada.[6] It involved a U.S. countervail action, the second in three years, which
eventually led Canada to impose, under intense pressure from the
U.S., an export tax against its own producers of softwood lumber.
The dispute arose after the U.S. ruled that some aspects of provincial stumpage fees constituted a subsidy. The softwood lumber
issue offered proof to pro-free traders of the need for a free trade
agreement, just as it proved to anti-free traders that the United
States could not be trusted.

The Canada-U.S. free trade agreement is one part traditional
trade agreement, and one part path-breaker. For better or worse,
the FTA is now one of Canada's *de facto* constitutional pillars, lodged
in the political pantheon alongside federalism, Parliamentary government, and the Charter of Rights and Freedoms. The continental
embrace has always been a part of Canada's historical reality, but
free trade has given the embrace new institutional form and unde-
niable substance.

PART II:
DOING THE DEAL:
A THREE-RING CIRCUS

5

THE UNITED FRONT

Managing the Canada-U.S. free trade negotiations was akin to running, and watching, a three-ring circus, but one that mixed juggling, combat, and dance. In one ring, the Mulroney government balanced its desire to limit provincial power in the negotiations with the need for a deal that earned provincial support, but did not require provincial legislative approval. In the centre ring, Simon Reisman and Peter Murphy squared off in what was billed as the main act. But while most eyes were fixed on the Reisman-Murphy duel, the origins of the circus could be found in the third ring where the Canadian government was engaged in a "pas de deux" with Canadian business. The lead partners on the government dance card were the Business Council on National Issues (BCNI) and the Canadian Manufacturers' Association (CMA).

MOUNTING A LOBBY

The BCNI enjoyed a high profile in the battle for free trade, and not just because its members are powerful CEOs of the most important corporations in Canada. Its visibility was also due to its president, Thomas d'Aquino. D'Aquino defines a very large role for BCNI, and himself, on the national policy stage. A smooth and tireless proponent of the business view, BCNI's own CEO clearly relishes his job and the influence it grants him in the nation's business. Though d'Aquino was trained in the law, most of his career before BCNI was spent as a consultant and political aide, learning the channels of influence in Ottawa. In pinstripe uniform, he speaks for the council not only on issues like the deficit, but also on others that go way beyond the traditional concerns of business, including the constitution, parliamentary reform, and foreign and defence policy. And beginning in 1981 when he became head of BCNI, d'Aquino set out to get Canada into a comprehensive trade deal with the United States. He did not see his task at an end once that decision had been made, however. The agenda and strategy for the negotiations remained to be set, and d'Aquino wanted to be at the centre of this process as well. After Simon Reisman set up the TNO early in 1986, d'Aquino handed him two black books that set out the BCNI view of what a comprehensive trade agreement might look like. These had been developed during several meetings of the BCNI trade task force with trade experts and officials. As Reisman had already done in his memorandum to Mulroney in October 1985, the books anticipated many of the topics that ended up in the final agreement. Reisman responded that the BCNI approach was not sufficiently broad and ambitious. In particular, it did not tackle the whole issue of subsidies to Reisman's satisfaction. In this respect, the proposal was deliberately restrained, however. The BCNI view was that the subsidy issue was too complex to deal with and, moreover, would fatally undermine political support for a free trade deal in Canada.

Subsidies were of special concern to the Canadian Manufacturers' Association as well. At an early meeting with the CMA board of directors, Reisman included a subsidies regime and national treatment as part of his vision of a big broad trade deal. A brave man, he told the manufacturers that it was even in Canada's economic interest to eliminate its own subsidies unilaterally, even if the U.S. did not respond in kind. The CMA directors were stunned by this typically bold Reisman rhetoric. They were also impressed, as intended, by his frank description of what an agreement should cover. He told them that tariffs would go to zero, national treatment would apply, and the deal would cover services. "Was the CMA prepared to live with that?" Reisman asked with characteristic bluntness. Despite obvious reservations, the CMA members present gave his strategy their official blessing. While the Canadian Manufacturers' Association was less aggressive than d'Aquino's BCNI in its efforts to influence the agenda and strategy for the negotiations, CMA support was actively pursued by Reisman through direct approaches, which he did not make to other organizations.

The CMA was more active than BCNI in efforts to shape the formal business-government consultative machinery for the conduct of the negotiations. It advocated and supported the two-tiered consultative system that was adopted, composed of the International Trade Advisory Committee (ITAC) and the Sectoral Advisory Groups on International Trade (SAGITs), and the SAGITs became a key channel of influence for the CMA into the negotiations. Both d'Aquino and CMA President Laurent Thibault also had frequent, often daily, contact with either Reisman or his deputy, Gordon Ritchie. This degree of access far exceeded that of other business interest groups, including the banks and energy interests. And BCNI enjoyed even greater leverage because of d'Aquino's political connections. Mulroney and his ministers called frequently.

BCNI and the CMA also played an important role in the negotiations through their efforts to shore up and energize an American coalition in support of free trade. The negotiations threatened to go off the political rails many times between the spring of 1986 and the summer of 1987. And a key factor in any derailment could have been the lack of pressure from the American business community on U.S. negotiators and key politicians. The lack of American business interest in the negotiations simply reflected the usual low profile of Canadian-American issues in the United States. But it was also due to the relative complexity of U.S. business affiliations on trade matters. The original post-war American business coalition in support of trade liberalization had become anti-free trade. Their credo was now fair trade. And the new pro-free trade coalition was geographically more diffuse and centred in the service sector, where the focus was on other American trading partners. In general, the coalition supporting free trade in the U.S. business community was distracted and sluggish.

This was evident in November 1986, when BCNI organized the first bilateral business meeting, attended by CEOs from corporate giants like General Motors, American Express, and IBM. While the obligatory joint communiqué was released, BCNI members came away convinced that there was only lukewarm support for free trade in the U.S., and no awareness of the Canadian view that the American negotiators were putting an agreement at risk by their refusal to negotiate in good faith. The CMA, sensing a similar attitude among U.S. manufacturers, organized a joint meeting with its American counterpart, the National Association of Manufacturers, in Washington in April 1987. When he addressed the Washington meeting, Laurent Thibault pleaded with his American colleagues not to paint Canada with the same unfair trade brush being used on other countries: "How many of your major trading partners are confident enough of the general fairness of their economic and trading system to offer to sit down and negotiate . . .?"[1] In July, a BCNI business delegation that included Peter Lougheed and Donald Macdonald met with Senator Lloyd Bentsen and other influential members of the U.S. Senate. D'Aquino's worst fears about U.S. inattention and Canadian mishandling of the negotiations were confirmed when Bentsen indicated that he saw little reason to give Canada any special treatment on the trade remedy issue.

A U.S. pro-free trade coalition finally did emerge in July 1987, under the title of the American Coalition for Trade Expansion with Canada. The catalyst for its creation was Jim Robinson, head of American Express and a leading advocate in the U.S. of trade liberalization in the service sector. A good friend of David Culver, the chairman of BCNI and CEO of Alcan, Robinson was also chairman of the BCNI counterpart U.S. Business Roundtable's committee on trade. He became the chief contact for efforts by the Canadian business lobby to exert pressure on the Reagan administration.

When Simon Reisman broke off the negotiations in September 1987, it was Robinson who was called to a meeting in Toronto with BCNI members. He was told bluntly that the Canadian business community supported Reisman's decision because the Americans refused to deal with Canada's central issue of trade remedies. BCNI also made it clear that there could be serious consequences for the U.S. as a result of the failure of the negotiations, including the defeat of Mulroney's government and its replacement with one far less friendly to business. Robinson delivered the message directly to Reagan and Baker within hours. Coupled with pressure by the Canadian government on the U.S. administration, the BCNI intervention helped to bring the negotiators back to the table for the final bargaining session in October 1987. This time, the ministers at the table included U.S. Treasury Secretary James Baker. American business finally had the ear of the Reagan administration. As for Robinson, in 1989 his American Express Company was given a licence by the Department of Finance to practise bank-like business in Canada, stimulating howls of protest from the big six Canadian banks.

The CMA and BCNI also attempted to influence particular, substantive areas of the agreement. However, since many of the FTA trade-offs were not made until the final weekend in Washington when BCNI and CMA were not present, their influence was not immediate but resulted from the expression of views throughout the entire negotiation. BCNI pushed very hard for the inclusion of the Auto Pact in the FTA because it was felt to be more secure inside than out. D'Aquino had also worked steadily on Ontario Premier David Peterson to get him to modify, or at least mute, his opposition to free trade. Inclusion of the pact in the agreement could offer a means to win Peterson's support. BCNI offices also became one of the main conduits for pressure from the beer industry to get its protective practices grandfathered under the FTA. Alarmed by the industry's threat to go public and mount an anti-free-trade campaign unless it was protected, BCNI executives urged appeasement to avoid a split in the united public front that business had managed to mount. In the event, the beer lobby got what it wanted. BCNI also supported the government in its efforts to secure an exemption from the agreement for Canada's cultural industries. American business interests identified culture with the entertainment business, and saw only Canadian efforts to protect another industry. BCNI made a serious effort to convince its American counterpart that cultural issues were a sensitive and legitimate element in the Canadian political equation.

CMA interventions were more subtle and numerous, because it had to be concerned with the details of numerous sectors, parallel to the SAGITs. It pressed the negotiators not to leave the food processing industry swinging in the wind, subject to injury from both American producers and Canadian agricultural marketing boards. CMA canvassing also raised the issue of temporary entry for business persons to a level of importance unanticipated at the start of the negotiations. Between the two major lobbies, BCNI is probably accurately credited with having had more influence in Ottawa, and marginally more impact on the FTA negotiations. The CMA nevertheless played an important federal role, and was also often better positioned to exercise continuous pressure on provincial capitals than was BCNI.

MANAGING THE LOBBY

The business community played its most significant role in getting free trade on the policy agenda. If business interests, led by the BCNI and CMA, had not changed their historic positions on the basic issue of free trade, the FTA would not exist.[2] And throughout the free trade saga, Canadian business interests were able to maintain a remarkably solid united front in public. But behind the united front, important struggles were taking place between contending business interests. Threats to "go public" against the FTA were used on several occasions by the beer industry and the food manufacturers. Business rescue missions were launched on a number of occasions when it appeared that the Mulroney government was mishandling the negotiations and the political marketing of the trade deal, and to prompt the American business community to step up its pressure on the Reagan administration.

In all major issues of Canadian public policy, the power and influence of business derives from two sources.[3] First, a privileged influence emerges out of the structure of any capitalist system, because of the obvious dependence of government on business to generate the great majority of jobs, as well as goods and services in the Canadian economy. A second source of influence is more directly political, and flows from the superior representation, lobbying capacity, and resources available to business. These multiple channels of influence include financial support for both the Progressive Conservative and Liberal parties, continuous interest group lobbying by business associations, the strategic influence of major companies, and policy think tanks largely funded by business. In the negotiation phase of the FTA, the dynamics of business-government relations became much more complex. These were played out through the formal consultative machinery, as well as in interest group strategies in specific sectors, such as food manufacturing, banking, and energy, in addition to the continuing role of major business lobbies such as the BCNI and the CMA.[4]

The designers of the FTA consultative process knew that they would face three imperatives regarding business and private sector involvement. They needed formal and non-partisan business political support to foster the legitimacy of the entire free trade initiative. They also required good advice to gauge the effects of alternative negotiated outcomes on specific industries. Finally, they needed a buffer to deflect demands for protection that would arise from numerous business interest groups. The formal consultative machinery established for the FTA process would answer all three needs. The 38-member International Trade Advisory Committee (ITAC) was designed to provide legitimacy, and the 15 Sectoral Advisory Groups on International Trade (SAGITs) were established to provide advice. Together they offered a buffer against demands for special treatment. This consultative machinery was the product of Canada's experience in the Tokyo Round of the GATT negotiations in the 1970s. Business interests were dissatisfied with the level of industry-specific advice that had been secured during Canadian preparations for the Tokyo Round. The two-level FTA machinery that was eventually put in place to remedy this deficiency was directly copied from the U.S. advisory system after Canadian Trade Minister James Kelleher had discussed the system with American officials and urged its adoption in Canada.

The ITAC-SAGIT system was conceived originally as a vehicle for general private sector consultation, including input from labour and education groups, and not just from business. But it became primarily a business consultative mechanism. Organized labour was involved in a limited way through the presence of members of the Canadian Federation of Labour (CFL), composed mainly of construction workers. But the far larger and more important Canadian Labour Congress (CLC) would not accept an invitation for its members to join. The CLC refused for the same reasons that it had opted out of other consultations in the late 1970s and early 1980s, namely, a fear of being co-opted by a system that they believed to be dominated by business. Even when CLC President Dennis Mc-Dermott mildly, but publicly, supported the appointment of Walter Light as chairman of ITAC, he faced strong censure from other key CLC executives, such as Shirley Carr and Bob White, who opposed free trade from the outset.

THE LIGHT BRIGADE

Walter Light's appointment as head of ITAC brought credibility and a vital channel into the private sector. The former head of Northern Telecom, Canada's largest high technology export-oriented company, and a major centre for research and development, Light took firm charge of his 38-member group. Task forces were launched on general issues such as adjustment assistance, interprovincial trade barriers, the scope of the agreement, and multilateral trade issues. ITAC members met about every 12 weeks and had a direct link to the TNO through the attendance at its meetings by Gordon Ritchie, the deputy chief negotiator, and, on occasion, Simon Reisman. It is difficult to gauge the exact influence of ITAC on Canada's conduct of the free trade negotiations. Since it was not fully operational until mid-1986, after negotiations had started, it cannot be said to have had a vital impact on the basic negotiating strategy, or on the scope of the negotiations, since these were set much earlier by Simon Reisman and Brian Mulroney. However, TNO officials derived constant comfort from the ITAC consultations, since ITAC strongly supported the FTA initiative. Its meetings, and many of the SAGIT meetings, were often a welcome relief from the hostile climate that prevailed in the federal-provincial and parliamentary-media domains. This was especially true during the long months of 1986 and 1987 when the negotiations were going nowhere.

The ITAC did influence the content of the FTA debate, as distinct from the negotiations, at a fairly early stage. It recommended to the TNO and the government that no special adjustment assistance was needed for Canadian industry, arguing that existing adjustment programs were satisfactory. ITAC also argued strongly that existing adjustment programs should be directed entirely to assisting workers and communities, rather than firms. The issue of adjustment assistance subsequently produced a basic tension between the substance and the selling of the FTA. In substantive terms, ITAC and the government were on solid ground in saying that special programs were not needed. This was because it was difficult to distinguish those workers who were adversely affected by free trade from those who were affected by general economic conditions. However, the task of selling the deal politically might have been made easier if the government had announced the creation of a special adjustment fund.[5]

The role of Walter Light in the ITAC "Light Brigade" was crucial because of his personal network, especially his connections with Peter Lougheed and Wendy Dobson. Dobson, who later joined the Department of Finance as associate deputy minister, was a member of ITAC in her capacity as head of the C.D. Howe Institute. She and economist Richard Lipsey played key roles in lobbying Mulroney ministers and officials for free trade early in 1985. Dobson shared many views with Light, including the conviction in 1986–87 that the Americans were not seriously engaged in the negotiations and that something had to be done about it. Light and Lougheed, the former Alberta Conservative premier, shared a common practical experience in dealing with the American Congress, rather than the U.S. administration. When American interest in the negotiations seemed at its lowest ebb, Light, Dobson, and Lougheed began knocking on the doors of key congressional and business contacts in Washington. The retired businessman, the retired politician, and the think-tank thinker were able to present themselves as a non-partisan group in their efforts to persuade the Americans to rescue the free trade talks. Later, in 1987, Light saw the need for a more broadly based coalition to support the deal, and this eventually took the form of the Canadian Alliance for Trade and Job Opportunities. The Alliance arose out of the conviction that the Mulroney government was losing the public relations battle at home. ITAC could not intervene in this fight directly, since it was supposed to be non-political. Light was among those who suggested that Peter Lougheed and Donald Macdonald head up a new alliance to fight for the FTA in Canada.

SECTORAL BATTLES AND THE POLITICS OF TRADE

The structure, operation, and influence of all 15 of the sectoral advisory groups, or SAGITs, cannot be fully considered here. But we can provide a sense of their dual role as a source of industry advice and a buffer against interest group pressures. In addition, the manoeuvring by groups over the structure and composition of their SAGITs provided a forecast of some of the later struggles that would take place among business interests as the negotiations proceeded. The SAGITs are generally given good marks by their members and by TNO players for their role in providing advice on specific industries.[6] In particular, they supplied essential advice on how rapidly tariffs ought to be reduced to zero in each sector and on the general technical aspects of each industry. This was especially vital in the FTA negotiations because the TNO was made up of quite senior officials, knowledgeable, but not hands-on experts in all 15 SAGIT sectors. Such experts do exist at the middle levels of government departments, but the TNO tried to shield itself from too much input from line departments for fear that it would become mired in the interdepartmental swamps of the Ottawa policy process.

The SAGITs were composed of members selected in their own personal capacity, rather than as formal representatives of interest groups. This enhanced their role as buffer, deflecting some of the pressures away from the negotiators. TNO sent any formal industry association briefs directly to the appropriate SAGIT for comment and discussion. This practice also arose out of experience with the GATT Tokyo Round, where many federal officials judged the industry briefs were not very good. The SAGITs did not insulate TNO from pressures from interest groups entirely, of course. Many groups had their own separate channels of access. And most tried, with only limited success, to see Reisman, Ritchie, and other TNO officials as well as their relevant departmental and regional ministers in the federal cabinet. The selection of the SAGIT members involved a long and cumbersome process that was rife with politics. The government canvassed more than 80 trade associations, as well as provincial governments, for suitable persons. This process generated more than 2,300 potential names. The politics of the selection process for the approximately 250 SAGIT positions required that the SAGITs be larger than originally intended. As finally composed, the 15 SAGITs ranged in size from 25 to 40 people. Alan Rugman and Andrew Anderson's classification of probable SAGIT orientations toward free trade as the negotiations began were not far off the mark.[7] Four of the SAGITs, including agriculture producers and auto parts and furniture manufacturers, were expected to lean against free trade, and they did. Six SAGITs would favour it, including minerals and metals, apparel and fur, and general services. And five groups would be mixed, including forest products, chemicals and petro-chemicals, and communications. In general, these were the patterns of support and opposition that prevailed. The politics underlying these patterns can be illustrated by looking more closely at three specific sectors.

FOOD MANUFACTURERS: SURROUNDED ON THE INSIDE

The sectoral group on agriculture, food, and beverages became the largest SAGIT because of the intense struggle that was waged from the outset to try to capture it. The Agriculture minister, John Wise, made every effort to stack the SAGIT with members committed to preserving Canada's system of supply management through marketing boards. TNO's two main agricultural negotiators — Peter Connell, a former deputy minister in Agriculture Canada, and Mike Gifford, an Agriculture Canada expert — were also supporters of marketing boards. However, food manufacturing and processing interests insisted that unless marketing boards were phased out, the food processing sector would be extremely vulnerable under free trade. This is because their input costs would be inflated by protected produce prices, while their American competitors would enter the Canadian market with much lower prices based on American input costs. Although the food processing industry was represented on the SAGIT, they were surrounded in the group by pro-marketing board interests.

Conflict in the agriculture SAGIT was not just between primary producers and food manufacturers. There were divisions within interest groups such as the Canadian Federation of Agriculture. The Grocery Products Manufacturing Association also had internal divisions between its dominant foreign-owned firms such as Nestle's, and Canadian-owned firms like McCains. In addition, the beer industry quickly developed its own channels of influence outside the SAGIT. But the issues of marketing board and supply management became the central concern.

The first time these two wings of the agri-food industry were required to deal seriously with the differences in their positions was during the SAGIT process. They had previously taken part in Ottawa's efforts to develop a national food strategy, but these discussions were never disciplined by the realities of a firm deadline. Under the FTA process, everyone knew that changes would come and that deadlines had meaning. The agriculture SAGIT had extensive contacts with the TNO and frequent meetings with Simon Reisman, who was familiar with the debate between the two camps. As a former member of the board of Weston's, Reisman knew a considerable amount about the competitive cost structure of the food manufacturers. When they pressed hard in favour of phasing out marketing board protections, Reisman, while sympathetic and probably agreeing in principle, countered that adjustments could be worked out later. Or he pointed out that such factors as cheaper Canadian sugar prices would offset claimed cost disadvantages for manufacturers.

But behind the TNO support for marketing boards was a simple political fact. Mulroney's cabinet ministers, led by Wise with support from senior ministers such as Joe Clark, had promised that supply management policies would be preserved under any agreement. This commitment was tested many times during the negotiations. Finally, in February 1987, matters came to a head when 15 food manufacturing companies sent a joint letter to Joe Clark, the External Affairs minister, indicating that they would have to reconsider their support for free trade unless the supply management practices were changed. Simon Reisman was sent to talk them out of their planned action, and he was successful. Much later in the process, the beer industry also threatened to go public against the FTA unless it was protected, a message that was carried directly to the prime minister. The beer industry was genuinely vulnerable to U.S. competition, and it possessed a real public relations capacity to seriously embarrass the government with an anti-free trade campaign. The industry prevailed. Food manufacturers did not fare as well. In the end, the supply management system was protected, ensuring that a key piece of the political coalition needed to secure passage of the FTA was still on side. But immediately after the deal was signed and the 1988 election won, food producers renewed their call for an end to marketing boards.

BANKERS: OUTSIDE LOOKING IN

Initial decisions about the structure and composition of the SAGIT on financial services provided an early signal to the powerful banking community that the banks might be traded off for Canadian gains in other areas of the negotiations. The SAGIT was broadly defined to include general issues of trade in financial services, and included only two members from the big six chartered banks. To the consternation of the banking community, the SAGIT also included a representative from a foreign bank, Lloyd's Bank of Canada. Canadian bankers doubted that any other country would allow a foreign bank to sit on an advisory group sworn to secrecy because of the sensitivity of its deliberations for the *national* interest.

The Canadian banking industry did not join the general movement toward free trade that occurred in 1983–85. This was partly because trade and banking had operated historically on separate tracks in the economy. International financial matters were the jealously guarded preserve of the Department of Finance in Canada and the Treasury Department in the United States. The history of banking policy in Canada since the Second World War revolved around a series of Bank Act reviews, occurring roughly every 10 years. For the big six banks, this made policy-making a fairly regular, and orderly, process. To preserve this order in the free trade negotiations, banking and finance issues would be kept away from the trade negotiators. This view was especially strong in the U.S., and the final deal on financial services was made directly by Treasury Secretary James Baker. Likewise in Canada, although Simon Reisman wanted to hold on to the banking sector for possible trade-offs, it was Michael Wilson who made the final decisions on the deal in financial services.

The banking industry itself was divided on the free trade issue during the negotiations and after the deal had been made. The Royal Bank, Canada's largest, supported the FTA because of its positive overall effects on economic growth, rather than because of its direct banking provisions. The Toronto-Dominion Bank, always Canada's most nationalistic, opposed the FTA, because it judged the banking provisions to be simply a bad trade-off. The Bank of Nova Scotia also opposed the deal, in part because its CEO, Ced Ritchie, had strong Liberal sympathies. Others withheld support because they believed in 1987 that an FTA would not be successfully negotiated. Because of these divisions in the banking community, the Canadian Bankers Association initially declined an invitation to join the Canadian Alliance for Trade and Job Opportunities.

During the negotiations, the banks were convinced from a very early stage that their sector would be traded off to secure gains in other areas of the agreement. They knew that both Simon Reisman and Bill Hood, the TNO negotiator for financial services, strongly favoured national treatment. In the banks' view, the national treatment concept was unbalanced. Granting it to American banks would gain little for Canada because the Americans could not deliver reciprocal treatment. This was because of the greater regulation of banks in the U.S. by state governments and the fact that the American banking system under Glass-Steagall legislation was much more decentralized and fragmented than the Canadian system, which was anchored to the branch banking system controlled by the big six banks. As one Canadian banker put it, with only mild hyperbole, "Banking and Glass-Steagall are to the Americans what culture is to Canada." In the TNO's strategic view, the banks were strong Canadian-owned institutions, capable of competing in world markets. They would gain from the greater economic growth that would result from the FTA. TNO also knew that the U.S. was already more open to foreign banking than Canada, and Canadian banks would simply have to give up some of their protection. When the TNO formally asked the Canadian banks to itemize their complaints about barriers to the American market, the relative openness of the American system was confirmed in the embarrassingly short list that the banks produced.

During the negotiations, relations between TNO and the banks were partly influenced by the perception in the banking community that Mulroney and his principal ministers were against the banks. The government had a number of ministers and MPs who blamed the Eastern Canadian establishment for permitting the Liberals to run Canada for the previous 20 years. Bankers were part of the establishment, and now that the "outs" were "in," they viewed the banks with mistrust. The Tory caucus also contained strong supporters of small business, and the small business lobby had been critical of Canada's big banks. The House of Commons Committee on Finance, headed by populist politician Don Blenkarn, made its reputation partly through "bank bashing." Even Finance Minister Michael Wilson, who would normally be an ally of the banks, was from the securities industry, a sector with a long history of conflict with the banks. Long accustomed to good relations with government, the banks found themselves in an unusual position, on the outside looking in.

The banks' position was made worse as a result of world-wide pressures for financial deregulation, especially concerning the relationship between the banking and securities industries.[8] In the 1980s, pressure for change was coming from the technical revolution brought on by computers that allowed capital to move around the world at breath-taking speed. Canadian banks were concerned that their world-wide share of business would decline in the face of the challenge from Japanese and German banks that had already been allowed into the securities business. Under North American financial legislation, the four pillars of the financial system — banks, trust companies, securities, firms and insurance companies — were prohibited from engaging in one another's business areas. This separation was designed to preserve probity and trust in the financial system, and to prevent concentrations of economic power. However, gradual deregulation in the 1970s had produced a new array of financial instruments that regulators could not keep up with. The pressures for deregulation had already resulted in a review of policy at the federal level in 1984–85; and in December 1986 in Ontario, the province with the most decisive role in securities regulation, the government announced that it would deregulate the securities industry and allow banks to buy securities firms. The specific stimulus for this pre-emptive move, which came just as the TNO was negotiating financial services with the U.S., was a report showing that the main securities firms in Canada were seriously undercapitalized.

The big banks had already been urging Ottawa to move in the same direction in their meetings with the Finance minister and the governor of the Bank of Canada in June 1986. These pressures triggered a classic federal-provincial quarrel. Following the British "big bang" deregulation of the London financial market, Ontario and Quebec found themselves in a competition to be the first to deregulate in Canada. In November 1986, the federal government passed an order-in-council giving permission to the Bank of Nova Scotia to establish a wholly owned subsidiary in the securities field in Quebec. This seemed designed to give Montreal an edge against changes expected in Ontario towards partial deregulation. The Quebec move prompted Ontario to announce a full-scale, rather than just a partial, deregulation. As a result of this abrupt policy shift, Canadian banks were given a one-year advantage over potential foreign buyers of securities firms. Thirteen takeovers of securities firms quickly occurred, with scarcely any consultation about the policy with the securities industry.

The Ontario decision to deregulate probably gave away some of Canada's bargaining leverage in the free trade negotiations. If the same changes had been offered later, it might have been in exchange for U.S. concessions. However, given Ontario Premier David Peterson's opposition to the FTA, such co-ordination might have been impossible. The reverse case could even be made, namely that the deregulation move energized the financial services negotiations, which up to that time offered little prospect of Canadian gains in the banking sector. It prompted Canada to press for any benefits that

might result from expected future changes in the Glass-Steagall legislation to merge the American banking and securities industries.

Banking issues loomed large in the final stage of the negotiations,
not only because they were "deal breakers," central to the two sides'
respective demands, but also because the key ministers at the table
were Michael Wilson and James Baker. Both men carried a special
brief for their own portfolios. A banking deal would be done, and
they would do it. Canadian banks were never won over by the deal,
however. In the 1988 election, the banks mostly stood aside from
the debate, and did not openly join the final rush of support by the
rest of the business community, preferring to remain on the outside.

ENERGY: CONSOLIDATING GAINS
WEST AND SOUTH

When she was opposition energy critic, Patricia Carney headed a
task force in 1983–84 to help develop the Tory energy policies that
paved the way for the pro-market energy accords in 1985 and 1986.[9]
Many of the members appointed to the SAGIT on Energy had been
associated with the Conservative task force, and saw the SAGIT as
a natural continuation of the policy process flowing from the accords. Energy interests in the oil and gas sector were also represented through bodies such as the Canadian Petroleum Association
(CPA) and the Independent Petroleum Association of Canada
(IPAC).[10] CPA represented the larger foreign- and Canadian-owned
integrated companies, and IPAC represented smaller Canadian
companies. CPA was concerned with both the upstream (exploration) and downstream (production) aspects of the industry, while
IPAC had a greater focus on the exploration sector, especially gas
exports. The industry protected its interests through strong links
with the governments of Alberta and Saskatchewan. Oil and gas
interests also had their own SAGIT, headed by Robert Pierce, vice
president of NOVA, an Alberta-based oil company, and CEOs of three
major oil companies were active in the BCNI. As a result, the oil and
gas industry was well represented in the negotiations.

The strategy of energy interests during the negotiations was two-pronged. First, they wanted to keep an extremely low profile for energy issues. Second, they wanted to consolidate and extend the gains they had achieved already under the Mulroney government, which had created virtual free trade in energy through its policies. The strategy was rooted in bitter memories in the oil patch about the 1980 National Energy Program (NEP), imposed on the industry by the Trudeau Liberals. The program had involved a massive federal intervention carried out in the wake of the 1979 energy crisis.[11] Though negotiations occurred in 1981 between Ottawa and Alberta, the NEP was seen in Western Canada as a unilateral, and illegitimate, action by Ottawa to favour Eastern consumers at the expense of the West. CPA and IPAC had been excluded almost entirely from the policy process surrounding the NEP and its aftermath, and were determined that this would not happen again. The free trade agreement would be used to ensure that there were no more NEPs. The industry also wanted to ensure that consultations for the free trade negotiations would be thorough, but discreet. They knew from the NEP experience that energy could easily get caught up in emotional nationalist issues about Canada's energy security, and this could thwart their free trade plans. To avoid the attention of energy nationalists, the CPA and IPAC decided not to join any national pro-free trade campaigns, such as that launched by the Alliance for Trade and Job Opportunities. In retrospect, it is remarkable that the energy issue did not surface more frequently and controversially during the free trade debate of 1986–87.

Discretion was crucial because the FTA offered an unparalleled opportunity to drive heavy nails into the NEP coffin fashioned by the Mulroney government immediately after taking office. In 1983–84, the Conservatives had worked hard to build bridges to the oil and gas sector, and committed themselves to undoing the Trudeau NEP. Determined to restore markets and cement the Western leg of its electoral coalition, the Mulroney government moved quickly in its first year in office to establish both the Western Accord and the

Natural Gas Accord. The Western Accord dealt mainly with oil and restored the continental energy market to a degree not seen since the years prior to the first energy crisis in 1973. The accord on gas significantly deregulated the natural gas industry and led to the elimination of the surplus test for gas exports, a requirement that producers set aside a 25-year supply of reserves for Canada's energy security. The absence of major political controversy over the elimination of the surplus test indicated that in the late 1980s energy could be dealt with like any other trade commodity. This had not been the case earlier in the 1980s. In their approach to the issue, industry and the TNO read the political climate accurately. Eastern Canadian worries about oil and gas security rise and fall with the price of oil. By the mid-1980s, energy prices were stable or declining, so there was political room to move.

The strategy to keep a low profile for energy was seriously challenged only once during the negotiations. In mid-1987, a few press reports surfaced indicating that there might be a separate chapter on energy, with a provision on proportionality. This produced a flurry of charges by the Pro Canada Network about an energy sell-out. To marshal a response, political advisers to federal Energy Minister Marcel Masse contacted energy interests about creating a public pro-free trade energy coalition. CPA and IPAC strategists advised against the move. Although several meetings were held, and would provide the foundation for public action in the last month of the 1988 election battle, the low profile prevailed for the negotiations, and the issue went away.

Both TNO and the industry concluded early on that Canada, especially the West, stood to gain from the elimination of border measures in the energy sector. Canada's energy trade balance was healthy, but Canadian negotiators knew that in previous decades the U.S. had erected numerous barriers against Canadian energy imports. TNO did not want to take the energy issue to the Americans, however, not only because of its potential for controversy, but also because gains to Canada would accrue naturally from U.S. efforts to reduce border measures. The Americans would take the lead on this issue and pay a price on other issues for changes that would benefit Canada anyway. Perhaps the U.S. would have paid even more had the pre-FTA Conservative moves toward free trade in energy been held back, to be traded during the negotiations for other concessions from the U.S. This did not occur because Conservative policy was driven by domestic, not bilateral, political imperatives, especially the desire to make good on election promises to Western Canada. In addition, both energy accords were concluded before the government had firmly made the decision to pursue the free trade negotiations.

Canada originally did not favour a separate chapter for energy in the FTA. The energy issue was handled by TNO official John Donaghy, who reported to Germain Denis, the assistant chief negotiator for market access for goods. Organized in this way, energy would be treated in the negotiations as just another commodity to which GATT-like regimes would apply, and the trade-off would be a straightforward one. If improved access to the U.S. market was to be achieved for Canadian energy products, it would have to be accompanied by assurances for the U.S. about security of contracted supplies. This trade-off led to the proportionality provisions, described in FTA Chapter 4. Canada could restrict supply for reasons of conservation, but contracted supplies could not be arbitrarily cut off. They could only be reduced proportionately, based on a three-year average of previous volumes. The American negotiators also had an interest in keeping the profile of the energy issue low because they had a serious political problem with energy at home. The U.S. energy lobby, centred in Texas, the home state of Treasury Secretary Baker, was opposed to increased Canadian imports, and its opposition could have been enough to scuttle free trade. Both CPA and IPAC spent as much time lobbying their counterpart U.S. organizations, the American Petroleum Institute and the Independent Petroleum Association, as they did lobbying in Canada. The American organizations were opposed to free trade in energy because they believed that Canadian oil and gas exports were subsidized. These pressures were balanced, however, by a

U.S. desire for the extra margin of energy security that Canadian supplies could provide in the long run.

The U.S. had gone along originally with Canada's desire to avoid a separate chapter on energy. But in the final weeks of the negotiations they changed course and insisted that there would have to be a separate chapter, realizing that the terms on energy would help them sell the deal to Congress and the American public. The basic provisions of that chapter were in place by the time of the last major bilateral negotiating session in Cornwall in August 1987. However, as they travelled up the TNO line along with other border measures, from Donaghy to Denis and from him to Ritchie and Reisman, the energy provisions were given the nod, but in a way that led to some later misinterpretation. The final rush to produce the energy chapter revealed the lack of clear communication in the TNO line. As a result, the presence of a separate chapter on energy with proportionality provisions, even though similar to normal GATT rules, caught the Canadian oil and gas industry and the federal Department of Energy, Mines and Resources off guard. There were numerous expressions of concern about just what had been agreed to. But most of these concerns were cleared up after TNO officials explained what had happened.

To no one's surprise, the Canadian energy industry supported the FTA and its energy provisions. Energy interests did not anticipate that the agreement would generate immediate increases in trade volumes, but they were confident of longer-term benefits, including improvements in the energy investment climate. There were some Eastern gas utilities that expressed concern about potential future shortages of supply, but dissidents were in the minority. To many energy players, the FTA meant that they now had virtual constitutional protection against unilateral meddling by some future government dominated by Eastern Canadians. Key energy interests also accepted without enthusiasm the grandfathering of Canada's foreign investment rules on energy projects on the Canada Lands. Former Energy minister Patricia Carney was at the table as Trade minister in October 1987, and she was among those who insisted on these grandfathering provisions. Without them, the energy provisions would have been much more vulnerable to attack.

Canadian business was instrumental in putting free trade on the national policy agenda, and its ability to maintain a united front throughout the long negotiations when the government was besieged by its critics enhanced its influential role. Behind the united public front, of course, there were substantial divisions between, and even within, sectors. Traces of these divisions were revealed in the formal consultative machinery, the tactics of sectoral interest groups, and in the continuous access enjoyed by both BCNI and the CMA. But they were papered over sufficiently to present a broadly united business front in favour of free trade. Although business did not exercise a decisive influence on the scope or core strategy of the negotiations, it was of crucial importance in shoring up the American business coalition at strategic times. Canadian business also provided a consistent ally for the beleaguered Mulroney government, even at those times when many in the business community thought the government was in serious danger of fumbling its free trade initiative.

6

NO SEAT AT THE TABLE

David Peterson moved restlessly about the Ottawa conference room where Canada's prime minister and the 10 provincial premiers, along with assorted officials, were meeting. Ontario's premier was feeling good. Always in a minority position on free trade at these gatherings of first ministers, he was finally being vindicated in his scepticism about Brian Mulroney's leap of faith. It was September 1987, and the free trade negotiations were clearly in trouble, with continued American stonewalling making agreement improbable. As well, Peterson and his Liberals had just crushed the Ontario Progressive Conservatives in a provincial election in which Conservative leader Larry Grossman had made support for free trade the main plank in his campaign. As the first ministers discussed the trade issue, Peterson rose a number of times to pour himself coffee, and then, balancing the cup and saucer in hand and sipping his coffee, he moved around the perimeter of the room, interjecting comments into the discussion, chiding his fellow premiers over their support for a losing cause. When finally he interrupted the comments of Newfoundland's feisty premier, Brian Peckford, in this fashion, Peckford, frustrated by 15 months of Ontario nay-saying on the negotiations, told Peterson in blunt language what he could do with his sly scolding. Following the meeting, in a statement to the press, he rebuked the Ontario premier further for using the endangered talks for his own political purposes.

The meeting of first ministers was the main act in the second ring of the free trade circus being managed by Ottawa. Federal-provincial negotiation is a tried-and-true way of making public policy in Canada, but the formal involvement of the provinces in Canadian trade policy is a relatively new thing.[1] Provincial participation originated in the Tokyo Round of multilateral trade negotiations that lasted from 1973 to 1979. With the achievement of substantial reductions in tariffs in previous negotiating rounds, the Tokyo Round was expected to move into new issues involving non-tariff barriers to trade that would touch more directly on areas of provincial jurisdiction. Recognizing this, provincial trade officials, especially those from Alberta, demanded to be consulted on Canada's position at Geneva. In response, Ottawa provided irregular briefings to provincial officials; and although the consultation was one way, the provinces nevertheless received reasonably detailed information about the ongoing multilateral negotiations.

The Tokyo Round experience raised provincial expectations about participation in future trade negotiations. And the prospect of bilateral free trade negotiations could be expected to touch off demands for more than one-way consultation, since the United States provided by far the largest market for the exports of every province except British Columbia (where the countries of Asia and the Pacific were equally important). As the government edged its way toward a free trade decision during the winter of 1984–85, however, the provinces as a whole were not a major preoccupation. But, at a meeting of first ministers in February 1985 following the release of the Kelleher discussion paper, the Alberta premier, Peter Lougheed, offered strong support for the idea of negotiating a bilateral trade agreement with the United States. Not hearing any explicit opposition to the idea, and placing considerable faith in Lougheed's political judgement, the prime minister took this as provincial assent to continue to move forward on the initiative. After the Shamrock Summit in Quebec City in March 1985, however, when some form of negotiation looked like a serious prospect, the provinces began efforts to define a formal role for themselves in the proceedings.

Not surprisingly, the call for provincial participation in any bilateral negotiation came first and loudest from the West, led by Alberta. Although Lougheed and Mulroney seemed to be on the same wavelength on free trade, the Western provinces were not about to trust their fate in a bilateral negotiation to a federal government that might be dominated by Ontario and Quebec interests. The surest way to avoid Central Canadian treachery would be to secure a Western seat at the table. And so, at a meeting in the spring of 1985, the four Western premiers, including Manitoba's NDP premier, Howard Pawley, expressed their support for bilateral trade liberalization, but requested "full provincial participation" in any negotiations. Ontario and Quebec, as Canada's largest exporters, also endorsed the concept of full participation in any negotiations that might come about, although they were much more cautious in their support for trade liberalization, especially Ontario. The Atlantic provinces, while supporting negotiations, were neutral on the question of full provincial participation. They were more inclined to rely on the federal government to protect their interests against Central Canadian predators.

SANDBAGGING THE PRIME MINISTER

The announcement of Mulroney's decision in September 1985 to initiate free trade negotiations with the United States, while not unexpected, nevertheless caught some provinces off guard. Provincial interests were not a major factor in the federal decision to negotiate, and no formal federal-provincial consultations on the issue had been undertaken, although there had been informal discussions between federal and provincial officials. Determined not to be shut out of the negotiation process itself, the Central and Western provinces set out to capture a role for themselves. Their opportunity came at a first ministers' meeting in Halifax in November 1985.

In reaction to the rancour that prevailed in federal-provincial relations during the Trudeau era, Brian Mulroney had committed his government to the principle of national reconciliation in federal-provincial relations through greater co-operation and communication with the provinces. But during his first year in office, with the exception of energy policy, there had been few opportunities to give the principle concrete policy expression. Free trade clearly involved provincial interests, however, and Mulroney would find it difficult to deny their claim to a right to participate on the issue. Moreover, the apparently unconditional federal commitment to co-operation with the provinces emboldened the premiers in their bid for expanded powers. The stage was set for an aggressive provincial effort to capture a seat at the free trade table.

Federal planning for the first ministers' meeting was handled by the Department of External Affairs on the trade negotiations issue, while the Federal-Provincial Relations Office handled general planning for the meeting. Neither was prepared for the ambush that awaited Mulroney in Halifax. There was no serious discussion with the prime minister in advance of the meeting about what the provinces were likely to demand, nor was there any serious advance planning about how to respond to the demands.

The provinces, on the other hand, had prepared well, co-ordinating their approach in advance. On the afternoon of the first day of the meeting, the Western premiers, supported by Ontario, insisted that the provinces should be full, and equal, participants in the upcoming negotiations. Ontario then upped the ante, proposing the creation of a joint federal-provincial secretariat to oversee the negotiations. The prime minister was on the spot, and External Affairs officials were left squirming. Simon Reisman, who had been appointed chief negotiator earlier in the month, was flown to Halifax the following day to put out the fire. Reisman's blunt rejection of provincial demands was enough to scuttle the Ontario proposal for a joint secretariat. But he was unable to shut the provinces out entirely, and External Affairs Minister Joe Clark put forward the deliberately undefined principle of "full provincial participation" in the negotiations in order to satisfy provincial demands.

The premiers left Halifax under the impression that they had secured their goal of substantial participation in the upcoming negotiations. They subsequently interpreted this to mean equality of participation, with Reisman operating under instructions from the 11 first ministers, plus a role in framing the negotiating mandate and a seat at the negotiation table. Although this was clearly unacceptable to Ottawa, Mulroney was reluctant to say so because of his loudly proclaimed commitment to co-operation in relations with the provinces. As a result, the provinces continued to press their case and Ottawa was forced to fend them off, without saying no outright. This ambiguity resulted in a significant diversion of the energies of the new Trade Negotiations Office being assembled atop the Metropolitan Life Tower in downtown Ottawa. Rather than assigning the bulk of his time and that of his staff to preparations for the substance of the upcoming negotiations, Reisman was preoccupied with the question of provincial participation during the crucial months leading up to the start of negotiations in May 1986.

In January 1986, provincial representatives designated by the premiers met with Reisman in Ottawa, and they agreed to hold regular, formal consultations. The group would be formalized as the Continuing Committee on Trade Negotiations (CCTN) and would meet on a monthly basis throughout the negotiations. This represented an unprecedented degree of provincial involvement in the trade sphere. For this reason, most provincial trade officials were satisfied to be consulted on a regular basis. However, some of the provincial CCTN representatives insisted that consultation did not go far enough, demanding instead a joint decision-making process. During the next few months, Joe Clark, accompanied by the TNO assistant chief negotiator, Alan Nymark, visited each premier to discuss the ways and means of provincial participation. At none of these meetings was equality of participation granted, but neither were the limits to participation clearly defined by

Clark. In March, the premiers proposed that provincial representatives should attend those negotiating sessions dealing with issues directly affecting provincial interests, but would speak only with Reisman's consent. The federal reply would come in June, in time for the first ministers' meeting.

A SEPARATE TENT

Although the provinces had managed to gain admittance to the free trade circus, Reisman and his officials would see to it that their ring was set up in a separate tent, several steps removed from the main acts featuring Canada-U.S. and business-government relations. Shortly before the first ministers' meeting scheduled for June 1986, the prime minister was persuaded to write each premier to say that there would not be equality of participation. Mulroney carried this message into the meeting on June 2. He promised full consultation, but told the provinces they would not be granted a formal role in the establishment of the negotiating mandate, nor would they have a seat at the table.

The provincial coalition collapsed in the face of federal resolve. First to defect were the Atlantic provinces, never convinced that a direct provincial voice was in their interests anyway, since it would probably be dominated by the larger provinces. They decided they would be better off to rely on indirect influence with the Feds to protect their position. The Western provinces, led by Alberta, had mounted an aggressive effort to capture a formal role in the proceedings in order to guard against Central Canadian perfidy. But they agreed to go along with the federal position for the time being, keeping a wary eye on Ontario and Quebec. Quebec's Bourassa also decided that equality of participation was not an issue worth risking isolation over, and he accepted the principle of full consultation instead. In the end, Ontario's Peterson was left isolated in his demand for a seat at the table, and he reluctantly decided to go along with the consultation alternative.

Mulroney had agreed to consult the provinces, and consultation they would get, in unprecedented proportions. Over the course of the negotiations, the prime minister and the premiers held three regular first ministers' meetings, plus eight special sessions on free trade. Reisman and his officials provided monthly and quarterly briefings on the state of the negotiations. Working group meetings on various sectoral issues were also held with the provinces. Finally, meetings of the CCTN were held before each plenary Canada-U.S. negotiating session, and after each session Alan Nymark briefed the provinces by telephone on developments in the negotiations. With all this activity, the provincial premiers could hardly claim they were not being consulted. The communication channel was viewed by some provincial officials as being largely one-way, however, and they suspected TNO of using CCTN principally for a "show and tell" exercise, where Reisman and his officials showed, and heard, only what they wanted.

Although first ministers' meetings provided the most senior political level for federal-provincial meetings on the negotiations, the CCTN provided the most important forum for consultations. At a meeting in late June 1986, the provinces were presented with the broad negotiating mandates on each of the major issues. The mandates had been discussed in general terms at a first ministers' meeting earlier in the month before going forward to the federal cabinet for approval. TNO officials presented this information to the provincial representatives, and asked for their views, but carefully avoided seeking either approval or agreement from the provinces. As the mandates evolved during the course of the negotiations, TNO took the changes back to provincial officials and first ministers, again for information. Reisman claimed to the provincial CCTN representatives that they were receiving more, and better, information about the negotiations than were federal cabinet ministers. That was undoubtedly the case, since the cabinet was not kept informed about the state of the negotiations, and only those federal ministers directly involved in the talks had more than the vaguest idea what was happening.

The CCTN also provided a forum for the expression of provincial concerns, usually about particular issues in the negotiations. And although the formal meetings of the committee were largely taken up by federal slide shows, they provided a foundation for subsequent informal, bilateral meetings between federal and provincial officials where provincial concerns could frequently be resolved satisfactorily. Nevertheless, CCTN representatives often complained that they were being "handled" by TNO, and that they were receiving only the information Reisman wanted them to have in "one-way" consultations. Furthermore, some provincial officials viewed the TNO approach as combative, seeing the provinces rather than the United States as the adversary in the negotiations. Their complaints about process fell on deaf ears, however, not only with Reisman and federal ministers, as might be expected, but also with most of the officials' bosses, the premiers. Process is the peculiar concern of bureaucrats who spend their professional lives embroiled in turf battles, and the majority of premiers were unwilling to get into another fight over the issue. So the endless consultations continued, while individual provinces set about guarding their flanks as best they could to protect themselves from being blind-sided in the negotiations. Provincial strategies in these protective efforts varied widely, reflecting both their positions on the issue of free trade and their relative power to influence outcomes.

WESTERN CANADA: READY, AYE, READY

Strongest and earliest support among the provincial governments for free trade was to be found in Western Canada, especially Alberta and British Columbia. Alberta Premier Peter Lougheed played a key role in influencing Mulroney's decision to negotiate free trade, and when he left office in October 1985 he continued his active support of the initiative, support that included a warning to David Peterson about the adverse consequences for national unity should Ontario cause the deal to be jettisoned. Alberta had been badly burned by the Trudeau government's National Energy Program in the early 1980s, and was hit hard by the recession that followed.

The Alberta government wanted a free trade agreement in order to secure access to the American market for the province's energy and agricultural products. Equally important, Alberta wanted to lock in the renunciation of federal interference in energy policy that had been achieved through the Western Accord in 1985.

Lougheed's successor as premier, Donald Getty, appointed Harold Millican as Alberta's trade representative to the CCTN in January 1986. Formerly Lougheed's executive assistant, provincial deputy minister of intergovernmental affairs, and executive director of the Canadian Petroleum Association, Millican was a smooth conciliator, determined to keep the Feds moving in the right direction, since Alberta's interests were well served by the free trade initiative. Familiar with Reisman from his years as Finance deputy, he knew that honey worked better than vinegar when dealing with the chief negotiator. Many in the Alberta bureaucracy, still angry over the NEP, were prepared to do battle with any federal agency, including the TNO. However, Millican preferred to keep his head down at CCTN meetings, maintaining constant surveillance over TNO activities, while holding frequent private dinners with Reisman and his people. Although the Alberta trade representative and his officials concentrated on the key agriculture, energy, and petro-chemicals sectors, they also supported Reisman's efforts in other sectors less directly related to Alberta's interests, such as services and banking.

On the crucial issue of energy, Millican preferred to keep a low Alberta profile as well. Recognizing that the question of secure energy supplies remained very sensitive in Central Canada, he believed it would not be in the province's interest to single out energy for special consideration, but instead to treat it as any other commodity in the negotiations. In this position he found common cause with Reisman, who was resisting American pressure to have a separate working group, and a separate chapter in any agreement, on energy. Alberta energy officials were anxious over this strategy, concerned that their key issue was being neglected, and pressed to have it raised directly, both in CCTN and in the bilateral negotiations. Millican's strategy to keep energy under wraps prevailed, however, and the issue remained a "sleeper" throughout the negotiations. When a separate chapter on energy did appear in the final agreement, it took many by surprise, as Millican had intended.

British Columbia, too, strongly supported the free trade initiative, but originally for different reasons. As already noted, the province was less dependent on trade with the U.S. than were other provinces, since it had strong trade ties with Asia and the Pacific. Growing U.S. protectionism did threaten investment in B.C. industry, however, and securing the American market would stabilize the investment climate in the province. And although U.S. tariffs were not a major concern in British Columbia, since many products were shipped duty free, industries in the province were adversely affected by Canadian tariffs, which increased their input costs. Negotiating the removal of these tariffs was in the provincial interest. For these reasons, British Columbia was an early supporter, and in August 1985 Premier Bill Bennett proposed a resolution in favour of free trade at the annual meeting of provincial premiers.

British Columbia's approach to the negotiations was fundamentally altered in October 1986, however, when a 15 per cent countervailing duty was imposed by the U.S. government on imports of Canadian softwood lumber. This case had been in the wind since the spring, when the lumber issue had nearly derailed the negotiations in the Senate Finance Committee. British Columbia was the largest lumber-producing province, and Bennett's successor, William Vander Zalm, had no stomach for a prolonged fight with the U.S. on the issue. British Columbia's interests had been hurt earlier in the negotiations when the U.S. imposed a five-year tariff on imports of Canadian cedar shakes and shingles. In that case, an angry Canadian reply, followed by retaliatory tariffs, failed to change the American position. Vander Zalm was determined to avoid yet another punitive U.S. trade remedy action, and the federal government was prepared to let B.C. take the lead on lumber. The federal strategy was also influenced by the fact that Patricia Carney, the federal Trade minister, was the senior minister from B.C. in the

Mulroney cabinet. At a meeting in Vancouver in November 1986, the first ministers agreed to raise export prices for softwood lumber through the imposition of a 15 per cent export tax, rendering the U.S. countervailing duty unnecessary. Ontario Premier David Peterson was the lone dissident, but his strenuous objections were insufficient to counter the influence of British Columbia's dominant position in the lumber industry.

During 1986, the proportion of B.C. trade that was subject to American countervailing duties grew from less than 1 per cent to 40 per cent. A free trade deal that would offer some protection against U.S. trade remedy actions was now essential to British Columbia's interests. But as the stakes increased, B.C. enthusiasm for the way the negotiations were being conducted by Reisman and the TNO declined. With an economy more diversified than that of Alberta, B.C. could not focus on a limited number of issues with the same intensity that enabled Alberta to keep a constant check on how its interests were faring in the negotiations. Reisman was carrying more of British Columbia's eggs in his negotiation basket, and provincial officials responsible for their safekeeping were being drawn into the consultation process, although at a lower level. Vander Zalm's deputy attended one meeting of the CCTN and never returned, leaving representation to officials from the ministries of economic development and intergovernmental affairs.

Although these officials were satisfied with the general consultative process afforded by CCTN and the Nymark briefings, they were less pleased with the federal-provincial consultations on specific issues that directly affected provincial interests, such as fish, fruit and vegetables, hydro-electricity, and wine, to say nothing of lumber. In addition, they were increasingly sceptical about Reisman's capacity to deliver the "big deal" he promised, and especially concerned that no fallback Canadian position was being prepared by TNO. Dubious about Reisman's ability to handle the sectoral issues and his claims of superior Canadian preparedness, and suspicious of being manipulated by TNO, they pressed for greater access to the process. However, their complaints were not well received in Premier Vander Zalm's office, where there was little interest in turf battles between federal and provincial bureaucracies. In the end, while still supportive of free trade, British Columbia was less enthusiastic about the course of the negotiations and their results than its Western neighbour.

ATLANTIC CANADA: PLAYING FROM THE PERIPHERY

Among the Atlantic provinces, Newfoundland and Nova Scotia were most fully engaged in the consultative process throughout the negotiations. Although generally supportive of the free trade initiative, they were less concerned than the Western provinces about the concept of full participation, partly because they were not adequately staffed to participate fully. Peckford's Newfoundland attempted to offset this disadvantage by concentrating its full attention on the issues that mattered most to the province, principally fish. Nova Scotia, on the other hand, with a more diversified economy, had to span a greater portion of the free trade agenda.

Nova Scotia had also been the target of a number of U.S. countervailing duties applied against its products, including fish and tires, two principal exports. The province therefore had a keen interest in an agreement that would restrain American use of trade remedies. To steer a safe course through the free trade shoals, Premier Buchanan chose Fred Dickson as Nova Scotia's trade representative to the CCTN. A Halifax lawyer and trusted adviser to Buchanan, Dickson co-ordinated a group of officials in the provincial Department of Industry, Trade and Technology.

More than most other provinces, Nova Scotia was concerned that the price for restraints on American trade remedy actions should not include limiting subsidies to industries for regional development purposes. Reisman was no fan of subsidy programs, however, and was propounding a big "national treatment" deal with the United States, involving subsidy disciplines in exchange for restraints on trade remedy actions. As presented to Nova Scotia officials at the start of the negotiations, Reisman's plan would open up the Canadian economy and subject it to a cold shower of competition. But a cold shower for Canada might result in pneumonia for Nova Scotia. Furthermore, should the federal government be persuaded to deal away regional development and supply management programs, the consequences for Nova Scotia would be dire. Dickson and his officials were wary.

An Atlantic coalition offered a measure of protection against both the TNO and the other provinces in these areas, so trade representatives from Nova Scotia and the other three Atlantic provinces met periodically to co-ordinate their positions. They also established their own working group on fish, after Reisman refused an Atlantic request for a federal-provincial working group on the issue, and the group prepared a proposal for submission to the TNO. Nova Scotia also took the lead in getting the Atlantic provinces to develop criteria for defining allowable regional development grants that would not be subject to countervail actions. They developed this proposal, and leaked it to the press, in order to prepare the ground for a defection in the unlikely event that Reisman was able to sell the Americans on his idea for a subsidies code. The proposal was deemed sufficient for protective purposes, since provincial soundings in Washington indicated that an agreement on subsidies had little chance of acceptance in the United States. Had it been otherwise, Reisman's proposal would have set off alarm bells in Atlantic Canada, where subsidies for regional development purposes were nearly sacrosanct. Nevertheless, the whole subsidies question had to be managed carefully by TNO because provincial opposition over this issue could have scuttled the entire agreement.

Within Nova Scotia itself, officials consulted early and extensively with industries to uncover problems with access to the U.S. market that would need to be addressed. They also identified particularly sensitive industries, vulnerable to competition from American imports. By the time negotiations began, Nova Scotia had identified the industries that needed protection. The results of the consultations, along with the list of vulnerable industries, were duly passed over to the TNO so that they could be integrated into the planning for the negotiations. As the negotiations progressed, however, provincial officials lost faith in the commitment of the TNO to the consultative process that was supposed to be under way. Instead, they came to believe that the principal TNO objective was to keep the provinces off balance and in line. To counter this, they tried to deal directly with Reisman on a more frequent basis. A meeting was arranged between Reisman and Michelin Tire executives to bring home to the chief negotiator the importance of incentives to locate industries in the Atlantic region. In addition, the first ministers' meetings became a more important channel to get across the provincial message, and Buchanan was briefed extensively on Nova Scotia's positions.

While ensuring its regional house was in order, Nova Scotia realized that, as always, Central Canada would exercise the major influence over outcomes in this federal-provincial game. The task for Nova Scotia, therefore, was to position itself somewhere between Ontario and Quebec, waiting to see which would influence the direction of the negotiations more. Although Nova Scotia was generally supportive of free trade, this strategy often required provincial officials to adopt a negative stance during Reisman's CCTN briefings, in order to preserve its middle position. The province declared beer and agricultural supply management programs non-negotiable, and insisted that regional development programs be preserved. With Quebec, Nova Scotia demanded that an adjustment program be developed to assist the transition to free trade, and with Ontario it demanded protection for cultural and social programs. The province maintained this balancing act throughout the negotiations as a means to protect its interests. Once the deal was done, Nova Scotia held out its approval in order to stimulate federal offers of incentives to sign on, and in the end was the last province to approve the agreement.

Quebec: Surprise Support

Quebec had long been thought to be the province with the most to lose from trade liberalization, with large numbers of inefficient industries concentrated in areas of declining Canadian comparative advantage. As a result, the province's opposition to free trade was a good bet. However, the Quebec position evolved from the "positively neutral" stance towards the initiative taken by the Parti Québécois governments of René Lévesque and Pierre-Marc Johnson in late 1985 to the strong support offered by the Liberal government of Robert Bourassa at the first ministers' meeting in June 1986.

Ministers in the Parti Québécois government, such as Jacques Parizeau and Johnson, before he became PQ leader, were moving early in 1985 to develop a trade strategy for Quebec. Free trade appealed to them on economic grounds because it offered a way to address the growing problem of American protectionism and to transform Quebec's economy, making it more competitive internationally. A new business class had emerged in the 1980s, Québécois entrepreneurs who were confident of their ability to compete and enthusiastic about the prospect of free trade. A free trade treaty would also guarantee an economic association with the United States, and could eventually do the same with Canada. The establishment of economic association would take care of an issue of considerable anxiety to many in Quebec, and the question of Quebec's independence from Canada could then be addressed in political terms alone, more fertile ground for Parti Québécois aims. Officials in the Department of Industry, Trade and Technology were more cautious than the ministers, and resisted the free trade idea initially. However, some basic research plus preliminary soundings in the business community revealed a basis for support. Trade policy officials, in particular, were concerned about the threat of growing U.S. protectionism to Quebec's economy, and they uncovered similar fears among Quebec industries. These larger considerations brought the bureaucracy into line. Thus, Quebec was already moving in the same general direction by the time of Mulroney's announcement of the initiative in September 1985. And although PQ leader Pierre-Marc Johnson was preoccupied with his electoral misfortunes at the Halifax first ministers' meeting in November, the federal offer of full provincial participation resolved the major remaining doubts of Quebec officials.

The landslide election of Bourassa's Liberals in December 1985 again raised the possibility of Quebec opposition to the negotiations. Bourassa had early concerns about absorption into a North American market, and some Quebec industries were worried about exposure to competition. But in general there was substantial support from Quebec business for free trade, as there had been in the larger Canadian business community. And of course the bureaucracy had already laid the groundwork on the issue, coming down on the side of free trade. This support brought Bourassa and his government on side. In March 1986, the cabinet approved a statement identifying Quebec's interests in the negotiations and in each of the major sectors. It also included a set of conditions that would have to be satisfied before the province could endorse any agreement. Nothing in an agreement should detract from Quebec's distinctness, meaning no restraints in the fields of culture and communications, nor should anything affect the division of powers between Quebec and the federal government. The agreement would have to preserve adequate room for the promotion of economic development, including the use of subsidies for regional development. The province also wanted the federal government to provide adequate adjustment assistance for the transition to free trade. Finally, Quebec insisted on participation in the Canadian side of the negotiation process, though no seat at the bilateral table was requested. These conditions were largely met in the final agreement, with the important exception of adjustment assistance.

To oversee Quebec's participation in the federal-provincial arena, Bourassa appointed J.W. (Jake) Warren as Quebec's trade representative to the CCTN. A former federal deputy minister, high commissioner in London, and ambassador to Washington, and the Canadian co-ordinator for the Tokyo Round negotiations, Warren was the most senior and experienced of the CCTN representatives, clearly a match for Reisman. As had been done in Alberta, British Columbia, and Nova Scotia, Warren held consultations with Quebec industries to uncover problems of access to the U.S. market and identify those industries that were especially vulnerable to competition from American imports. This information was provided to the TNO for planning purposes. Quebec also undertook a number of sectoral analyses on its own initiative, and provided the results to TNO.

Quebec's sensitivities were also aired at the CCTN briefings, where Warren's stature made it difficult for Reisman to dismiss them as ill informed, as he did some of the interventions of other provincial representatives. His stature also cast Warren in the role of spokesman for general provincial opposition to aspects of the conduct of the negotiations by the federal government. Warren's job was made easier, however, because Quebec was in basic agreement with the federal position. This left him the relatively more straightforward task of working changes at the margin, rather than bringing about fundamental changes in federal positions.

Bourassa himself was well briefed and knowledgeable about the details of the issues in the negotiations that most directly affected the province, and he used this knowledge to ensure that Quebec's interests were addressed at meetings of first ministers. Bourassa also had an excellent personal relationship with Brian Mulroney, a matter of no small importance on free trade issues that were close to Quebec's heart, like James Bay hydro-electric exports. At the same time, however, the Quebec premier tried to play a facilitator's role in the process, smoothing over federal-provincial differences in an effort to keep the negotiations on track. In many respects, on free trade Quebec assumed the leadership role in both CCTN and first ministers that Ontario had played traditionally on national issues, speaking for the provinces on matters of general concern while searching for enough common ground with the federal government to preserve forward movement. More important, Quebec's support for free trade was crucial in view of the position adopted by Ontario towards the negotiations. In March 1986, Ontario proposed that the two provinces form a common front to face the federal government. Quebec declined the proposal, however, replying that its alliances would depend on the issues at hand, and Quebec's interests on them. Certainly, if Quebec had joined Ontario, it is likely that the free trade initiative would have been dropped, or defeated, in the face of Central Canadian opposition.

ONTARIO: SITTING ON THE SIDELINES

If Quebec's position on free trade was a surprise, Ontario's position was an absolute puzzle to many. The ambivalence of the province's Liberal government on the issue was signalled early on. Attending his first premiers' conference in St. John's in August 1985, David Peterson resisted pressure from Peter Lougheed to get on board the free trade bandwagon. Instead he called for a delay in the decision to negotiate until a thorough analysis of the impact of free trade could be completed. Peterson's initial caution was influenced not only by the minority status of his government, dependent on support from the Ontario New Democratic Party, but also by the opposition to free trade in the Ontario bureaucracy, where the deputy minister of Industry, Trade and Technology, George Mac-Donell, was strongly opposed because of concerns about job losses. Following the federal decision to pursue negotiations, Peterson appointed Bob Latimer as Ontario's trade representative to the CCTN. A former federal assistant deputy trade minister, Latimer was well connected in Ottawa and had extensive experience as a trade negotiator. As his immediate assignment, Latimer was to asked to attempt to reduce the acrimony that was developing in the Toronto-Ottawa exchanges over free trade.

The Peterson government's continued strategy of sceptical disassociation from the federal initiative put Latimer in a difficult position, however. There were three elements to the Ontario position. First, and most important, the government believed that negotiating bilateral free trade was simply a very bad idea. Second, if

the federal government insisted on going ahead with the negotiations, Ontario knew that it would be the province with the most to
both gain and lose from free trade. Some sectors in the province
would prosper, but others would suffer enormous adjustment
costs. For this reason, the principle of "full provincial participation"
was an essential third element in Ontario's position, for if Ottawa
proceeded with the negotiations, then the province had to be a full
participant in the process in order to protect its interests.

After the federal government had made the decision to negotiate,
and then denied the provinces any direct participation, Ontario was
left with only the first element in its position, that the negotiation was
a bad idea. There was some support for free trade in the Ontario
Treasury Department, but Patrick Lavelle, another opponent of free
trade who had succeeded MacDonell as trade deputy, cut Treasury
out of the policy process. And in order to avoid bestowing legitimacy
on the initiative, Lavelle sharply limited Ontario's participation in the
federal-provincial policy process, refusing to permit discussions between provincial officials and their Ottawa counterparts on the development of federal negotiating positions. As a result, Latimer's role at
CCTN was to question federal plans and positions, but he could not
put any Ontario alternatives forward. This made him a special target
of Reisman's outrage, to the frequent embarrassment of the other
provincial representatives. The fact that Latimer had once worked for
Reisman in the federal bureaucracy gave a special edge to his attacks
on the Ontario representative. Despite Reisman's abuse, Latimer
remained stoic, accepting the slings and arrows as the inevitable price
of representing an unpopular position.

Ontario judged the free trade negotiations to be a bad idea on a
number of counts. First, the federal decision to negotiate was seen
to have more to do with Mulroney's search for an agenda than any
compelling economic reasons. Second, although provincial officials
acknowledged that Ontario could gain from free trade, they also
insisted that the province was already prospering without comprehensive free trade. In the Ontario view, fears about U.S. protectionism were overblown, and in any case the Auto Pact protected

Ontario's principal export. Free trade would remove tariffs and drive up the value of the Canadian dollar, making Canada's exports more expensive. It could also threaten the use of support programs for industrial development and the right to screen foreign investment. There were also strong reservations about Reisman's capacity to negotiate a deal that would be in Canada's interests. This scepticism was reinforced by reports from Ontario's Washington consultants that suggested the federal government was being outfoxed by the U.S. in the negotiations. Finally, Peterson and his officials were convinced that the Mulroney government intended to isolate the province anyway, determined to bash Ontario as part of its Western Canada–Quebec strategy.

For these reasons, throughout 1986 Ontario maintained its stance of non-co-operation, refusing to use the CCTN consultative process to present positions to the TNO on the various issues under negotiation. Latimer was told by his Ontario principals to use the consultations to find out as much as he could about what was going on, but never to commit the province to anything. The provincial government also undermined Canada's position in the negotiations by giving away a major piece of the Canadian financial services market that was on the bilateral negotiating table. Without consulting the TNO, Ontario opened its financial services sector to participation by foreigners, including Americans. This was partly in retaliation for a federal decision to permit the Bank of Nova Scotia to establish a wholly owned subsidiary in the securities field in Quebec.

At the end of 1986, the worst fears of Ontario officials were confirmed in what they saw as the debacle over softwood lumber. Peterson urged the federal government and his fellow premiers to stand up to the U.S. and contest the ruling that Canadian exports were subsidized. He argued that the imposition of an export tax equivalent to the countervailing duty would admit wrong where none existed and set a terrible precedent for Canada. These objections were ignored, however, and Peterson was left isolated in his opposition to the federal position, facing a coalition of Western provinces and Quebec. The episode created considerable bitterness.

In the Ontario view, Canada's interests on the issue had been sacrificed by a federal minister from British Columbia, Patricia Carney, under pressure from the B.C. government and from Canada's ambassador to Washington, Allan Gotlieb, whom Ontario officials considered unable to stand up to American pressure. On the merits of the softwood lumber case alone, Carney's decision to capitulate is difficult to understand. But the case could not be judged in isolation, because it was an integral part of the political dynamics of the free trade negotiations, resulting in additional pressure on the Canadians to settle the issue. Of course, this confirmed Ontario's scepticism about the entire free trade process. The more general lesson for Ontario was that the federal government simply could not be trusted to deal with the United States on trade. Lumber confirmed to Peterson, his senior adviser Herschel Ezrin, and Lavelle that the Mulroney government was more than willing to sacrifice the Canadian lumber industry, and Ontario's interests, in order to get a free trade deal with the Americans. On this point, the Ontario instinct was quite correct.

But, despite this evidence of the federal government's commitment to securing an agreement, Ontario still did little to protect its interests. It was early in 1987 before the government began the consultations with individual industries that had been undertaken by other provinces prior to the start of negotiations. And it was not until February 1987 that the Ontario cabinet finally decided that various ministries should begin preparing provincial positions on specific negotiating issues. By the time the results of this process were conveyed to the TNO in a series of letters from Latimer in the late spring of 1987, however, Canadian positions had already been fully developed on the issues. In any case, the Ontario submissions mainly raised more questions and concerns, but did not put any specific proposals on the table. After a full year of negotiations, the province was apparently still engaged in a debate about whether there should be a negotiation, rather than attempting to shape Canadian positions on specific issues.

By mid-1987, relations between Ontario and the TNO had broken down almost completely, with each side suspecting the worst of the other. Although Reisman and Peterson met for discussions on the important automotive issue, mutual bad faith prevailed. Patrick Lavelle arranged a meeting for Reisman with automobile and parts manufacturers, plus union representatives. The occasion was ostensibly to permit Reisman to learn about the industry; however, its real purpose was to sandbag the chief negotiator, exposing him to attack from opponents of free trade. But Reisman was far too wily to let Ontario determine public perceptions of the encounter; he distributed his own press release on the meeting *before* it took place, to the consternation of provincial officials.

By the time the provincial election campaign got under way late in the summer of 1987, free trade had become an intensely partisan issue in Ottawa-Toronto relations. The Peterson government's opposition to the negotiations was under direct attack by Grossman, with the encouragement of federal Conservatives. Peterson's response to the attacks was cautious. He set out six conditions that would have to be met before Ontario could approve any deal. These were moderate demands, however, since the six corresponded to the negotiation objectives identified in the federal position papers that had been presented to the CCTN. Peterson had left his options open. In the event that an agreement was negotiated that met those federal objectives, Ontario could go along without giving in. By the time the first ministers gathered in Ottawa in mid-September, however, it was clear the negotiations were in serious trouble, and Peterson's opposition began to harden.

FOLDING THE TENT

As the free trade negotiations faltered in the late summer of 1987, the main act in the separate federal-provincial tent had been reduced largely to first ministers' meetings. TNO briefings of the provinces had become less frequent and CCTN meetings less informative. Reisman had never been enthusiastic about consulting the provinces, and his irritation grew with Peter Murphy's obstinacy.

Complaining that the CCTN took too much of his time, he took to departing shortly after meetings began, leaving the briefings to his officials. They had little of substance to report, however, since the negotiations were at a virtual standstill. Although provincial officials were unhappy over this turn of events, their political bosses were not. At the first ministers' meeting in mid-September, the premiers were told what most already knew, that the talks were in trouble and the chances for a big deal slim. That information made continued federal-provincial consultation less necessary, and certainly less attractive. If the free trade initiative was going to end in failure, then the premiers were better off putting some distance between themselves and the initiative, so that the failure would stick to Brian Mulroney.

For Ontario, this meant that David Peterson could become more outspoken in his opposition to the negotiations, since they now had little prospect of success. After the breakdown in talks towards the end of September, there was virtually no further consultation with the provinces concerning the terms and conditions for their resumption. In fact, on the day the two sides resumed negotiations, Friday, October 2, the first ministers had assembled again in Ottawa to receive the details on the permanent suspension of the free trade initiative. Instead, they were hastily informed of the resumption of the talks. That was the extent of federal consultation with the provinces at this crucial stage of the negotiations, however. Throughout the negotiations that took place during that weekend in October, Canadian negotiators had enough problems to handle, without concerning themselves with the requirement of federal-provincial consultation.

When the premiers travelled to Ottawa again the following week, it was to hear details of the deal that had been done. For most, the value of the agreement hinged on a select number of issues of central importance to their provincial interests, and most were satisfied with what had been attained. This in itself was a major achievement politically. Although Ottawa claimed that it could proceed on its own, since international trade was a federal matter and because the agreement touched few areas of provincial jurisdiction, nevertheless the FTA was a quasi-constitutional agreement. It was generally agreed that seven of the 10 provinces would have to be on side, in conformity with the constitutional amending formula, to make the deal politically acceptable. In the end, seven were there. While Pawley of Manitoba and Ghiz of Prince Edward Island joined Peterson in opposition, not surprisingly, it was Ontario that objected to the deal most strongly. Having never truly participated in the consultative process, the province had very little direct input into the Canadian position. Even on the crucial issue of the Auto Pact, while Ontario had been consulted, it had never agreed to the federal decision to eliminate duty-remission programs from the Pact. In the end, Ottawa overrode Ontario's objections, and provincial officials were simply informed of their removal.

However, if Ontario's non-participation had been based on a calculation that there would be no agreement, then Peterson and his advisers had guessed wrong. Too late, some provincial officials concluded that the decision not to participate had been a strategic error, and the time had come to do whatever possible to minimize its ill effects for their province. Between October and December, 1987, when the final terms of the agreement were hammered out between the two countries, the large Ontario bureaucracy was finally activated and allowed to engage its substantial expertise in an effort to influence the detailed legal text of the agreement to Ontario's benefit. This was little more than a rearguard action, however. Canada's largest, and usually most influential province, had already taken itself out of the game. Asked to explain how Ontario could have allowed the trade deal of the century to be done with the province sitting on the sidelines, one official said ruefully, "I guess we were just incompetent."

NEW PROVINCIAL INFLUENCE

Although the federal-provincial ring in the free trade circus was put in a separate tent of dubious fabric, nevertheless the provincial role in Canadian trade policy was probably altered by the process.

While the provinces had no seat at the table, they strongly asserted their right to be consulted on trade matters, and consultation occurred to an unprecedented degree, even if there was some cynicism about its effectiveness. Participation in the FTA negotiation also produced an enhanced trade policy capacity in the provinces, and created new room for them in the trade policy field. The precedent of provincial participation will be difficult to roll back, and the CCTN model will be available for future trade negotiations.

The main provincial players in future ventures into the trade policy arena will be Quebec and Ontario. Both will push aggressively for continuation of the formal consultative process that was put in place for the free trade negotiations and each will vigorously press its views on trade issues. They will do so for very different reasons, however, and the mix may spell trouble for federal trade officials. For Quebec, the FTA event was an important, in some ways formative, experience. When Ontario removed itself from the game, Quebec found itself in an unaccustomed position, playing the lead role on an issue on which it was in substantial agreement with federal aims. The Ottawa-Quebec combination proved to be a potent force, and Quebec officials were more than a little pleased at the extent of their influence over Canada's negotiating positions in a number of critical areas. As a result of this experience, Quebec will expect to be treated as something close to an equal partner by the federal government on future trade matters, and to see its views prevail.

In the aftermath of the free trade experience, Ontario officials were still smarting over the way they had been out-manoeuvred by the Feds. From their perspective, the province had been cut out of the process deliberately by the Mulroney government, part of its Ontario-bashing strategy. The province's response to this perceived federal strategy erred badly, however, first in assuming that Ontario could stop the negotiations, then in betting that there would be no agreement and, most important, in deciding to play the role of a spoiler only, rather than attempting to shape the Canadian negotiating position. Badly burned by the free trade experience, the province is likely to enter future federal-provincial trade consultations determined to reclaim its leading role and push Ontario's interests to the top of the Canadian trade policy agenda.

While the federal-provincial drama was unfolding, the main act in the free trade circus was appearing in the centre ring, where Canada and the United States conducted their negotiations. Unhappily for the Canadian players, the United States showed little interest in being a part of the act during the first 15 months of the negotiations. Our account now shifts to the centre ring, and an analysis of the bilateral negotiations.

7

PLAYING OUT THE STRING

"Simon, I know where you're coming from, I know what you want, I know what you need, and we're still talking." The words rang in Simon Reisman's ears as Peter Murphy repeated his litany of reassurance over and over. Reisman's problem was that while Murphy would talk, he would not negotiate. Instead, the chief U.S. negotiator encouraged his Canadian counterpart to lay out Canada's negotiating positions in exquisite detail, but refused to stake out American positions in return. In Reisman's own words, the American game was "drawing you out, getting you to undress while they were sitting there looking you over to see whether they were interested." In U.S. negotiating parlance, Murphy was simply "playing out the string" on Reisman, holding back on American positions, forcing the Canadians to reveal more and more details about their own positions as they tried to draw Murphy out. As we shall see, Murphy was not to be drawn out, and Reisman's frustration would grow to the breaking point.

A BIG DEAL

In contrast to the U.S. approach, the Canadians were open about their preference for a comprehensive agreement from the beginning. At the very start of the negotiating sessions in May 1986, Reisman proposed that Canada and the United States should negotiate a "big deal," one that would remove virtually all barriers to trade between the two countries by the end of the century. This was the vision of free trade that he had sketched for the prime minister in the October memorandum that won him his job. As negotiations proceeded, the chief Canadian negotiator fleshed out his concept of a big deal with the overarching principle of national treatment. As described by a senior TNO official:

> Reisman came armed with a single vision of a comprehensive agreement that would establish the rules of the game for Canada-US trade relations for the next few generations. He wanted to establish national treatment as the norm for the movement of virtually all goods and services between the two countries. If the US was prepared to accept his vision, he was prepared to extend this principle of non-discrimination to the US priorities of investment and intellectual property. . . . All that remained was for the Americans to agree and translate the vision into the detail of an agreement.[1]

Not incidentally, national treatment would exempt Canada from important elements of U.S. trade remedy law. This was important because the key Canadian objective in the negotiations was security of access to the American market. From Canada's perspective, the principal threat to secure access was U.S. action under its trade remedy laws, called contingency protection by Canada. Canadian concerns centred on the use by the Americans of (1) countervailing and anti-dumping duties against imports from Canada that the U.S. considered to be subsidized, as in the case of softwood lumber, or sold at less than cost, and (2) safeguards, used where there were sudden increases in imports, as in the case of cedar shakes and shingles. To achieve secure access, Canada had to negotiate a way to avoid these U.S. trade remedies. National treatment would significantly reduce their application to Canada, since Canadian imports would be treated the same as goods produced in the U.S.[2]

The U.S. was not ready to deal away its trade remedy laws,

however. Although Murphy and U.S. Trade Representative Clayton Yeutter had agreed, in a preliminary April 1986 meeting with Reisman and his deputy, Gordon Ritchie, that a comprehensive agreement was desirable, the Americans were not prepared to buy Reisman's national treatment vision. Murphy argued that U.S. trade remedy laws were directed at unfair trading practices, especially subsidies, and they were sanctioned by the GATT. In the U.S. view, it was unnecessary to negotiate either subsidies or trade remedies: if Canada wanted to avoid the application of countervailing duties against its products, went the American argument, then it should put an end to government subsidies.

These divergent approaches coloured negotiations from the start of the exploratory plenary sessions that ran from May through September of 1986. The purpose of these five meetings was to identify issues that would be negotiated subsequently, and to establish working groups to consider the issues in greater detail. At the second meeting in Washington in June, the two issues up for discussion were trade remedies and government procurement, two key ingredients in the Canadian design for a "big deal." Murphy informed the Canadians that the U.S. was not ready to discuss these issues at the meeting, requiring more time for preparation.

In fact, the Americans would never be ready to discuss the two issues, since they had no mandate to negotiate agreements on either procurement or trade remedies. Although Murphy would eventually agree to place the procurement issue on the table, he would do so as a means of securing a discussion of other issues of interest to the U.S.; he was never authorized to negotiate a comprehensive procurement agreement. As for trade remedies, there had never been any ambiguity in the American position. The Canadians had been told unequivocally by members of both the executive and legislative branches of the U.S. government that negotiating limits on the application of U.S. trade remedy laws was a non-starter because of almost certain congressional opposition. Nevertheless, the trade remedy issue was again on the agenda, along with agriculture, for the third plenary meeting at Mont Tremblant in July.

A Subsidies Code

At the July meeting, the Canadians tried another approach to the problem of secure access, one that played off the American preoccupation with subsidies. Reisman proposed that the two governments establish a regime to govern the use of trade remedy laws by defining new joint rules to discipline the practices that provoked the use of trade remedy actions by the U.S. in the first place. A central element of the regime would be a subsidies code that would define exactly which subsidy practices were prohibited and which were permissible. While a Canadian proposal for a regime to discipline its own subsidy practices may seem perverse at first glance, a subsidies code would allow Canada to sidestep *unilateral* U.S. definitions of what was subsidized, and therefore countervailable. Practices prohibited by the code would not be permitted under an FTA, but those deemed permissible would not be subject to countervailing duties. American recognition of a class of acceptable subsidy practices would achieve some measure of secure access for Canada, especially since the Canadians intended to negotiate sufficient room to continue what they considered to be defensible subsidies, such as those used for regional development.

Once again, the Canadians got little time for their vision of a subsidies regime from the Americans. The problem, and solution, rested with Canada, argued Murphy, since it was Canadian subsidy practices that required disciplining, not American. Murphy maintained that the U.S. had already eliminated most federal subsidies, and as evidence he pointed to the absence of Canadian countervail actions against American producers. Canada had recourse to the same countervailing duties against subsidized imports as did the United States, but obviously had not required them. Therefore, American subsidies were not at issue. Since the problem, in the American view, was one-sided, it was not necessary to negotiate a subsidies regime; Canada could solve its problem by disciplining its own subsidy practices. Nor did the Americans feel it was necessary to negotiate to impose self-discipline on Canada, since the U.S.

already had a solution to Canadian subsidies in its trade remedy laws. Stonewalled, the Canadians could only insist that any agreement had to address Canada's problem with trade remedies, and a subsidies regime offered a route that could satisfy the interests of both countries.

At the final exploratory meeting in Washington in September, Murphy raised investment, a central issue for the U.S. in the negotiations. Although the Americans rejected Reisman's vision of national treatment for the movement of goods and services between the two countries, they nevertheless proposed the adoption of the principle for investment. Reisman turned them back, however, asserting that Canada had never agreed to include investment in the trade negotiations. Before he could even contemplate seeking a mandate to deal on investment, the Americans would have to come around to the comprehensive agreement across the full range of issues, including trade remedies, that Reisman was attempting to place on the negotiating table.

At the conclusion of the exploratory meetings in September 1986, the two chief negotiators had agreed to the creation of a number of working and fact-finding groups to press ahead with the detail work on the issues, but they had found little else to agree on. And in the world beyond the negotiating table, U.S. protectionist harassment of Canada escalated sharply. On May 22, during the opening round of negotiations in Ottawa, the U.S. imposed a 35 per cent safeguard duty on imports of Canadian cedar shakes and shingles. At the same time, the American lumber lobby touched off an even more acute conflict when it filed a countervailing duty petition calling for a 27 per cent duty on imports of Canadian softwood lumber. As this case unfolded over the remaining months of 1986, the Canadian government was forced onto the defensive, insisting it would neither negotiate with the Americans on the countervailing duty nor institute its own export tax to forestall the imposition of a duty, but then doing both.[3] Murphy's refusal to deal with the issues combined with the timing of the protectionist onslaught threw the Canadians off balance, and led to sober second thoughts

about American purposes in negotiating free trade. The tir
the countervail actions may have been fortuitous, although
ing that they were not timed deliberately required as much wishful
thinking as it did good faith. The stonewalling, however, was a
deliberate strategy designed to force the Canadians, as the party
seeking the negotiations, to play the role of *demandeur*.

EARLY STAND-OFF

The exploratory negotiating rounds had revealed the basic struc-
tural problem that would dog the negotiations and, in the end, very
nearly prove their undoing. The principal Canadian goal in the
negotiations was to achieve enhanced and secure access to the
American market. Improved access would be achieved by removing or easing a number of barriers to trade, especially in the huge
U.S. government procurement market. Security would be achieved
through the imposition of restraints on U.S. trade remedy law
actions. The U.S. negotiators, however, were unable to enter into a
significant agreement to either restrict trade remedies or liberalize
procurement. They were pursuing a different agenda in the negotiations. The Americans had a long-standing interest in free trade.
The elimination of tariffs, a minimum achievement for the negotiations, was an important goal, since the Canadian average tariff on
dutiable imports was about double that of the U.S. In addition, the
Americans wanted to explore new ground on the issues of intellectual property and trade in services. The bilateral negotiations
would also serve notice on other trading partners that if no progress
were made in the multilateral trade talks, the U.S. could strike
bilateral deals.

These were not the top U.S. priorities in these negotiations,
however. Instead, the key American goals related directly to the
Canadian energy and investment policies that had touched off such
intense bilateral conflict earlier in the decade. The U.S. was determined to use the negotiations to ensure that they would never again
be a target of discriminatory actions like those embodied in the

National Energy Program and the Foreign Investment Review Agency. This could be done by securing the adoption of the principle of national treatment on investment. On trade issues, the American priority was to resolve a number of irritants by achieving disciplines on specific Canadian subsidy practices. The Canadians, however, were unwilling to consider investment until the U.S. agreed to a serious discussion of trade remedies, nor were they receptive to the one-sided American view of subsidy sins. This structure of interests provided a sure formula for prolonged standoff, and that is precisely what ensued over the next 12 months.

As the talks moved from the summer exploratory sessions into the second stage of substantive negotiations in November 1986, the Canadians remained perplexed by Murphy's approach. The establishment of working groups had done little to advance the process, for example. Reisman and his team viewed the working groups as a mechanism to negotiate the details of a potential agreement in each particular issue-area, going back to the plenary table for instruction as necessary. The Americans, on the other hand, were still unprepared for substantive negotiations, and used the groups primarily as a vehicle for information exchange. Nevertheless, there was marginal progress in process, if not substance. The trade remedies issue was recognized as separate and differentiated from subsidies, although Murphy would not agree to assign the new issue to a working group, proposing instead that it be handled by the two chief negotiators. Canadian demands for a separate working group were blunted by their own refusal to agree to a working group on energy, as requested by the U.S. The former Energy minister, Patricia Carney, had moved into the Trade portfolio, with responsibility for the FTA, and she still regarded energy as "her issue." The Americans believed that Reisman's reluctance to have an energy working group stemmed from his desire to assert control over the energy issue, by keeping it in the plenary arena. For this reason, the Americans were careful to link their refusal to agree to a working group on trade remedies to the Canadian refusal on energy.

At the insistence of the U.S. Treasury Department, financial services were separated from the rest of the negotiations on services. In Treasury's view, the regulations governing financial services industries, like banking, were too complex to be left to "mere" trade negotiators, requiring instead their own independent negotiating track, managed by Treasury officials. Reisman was unhappy with the separation, because it hampered his ability to exact a price from the Americans on other issues for Canadian movement on financial services, but he had little choice in the matter. He did make it clear that any agreement on financial services would have to be considered as part of an overall trade agreement, with appropriate trade-offs on other issues. However, Canada's ability to exact trade-off payments on this issue had already been severely compromised by the decision of the Ontario government to open its financial services sector, the largest in Canada, to participation by foreigners. For his part, Murphy was content to let Treasury take responsibility for the issue; he met with Treasury officials to keep informed about developments in the financial services negotiations, but made no effort to co-ordinate the two negotiating tracks.

There was also early movement on the significant issue of energy. Although Reisman, as we have seen, would not agree to assign the issue to a working group, a bilateral fact-finding group was established to explore the energy sector. That group concluded that government intervention had been reduced significantly in recent years and that as a result, energy trade had already been freed up substantially. An American inter-agency group had been formed earlier in 1986 to plan for negotiations in the energy sector. Although their focus had been on Canadian sins of intervention, especially the NEP, they concluded that in the past both governments had intervened excessively in energy trade for largely political reasons, to serve special interests, and with largely negative results. The American group identified the establishment of a clean system for trade in energy as a primary goal, a system that would provide stability for U.S. investors. This was consistent with changes in Canadian energy policy that had been under way since 1984. The result was concurrence between Canadian and American members of the fact-finding group that they should aim to establish free trade in energy. As had been the case with financial services, Murphy was content to allow the energy negotiations to proceed at their own pace, rather than attempt to integrate developments into a broader negotiating track. In the case of energy, however, this laissez-faire attitude stemmed from the conviction in USTR that free trade in energy represented too good a deal to hold back on. Accordingly, Murphy gave his energy negotiators their heads. In the end, the energy issue became, in the words of one senior U.S. official, "a real sleeper," where the Americans saw themselves achieving substantial gains, and the results, especially the non-discriminatory pricing and proportionality provisions, were controversial in Canada.

As a last act of 1986, Canada proposed principles for the establishment of dispute-settlement procedures to govern the operation of any negotiated agreement. To go along with the big deal they were trying to sell to the Americans, the Canadians proposed elaborate dispute-settlement machinery that would render binding decisions in the administration of an agreement. Anticipating limited machinery for a limited agreement, the Americans were unprepared for Canada's comprehensive proposal. The two sides could only agree to strike another working group to consider the issue in greater detail. Aside from these areas of progress, the Canadians had very little to show for more than six months of negotiation. Murphy had pressed hard for the inclusion of investment in the negotiations and Reisman had insisted that he had no mandate to discuss investment. He demanded that substantive American proposals be put forward on the issues that already occupied the table before he could consider seeking a mandate on investment. But Murphy preferred instead to continue to play out the string.

KNOW WHEN TO HOLD

The American approach could not have been a surprise to the Canadian negotiators. Canada was in the classic role of *demandeur*.

In the first place, the negotiations were a Canadian initiative. Under the terms of U.S. fast-track legislation, the request for free trade negotiations had to come from the other country. In any case, the U.S., aware of Canadian political sensibilities, would not take the public lead in promoting such a radical policy shift on the part of Canada. Most important, it was Canada's interest in enhanced and secure access to the American market, and not the reverse, that touched off the negotiations. Second, not only did the Canadians initiate the free trade negotiations, but they had the most to gain and the least to give in any potential deal to promote the free movement of goods. Under these circumstances, with Canada as the *demandeur*, the Americans could be expected to sit back and wait to hear what the Canadians wanted, and what they were prepared to offer to get it, before laying any of their own cards on the table. This should have come as no surprise.

What did puzzle the Canadian negotiators was the persistence of Murphy's refusal to engage on the issues. From the first meeting in Ottawa in May, the Canadians laid out their opening positions in considerable detail, only to be met with Murphy's assurances that he knew where the Canadians were coming from, and what they wanted and needed; but for some reason he couldn't or wouldn't set out U.S. positions in comparable detail. Perplexed and annoyed, the Canadian negotiators decided that their American counterparts were simply ill prepared. It was obvious to the Canadians that the Americans had not developed positions on the various issues, and this failure could be accounted for by the obvious lack of resources available to Murphy for the job at hand. While this interpretation helped the Canadians account for U.S. behaviour, it was only half right. It was true that Murphy did not have detailed positions at hand in the early stages of the negotiations, because on many of the issues they had not been prepared. But the Americans were not unduly concerned about the lack of preparation, because they believed the U.S. was dealing from a position of strength in the negotiations and could afford to continue to stall the Canadians. And it was also true that even when the

American preparations had been completed, Murphy chose not to present detailed positions to Canada, preferring instead to continue to string the Canadians along. Murphy's strategy of intransigence may have been born of necessity, but it was nevertheless his preferred strategy, and he held to it even after the Americans had prepared their detailed briefs on the various issues.

As 1987 opened, the U.S. strategy paid off when Canada blinked in the standoff over who should make the next move. The two issues of trade remedies for Canada and investment for the United States were emerging as the linchpins of any potential agreement. Although Reisman had no mandate to negotiate investment, the Canadians had believed from the outset that concessions on investment would be required to secure American action on trade remedies. At the very first preliminary negotiating session in May 1986, Murphy had put investment on the table and told the Canadians it was a *sine qua non* for any comprehensive agreement. The issue remained on the back burner until early in 1987, when the Americans began to press again to include investment in the negotiations, this time getting Treasury Secretary Baker to bring pressure to bear at the political level in Ottawa. Although Reisman was prepared to use the investment issue as a trump card to secure Canadian goals on trade remedies, he had insisted on some U.S. movement on the trade remedies issue before he would even seek a mandate to negotiate investment. Faced with Murphy's continuing refusal to engage on the trade remedies issue, however, Reisman decided to ante up investment as an additional incentive to move the Americans in the desired direction.

In February, Reisman and his deputy, Gordon Ritchie, met informally with Murphy and his deputy, Bill Merkin. Over dinner, the four discussed investment, exploring U.S. interests and Canadian concerns, each side trying to get a sense of the terms that the other might be after on this issue. Based on the discussion, Reisman agreed to seek a mandate from cabinet to include the investment issue as part of the negotiations and to authorize informal discussions between TNO and USTR staff on the issue. An American proposal was finally presented by senior Treasury official Robert Cornell at a plenary meeting in the spring of 1987. The Americans went for the moon, demanding full national treatment. Reisman was infuriated by what he saw as American perfidy, and he refused to accept the U.S. proposal. Telling Murphy that it was so outrageous that it would be better to proceed as though no proposal had been tabled, Reisman handed it back! His forceful rejection of the U.S. proposal would pay important dividends later, when Cornell once again had to manage the investment issue through the final stages of the negotiation, the memory of Reisman's outrage, and the abusive language that went with the famous temper, fresh in his mind.

Murphy's personal integrity was not entirely undermined in Canadian eyes by the investment episode, since this issue, like financial services, was being managed by Treasury and the Canadian negotiators assumed it was largely beyond Murphy's control. The episode did fit with Murphy's approach on other issues in the negotiations, however. The chief U.S. negotiator had a habit of agreeing to certain principles for discussion in his informal meetings with Reisman, and then ignoring, or forgetting, the agreements in subsequent plenary meetings. This practice disconcerted his own staff almost as much as it angered Canada's chief negotiator. Murphy was playing deliberate hardball with Canada, refusing to engage in substantive discussions on some issues, and adopting extreme positions on others. The Canadians were perplexed. Only a complete lack of preparation could explain the chief U.S. negotiator's refusal, or failure, to match Canada's approach to the negotiations.

UNEQUAL RESOURCES

The conclusion that the Americans were unable to set out detailed positions because they were unprepared was easy to reach if one simply compared the resources allocated by the two sides to the conduct of the negotiations. Canada had made free trade the centrepiece of foreign and domestic policy, and the government adorned it with a large bureaucracy specially created to undertake the negotiations. Following his appointment late in 1985, Reisman moved quickly to remove the mandate for free trade from the Department of External Affairs, where preliminary preparations had been centred. He was supported in this effort by the Department of Finance, where international economics officials were anxious to limit the authority of External Affairs on the international trade issue, a mandate External had acquired in the 1982 government reorganization. Reisman was determined to have an independent Trade Negotiations Office with his own staff. He recognized the magnitude of the task ahead of him and, with considerable resentment in Ottawa over his plucking of the free trade plum, he simply could not rely on other departments to get the job done. Reisman also could not abide the "interdepartmentalitis," endless consultations between departments, that friends on the inside told him had come to plague Ottawa policy-making since his departure from the federal bureaucracy. In organizing and staffing the TNO, however, Reisman initially planned to follow past practice and work with other departments, getting a few key people seconded to his staff who would draw on their home departments for additional support. He wanted to appoint three of the top people in Ottawa as his deputy chief negotiators — Derek Burney, from his position as associate under-secretary at External Affairs, to manage the Canada-U.S. dimension of the negotiations; Gerry Shannon, then assistant deputy minister of international trade and finance in the Department of Finance, to focus on the domestic economic policy dimension; and Gerard Veilleux, then secretary to the cabinet for federal-provincial relations, to handle consultations with the provinces. In each case, his request was denied, as deputy ministers tried instead to send him people they wanted to be rid of. As a result, Reisman concluded that co-operation with line departments would not be possible, and he set off to create and staff a much more independent organization. In the end, the Department of Finance would regret its role in creating an organization beyond the reach of even its substantial influence.

TNO was soon the place to be in Ottawa, and recruitment became a mark of status. The chief negotiator created TNO in his own image, choosing bright and aggressive people who were convinced of their ability to take on the Americans and best them with superior organization and skills. Unable to secure his triumvirate of deputies, Reisman opted for a single deputy chief negotiator, in the person of Gordon Ritchie. Ritchie had followed the fast track to a senior position in the federal bureaucracy before falling out of favour with the new Tory regime, resulting in a transfer to Toronto by his former Department of Regional Industrial Expansion. Reisman had a longstanding relationship with Gordon's father, Ed Ritchie, an Ottawa mandarin in the 1960s whom Reisman had served when Ritchie the elder headed up the negotiations that resulted in the Canada-U.S. Auto Pact. In a sense, Reisman rescued Ritchie the younger's civil service career by bringing him over to TNO, where he quickly established both his command of the free trade issues and his authority over the organization. Reisman also received a second nominal deputy in the person of Sylvia Ostry who was moved into the TNO from External Affairs to be in charge of the machinery for Canada's participation in the GATT round of multilateral trade negotiations. Although Ostry (over her strenuous objections) reported to Reisman, the move was more for reasons of organizational symmetry than substance, and Reisman's overwhelming preoccupation was with the bilateral negotiations.

Several assistant chief negotiators were selected to staff the layer underneath Ritchie. To serve as general counsel, the TNO's chief lawyer, Reisman chose Konrad von Finckenstein from the Department of Justice. Germain Denis, a seasoned trade negotiator, moved over from External Affairs, first to handle the multilateral negotiations, then moving to issues of market access, and he was followed from External by David Lee, who took over responsibility for the multilateral negotiations. Alan Nymark, who had served as director of policy for the Macdonald Commission, took on responsibility for federal-provincial relations, while Charles Stedman shifted from Regional Industrial Expansion to manage liaison with industry. Andrei Sulzenko was also seconded from Regional Industrial Expansion, first to serve as Reisman's chief of staff in the initial stages of setting up the TNO, after which he took on responsibility for services and investment. Not everyone at this level was an experienced trade negotiator. Responsibility for individual issue areas, such as agriculture, energy, government procurement, and tariffs, which corresponded roughly to the chapters in the agreement, rested at the next level down in the TNO organization chart. Many, but certainly not all, of these people had negotiating experience, though frequently in the multilateral arena, where the dynamics of negotiation differ significantly from those in a bilateral setting.

All in all, Reisman drew deeply from the bureaucratic well to assemble what amounted to a new department of government. Its more than one hundred staff were housed in luxurious — by Ottawa standards — offices at the top of the Metropolitan Life Tower; and the resources and authority commanded by the TNO made it the envy, and frequently the target, of officials who toiled away in regular government departments. With a large staff working full-time on the negotiations, Reisman was able to prepare detailed Canadian positions on the various issues, and he was eager to present these to the Americans once talks got under way.

By contrast, the U.S. was treating the whole affair as business as usual. Although Murphy was the chief negotiator, he carried other responsibilities in USTR as well, even as the negotiations proceeded. His deputy, Bill Merkin, who had worked on Canada-U.S. trade issues since 1981, did spend the bulk of his time on the free trade negotiations. But for additional staff support at USTR, Murphy had to draw on officials who dealt with the Canada-U.S. issues only as part of their wider responsibilities in the agency. Beyond these meagre USTR resources, Murphy was forced to depend on officials in line departments to develop American positions on the various issues, and they did so as part of their continuing departmental responsibilities. Not only did this make control over the pace of developing U.S. positions more difficult for Murphy, but it allowed the departments to protect their policy turf more effectively.

These different approaches to the negotiations were reflected in arrangements for the alternating negotiating sessions. At the opening session held at the lavish TNO facilities in May 1986, the Canadians proudly ushered the American delegation into the conference room, decorated with wood veneers and leather, that had been created especially for these negotiations. Beyond a door at one end of the room was a full kitchen, from which the Canadians dispensed generous hospitality to their American guests. These surroundings gave off a clear message: the negotiations were a very big deal in Ottawa, and Canada was prepared to commit substantial resources to their conduct. In contrast, the Washington sessions were held at USTR headquarters in the Winder Building on 17th Street, where USTR staff were forced to share cramped offices. Located across from the ornate Old Executive Office Building, the Winder Building gives new meaning to the term nondescript. Even with appropriate hospitality, the Arborite-and-plastic conference room where negotiating sessions took place would have seemed inhospitable, and hospitality was rarely offered. As one senior Canadian official noted ruefully, one of the most finely honed American negotiating skills is their ability to make you feel utterly insignificant. The Winder Building was an excellent prop for this purpose. The inescapable message was that free trade was no big deal; the Canadians were just one more trade delegation among many that were routinely handled on 17th Street.

A QUESTION OF COMPETENCE

The arrival of spring in 1987 brought another summit meeting between the prime minister and the president, an event that Reisman saw as an opportunity to outflank Murphy in his stubborn refusal to negotiate. The Canadians would attempt to enlist the U.S. president in their campaign to flush Murphy out, by having the two leaders reaffirm the basic components of Reisman's big deal. If

Murphy was insufficiently prepared to conduct serious negotiations, then the Canadians would use the president to force his hand. Engaging the politicians was becoming Canada's *de facto* strategic response to Murphy's strategy. The Canadian response was based on a belief that somewhere in Washington there is actually a decision centre that can be used to gain control over the policy process. The near-death of the free trade initiative at the hands of the Senate Finance Committee the previous spring should have cast doubt on this belief. It was a strategy that alarmed USTR officials nonetheless. They sweated through each conversation between the two leaders, fearful that the president would unwittingly undertake a commitment that would prove unacceptable to Congress, undermining the prospects for agreement.

Not even presidential reaffirmations could move Peter Murphy, however. Following the summit, Murphy not only choreographed the presentation of the perfidious Treasury proposal on investment, but also used the occasion of yet another informal dinner to convince Reisman that he was finally prepared to engage fully on all the issues. Then, in the following plenary negotiating session, Murphy presented the same investment proposal that had so outraged Reisman previously. In the face of the continuing U.S. refusal to get on with serious negotiations, the Canadians were simply unable to believe any longer that a lack of preparation could account for the absence of any American substance. Instead, they concluded that unlike their own champion, Peter Murphy lacked the status necessary to command sufficient attention in official Washington to obtain a negotiating mandate. Thus Murphy could talk, but without a mandate he could not negotiate, and this would account for his behaviour.

As the non-negotiation dragged on, however, Canadian annoyance turned to contempt. The different Canadian and American approaches to the negotiations were judged to reflect a fundamental difference in the competence of the two teams. One senior member of the Canadian Trade Negotiations Office expressed this view, which was widely shared in TNO:

The American team would arrive and would say: "Well, if you could excuse us for an hour, we'll have a meeting and decide what we can talk to you about, or what our position is going to be." Literally, we would introduce the American delegation to each other. We would have been working our asses off preparing for these meetings. These were monthly meetings — not very hard to get organized.

It's all part of a tragic situation — the average US bureaucrats are very weak, very badly paid, very badly equipped, and don't have the capacity to do a good job.[4]

It is conventional wisdom to avoid underestimating the shrewdness of your adversary in a negotiation. But it is equally true that negotiators too rarely look at events from the perspective of their adversary. Instead, they try to explain the failure of the other party to "see reason" by convincing themselves that it does not properly understand its own interests, or is incompetent. The greater the frustration experienced during the negotiation, the greater the likelihood that such beliefs will surface. The Canadians were frustrated almost beyond endurance by the Americans' approach to the negotiations, and they found it satisfactory, on a number of counts, to attribute this behaviour to incompetence. Condescension in negotiation may be perilous, however, especially if one is dealing with a Yankee trader that is also an economic superpower.

AN AMERICAN POLITICAL EQUATION

There was a strategy behind the American game of non-negotiation, and it was one that the Canadians perceived, and understood, to some extent. However, Canada's negotiators simply could not support for very long an interpretation of American behaviour that suggested the U.S. was deliberately putting the negotiations at risk, because they were so important to Canada. And since the Canadians believed their approach offered the best prospect of achieving an agreement, the U.S. failure to adopt a similar approach had to be due to inadequate preparation or incompetence, or both.

The problem with this interpretation of American behaviour was that it assumed that the U.S. focus was on its relationship with Canada, and it superimposed Canadian attitudes on the American negotiators. The decision to pursue free trade had been a significant one for Canada, and its promoters had no alternative in mind should the negotiations fail. Without any attractive non-agreement alternatives before them, the Canadian negotiators were ready to make concessions to avoid failure. Peter Murphy was counting on this, and he was more willing to risk non-agreement by holding back concessions. Furthermore, Canada was not at the centre of Murphy's thinking. That special place was reserved for the U.S. Congress, and the key relationship for the political equation that Murphy was attempting to construct was between Congress and the Reagan administration. Although Canadians might not like it, the domestic politics of American trade policy, not Canadian-American relations, are central to an understanding of the U.S. approach to the free trade negotiations with Canada. With the Americans negotiating "inside out,"[5] the Canadians were left to wonder when the negotiations would begin.

The answer to that question was not entirely under Peter Murphy's control, however, and he knew it. While Murphy was playing out the string on the Canadians, getting them to lay out the whole of their negotiating position while holding back as long as possible on the presentation and development of his own positions, it was a highly risky game he was playing. Operating on the assumption that the crucial components of any agreement would have to be constructed at the political level, rather than by Reisman and himself, Murphy was determined to hold back concessions for as long as possible. When the talks were then bumped up to the political level, his principals would be in a favourable position from which to begin dealing. Murphy wanted an agreement, but one that he judged would prove acceptable to Congress. If the deal was going to be struck ultimately at the political level, as he believed it must, then Murphy had to anticipate political concession-making. This meant he had to hold out on key issues in order that the concessions ultimately made would still be within his estimate of the congressional acceptance range.

The chief U.S. negotiator's strategy of stonewalling was applied not only to the Canadians, but to most other players on the American side as well. Murphy gave occasional briefings to the cabinet-level U.S. Economic Policy Council, but provided few details regarding the actual state of the negotiations. His boss, U.S. Trade Representative Clayton Yeutter, was regularly reduced to asking other staff in USTR what Murphy was up to. In a town where knowledge is power, the chief negotiator was keeping his cards extremely close to his vest, largely to protect his own freedom to manoeuvre in the negotiations. Murphy believed that if the most difficult issues surfaced too early in the negotiations, this would provide an opportunity for opposition to mount either in Congress or in line departments on whose turf Murphy would be treading. He needed two things — time to build a consensus where he could, and surprise to overcome opposition where consensus was not possible. Even members of Congress were largely unaware of Murphy's activities. This was partly because they were not interested, but it was also partly due to the fact that the chief international trade counsel, Jeffrey Lang, was applying the knowledge-equals-power maxim to the Senate Finance Committee. Murphy was briefing Lang on developments in the negotiations, but Lang was withholding the information from the staffs of Finance Committee members.

The logic of Murphy's strategy may have made sense, but its execution was fraught with risks. In the first place, he had nothing to offer to the Canadians on their key subsidies-trade remedies issue. Forcing concessions from Reisman on the investment issue by holding out on the deal-breaking issue of trade remedies could only embitter the Canadians when the Americans ultimately refused to deal. Second, Murphy seemed inclined to stand pat until the negotiations were moved to the political level, willing to risk failure at this stage of the game in order to avoid concessions. But time was running out on a fast-track calendar that required agreement by early October. And while Murphy's strategy was focused on preventing a shift to the political level for as long as possible, it did not include a means to engage the politicians. In the end, Reisman would have to supply the means.

No Big Deal

Misperceptions of Canadian strategy also plagued American negotiators. While Reisman may have been sincere in advocating national treatment, the Americans never found the proposal credible. Unable to believe that Canada would take such a step, politically or economically, Murphy took Reisman's "vision" to be nothing more than the standard fare of negotiation posturing. The Americans also failed to gauge accurately the Canadian determination to secure some relief from the application of U.S. trade remedy law. From the Americans' point of view, Canada had been told repeatedly that no exception was possible on trade remedies, and yet the Canadians continued to negotiate. The U.S. negotiators therefore concluded that a deal without the trade remedies issue in it must be a possibility. Given this reasoning, the Canadians would be unable to convince the Americans that the trade remedies issue was a deal-breaker as long as they stayed at the table and continued to negotiate.

When the Americans refused to buy into Reisman's national treatment concept, the Canadians proposed that the two parties negotiate a subsidies code that would govern the application of trade remedy laws. Here again, Canada was the *demandeur*. In the view of the U.S. Commerce Department, responsible for the administration of trade remedy law, subsidies were already taken care of through countervailing duties. A subsidies code was, therefore, not only unnecessary, but would probably be unacceptable to Congress as well. Nevertheless, in the face of Canadian insistence that some movement on the subsidies issue was a prerequisite for agreement,

Commerce officials were persuaded to attempt to fashion a code that Congress could accept.

The U.S. counterproposal on the issue was presented at a week-long negotiating session held at the Transport Canada Training Centre near Cornwall in August 1987. The Canadian proposal on subsidies had taken an approach that was likened to a traffic light. Certain practices would be declared unacceptable, or subject to a red light, but other practices would be deemed acceptable, and subject to a green light. Ambiguous practices, in the yellow zone, would be assigned to a binational panel to determine their acceptability. The Commerce Department trade lawyers countered with an approach that focused on "bright lines and safe harbours." The bright lines would function like a red light, providing a clear signal of the types of Canadian subsidies that were unacceptable, while safe harbour would be granted to a very small number of specific programs that would be exempt from trade remedies, equivalent to a green light. Most important, countervailing duties would take care of any ambiguous practices. The proposal also distinguished between subsidies with an export effect and those that were purely domestic, the former requiring disciplines, the latter not. The consequence of this particular twist was not lost on the Canadians. It meant that U.S. subsidies directed to companies serving the huge American domestic market would be exempt, despite the fact that their effect was to displace imports. Under the American proposal, only Canadian subsidies would be targeted. In addition, the subsidy practices embodied in American defence spending were ruled off limits, on the grounds that trade policy could not be allowed to drive defence policy.

The deliberate intent of this proposal was to establish disciplines on subsidies tougher than those under existing American trade remedy law. Furthermore, the effect of the proposal was that the disciplines would apply to Canada, but not to the U.S. It was an approach designed more to win congressional approval than Canada's acceptance. But the Canadians were under intense pressure to get a deal, and after so many months of trying they finally had an offer on the table from the Americans. As a result, some senior TNO officials insisted on taking a serious look at the American proposal. And Reisman gave them a hearing. Generally unsympathetic to the whole subsidies game, he was ready to give up certain Canadian subsidy practices in return for American guarantees not to countervail others that both parties agreed were acceptable. But others in TNO argued that the American proposal was so unbalanced and one-sided, and it cut so deeply into Canadian subsidies, that it would provoke strong opposition in Canada. Provincial governments had been given ironclad assurances that the integrity of regional development programs would not be placed at risk in the negotiations, but the bright lines in the American proposal signalled clearly that they would be unacceptable. In the end, Reisman concluded that American safe harbours offered no security for Canada, and the Cornwall meeting broke up with little progress.

KNOW WHEN TO FOLD

With no American movement on the subsidies–trade remedies issue, and none possible on government procurement, coupled with a Canadian refusal to move any further on investment, the negotiations had reached an impasse by late August 1987. A solution appeared to be beyond the grasp of the two chief negotiators. Fifteen months of unproductive negotiations had created hard feelings on both sides of the table. Normally, the personal relationship between the two chief negotiators would not be expected to influence the course of negotiations unduly. But the rancour between Murphy and Reisman went beyond the usual friction that results from opposing interests, and it spread through their respective organizations. TNO perceptions of Murphy's incompetence had blossomed into contempt, while tolerance in USTR for Reisman's short fuse and abusive language had diminished to zero. The inherent bad faith images that had developed between the two sides made fruitful communication difficult. To make a bad situation worse, Reisman and the TNO were under fire in Ottawa, where critics were emboldened by the prospects of failure in the negotiations. The resulting siege mentality in TNO sharpened images of Murphy and the Americans as the villains in the piece.

After the failure to make progress in Cornwall, the Mulroney government decided that an end-run was required to get around the logjam that Reisman and Murphy had apparently created. Early in September, the prime minister's chief of staff, Derek Burney, executed the end-run by writing to his counterpart, White House Chief of Staff Howard Baker. Burney suggested that a meeting of senior officials from the two governments be held to attempt to resolve the impasse in the negotiations. Whereas the previous Canadian strategy had been to attempt to engage the politicians to pressure Murphy, Burney was now proposing that the negotiations be formally transferred to the political level. Baker rejected the initiative, primly pointing out that Burney was communicating with the wrong Baker. It was Reagan's treasury secretary, James Baker, who had the mandate for the negotiations, and he was the appropriate channel for such communications.

Rebuffed, the Canadians had little choice but to permit the Reisman-Murphy stand-off to continue. By now, there was little hope that the chief negotiators could resolve the impasse. Reisman's political masters had been unsuccessful in their efforts to bring political pressure to bear on Murphy, who seemed content to continue to play a waiting game, despite the ominous ticking of the fast-track clock. In some respects, the negotiations were not just standing still; they were regressing. When the Canadians finally got a glimpse of Murphy's position on government procurement, it offered very little of the U.S. market to Canada. On the deal-breaking subsidies–trade remedies issue, the Americans went back to insisting that the principal problem lay with Canadian subsidy practices; stop subsidizing and there would be nothing to fear from trade remedy laws. Murphy was still playing the strong U.S. hand, holding out to the bitter end. Time was on the American side, of course, since a hurried deal was more likely to be a limited deal, with maximum pressure on Canada to come to terms. Equally important, if the politicians took over the negotiations, they would start off from a position of strength as a result of Murphy's refusal to negotiate on key issues.

The flaw in this scenario lay in Peter Murphy's reluctance to reveal his hand even to his own political masters. They continued to believe that agreement by the October deadline could be achieved by the two negotiating teams, and dismissed Canadian alarms over an impending breakdown. Frustrated by this continued complacency, the Canadians decided they had to find some way to get an urgent message to Washington. There appeared to be only one way to deliver the message. Reisman was instructed to break off negotiations if the Americans showed no inclination to engage on the key issues at the next plenary negotiating session in Washington. In the event, Murphy continued to play the same hand and, early on the afternoon of September 23, Reisman announced that he was suspending the negotiations. The Canadians returned to Ottawa that same day.

Canada had gone into the historic negotiations insisting that it had to achieve some measure of secure access to the U.S. market. And from the beginning, the Americans had insisted that there could be no exemption from their trade remedy laws. On this key issue, the positions of the two parties were non-negotiable, and apparently irreconcilable. It was over this fundamental difference that the negotiations had finally foundered, when the impasse could not be resolved by Simon Reisman and Peter Murphy. The suspension of negotiations by Canada was a tactic intended to force American movement, but the impasse itself was real.

Reisman had negotiated with the U.S. on a number of other occasions, but he had not experienced the bearpit of American trade policy in the 1980s, where a resurgence in congressional influence produced more checks than balance. Nor had he ever come up against anyone like Murphy. Despite everything he tried, Reisman could not move the American, and his frustration was as real as the deadlock in which the two men were mired. Both during and after the negotiations, Reisman told his TNO colleagues how bitterly disappointed he had been at the choice of Peter Murphy as the American chief negotiator. "Murphy wasn't my match," he told one staffer, "I would have liked to have gone against their best, someone like Jules Katz or Bill Brock." He later confided to another old Ottawa hand that he had tried in so many different ways "to get Murphy to move off the dime," but he could "never figure the guy out." Resigned to what had happened at the end, Reisman opined, "Who knows, the whole thing might have been a strategy on their part." It was.

Reisman was left with little choice but to break off the talks, but the action must have stuck in his throat. Because if the tactic was successful, Reisman knew he would lose control of the negotiations when they passed to the political level, and his chance to be the godfather of free trade would pass, a victim of Murphy's obstinacy, or incompetence. In breaking off the talks, Reisman set the stage for the political negotiations that Murphy had anticipated for so long. But getting from here to there would offer a new chapter in the free trade story, and a perilous journey for Canada.

8

A WEEKEND IN WASHINGTON

Sam Gibbons decided to call Canada's ambassador. The chairman of the trade subcommittee of the U.S. House Ways and Means Committee was upset over the suspension of negotiations, and he wanted to discuss the problem with Allan Gotlieb. The Florida congressman took a special interest in Canada, and he was a staunch supporter of the negotiations. And Gibbons had a bright idea. In a meeting of American officials in May 1987 that included Peter Murphy and some of his USTR staff, Gibbons had floated a proposal to resolve the impasse that was developing over the subsidies–trade remedies issue. In situations where there were disagreements over the application of U.S. trade remedy law, suggested Gibbons, why not have the two countries simply get together and negotiate a joint determination. The jaws of the trade lawyers in the meeting dropped at the notion of the U.S. "negotiating" the application of its laws with a foreign government. Not only did Murphy and his people feel the suggestion was a bad idea for the United States, certain to be viewed dubiously by the Congress, but they also believed that it would not meet Canadian needs on the trade remedy issue. The suggestion was not taken up. Now, four months later, with negotiations suspended, Gibbons wanted to try out his idea again, this time on Gotlieb. The prospects for a resumption of the talks did not look good, however.

The Americans had no doubts that Reisman's suspension was a

tactic, and that Canada was eager to resume the negotiations. There was still time for the kind of limited agreement the U.S. had been looking for all along, so the task at hand was to coax the Canadians back to the table and nail down the elements of a deal before the expiry of the October 3 deadline stipulated by the fast-track procedures.[1] As Peter Murphy had so long anticipated, it was time for the negotiations to move to the political level. The principal player at this level would not be Clayton Yeutter, Murphy's boss and the cabinet officer responsible for the trade brief, however. Instead, cabinet heavy hitter James Baker, secretary of the Treasury, would get the nod. As chairman of the cabinet's Economic Policy Council, Baker had been handed the negotiation brief by Ronald Reagan earlier in the summer. Now it was time for him to get actively involved.

Supplanting Simon Reisman at the political level on the Canadian side would be neither Yeutter's counterpart, Trade Minister Patricia Carney, nor Baker's counterpart, Finance Minister Michael Wilson, although both would be part of the political team that would face the Americans. Instead, the familiar face of Derek Burney surfaced once again to handle the negotiations. Burney had become Mulroney's chief of staff early in 1987, and he quickly made the free trade issue his own. As one senior official put it, "Burney *was* the prime minister on trade issues." Baker's first approach to Burney reflected the U.S. view that Reisman's walkout was simply a tactic. By telephone, he repeated Murphy's positions on the issues, and urged the Canadians to come back to the table. Burney was not prepared to resume talks on that basis, however. Without some kind of movement from the Americans on the subsidies–trade remedies issue, there would be no resumption of the negotiations.

THE GIBBONS PROPOSAL

The proposal that Sam Gibbons outlined to Allan Gotlieb had two elements, although they were not sharply defined. First, he proposed that the contentious subsidies–trade remedies issue be put aside for further negotiation, and that existing trade law continue to apply in the interim. Second, he suggested that some form of appellate procedure could be used to review applications of national trade remedy law, where necessary. This proposal offered a route back to the table, although it took the parties some time to find their way. Following their telephone conversation, Gotlieb and Gibbons agreed that each would put the proposal forward for consideration. In response to a telephone call from Gotlieb, Burney requested something in writing, and Gotlieb responded with a proposal for a tribunal. Baker, too, requested a written proposal from Gibbons. Late one afternoon, the Congressman called George Weise, staff director of the trade subcommittee, into his office and dictated the basic elements of his idea for a dispute-settlement mechanism. He then instructed Weise to deliver the note to the treasury secretary by taxi. Having provided Baker with the basic idea that would salvage Canada-U.S. free trade, Gibbons left Washington that evening on a routine speaking tour.

Initial reaction to the Gibbons proposal was unpromising. The Canadians were not convinced that the concept addressed their security-of-access problem in any meaningful way. And Baker and his people were sceptical that the idea would find favour in Congress. Nor did they believe it satisfied Canada's demand for American movement on the trade remedies issue. The negotiations over whether to negotiate continued. At the end of the last week in September, Michael Wilson, in Washington for the annual meetings of the International Monetary Fund, met with Baker, and they agreed that their groups should meet to try to identify a basis for resuming the negotiations. At the beginning of the following week, Burney, Wilson, and Carney travelled to Washington to meet with Baker, his treasury deputy, Peter McPherson, and Clayton Yeutter. Despite extended meetings, the two sides remained far apart, and Burney and Baker were unable to identify a basis for resumption. The Canadians returned to Ottawa to report the continued stalemate to the prime minister and cabinet. Burney, Wilson, and Carney set up a command post in the Langevin Block across Wellington Street from Parliament Hill, and from there they continued their negotiations with Baker and his people by telephone and fax.

On Thursday, October 1, Burney and the ministers arrived back in Washington for a last-ditch effort to salvage the negotiations. Throughout the period since Reisman's departure on September 23, the two countries had continued to wrestle with the seemingly intractable subsidies issue. The Americans were unwilling, or unable, to improve on their safe-harbours concept in any meaningful way, and the Canadians were unwilling to return to the table without significant change in the U.S. position. Now, with the negotiations seemingly at a dead end, the two sides reviewed the other issues, beyond subsidies, to see whether they provided a sufficient basis for an agreement. With the U.S. still looking for the inclusion of provisions on investment, and Canada insisting that trade remedies be addressed in some way, no basis could be found. The Gibbons proposal offered an entirely different approach to the issue, focused not on changing rules governing the use of subsidies or remedies, but on disputes over the application of the rules already in place. But with time running out, only Gotlieb on the Canadian side saw the proposal as a solution to the impasse. As for the U.S., Baker remained unreceptive to the proposal. On Thursday, at the end of day, Burney informed Baker that the talks could not proceed, and he and the rest of the Canadian group returned to Ottawa where Burney would report their failure to achieve the breakthrough necessary to resume the negotiations.

Baker's lack of interest in the Gibbons proposal stemmed largely from opposition to the idea by members of the Senate Finance Committee, where any agreement must ultimately land. The committee's opposition was led by John Danforth, chairman of the subcommittee on international trade, with support from Montana's Max Baucus, a principal in the April 1986 effort to deny fast-track authority to Reagan. Danforth did not speak for the entire committee, however. Another member, Bill Bradley of New Jersey, supported Baker's efforts to find a *modus vivendi* with Canada. Allan Gotlieb, working non-stop to promote the proposal Gibbons had brought to him, called Bradley and asked him if Danforth's position reflected the sense of the Senate on the issue. When Bradley said that in his view it did not, Gotlieb urged him to call Baker and let him know this. Not only did Bradley call, but he also arranged to have a number of other Finance Committee members express their support for Gibbons's proposal to Baker and Yeutter.

On Thursday evening, Burney briefed Mulroney at the prime minister's Harrington Lake summer residence, where he was preparing for a gathering of first ministers the following day, and Mulroney made ready to announce the failure of the talks to the provincial premiers and to the country. Back at the Langevin command post in Ottawa, Burney received a call from Gotlieb. Having laid the ground in Washington for a reconsideration of the Gibbons proposal, Gotlieb now did the same with Burney, arguing that it was the only means to rescue the talks. Late that evening, the Canadian group met to reconsider the proposal. In the middle of their meeting, Baker phoned to say that the U.S. was prepared to take another look at the countervail issue, this time through the lens of Sam Gibbons's proposal. Baker also said that he would personally run the negotiations for the U.S. That was good enough for Burney. As midnight approached, Reisman was ordered to reassemble his TNO troops for an airlift to Washington early the next morning. The negotiations were back in business.

RISKY BUSINESS

At 6:30 on the morning of Friday, October 2, the TNO staff departed Ottawa for Washington for a last-ditch effort to salvage an agreement. Burney and the ministers, along with Reisman and his deputy, Gordon Ritchie, followed later in the morning. Canada returned to the free trade negotiations in an unenviable position. In the week following suspension of the talks, it had been the Canadians who shuttled in and out of Washington for meetings, and now they were once again coming to the Americans. Although there had been no doubt throughout the negotiations that Canada was the *demandeur*, while the U.S. was dealing from a position of strength, this pattern of travel provided highly visible confirmation of that status. And while the Canadian airlift to Washington may have seemed inevitable — nobody on either side seemed to expect Baker and his people to venture north — the fact remained that these negotiations, so crucial to Canada, would take place on American turf, with whatever benefits might be conferred on the home team denied the Canadians.

Not only would the negotiations take place on U.S. turf, but they would also be driven by American deadlines and agenda. To conform to the fast-track requirements, an agreement had to be concluded by midnight the following day, Saturday, October 3. As a result, the Canadians would be under tremendous pressure to do a deal with little opportunity for a full consideration of issues that were of fundamental importance to the country. At a stroke, all the advantage gained by Canada's painstaking preparation for the free trade negotiations had been diminished, if not swept away, as Canadian negotiators were forced to scramble to meet the U.S. timetable. Furthermore, with timelines so short, Baker would have the agenda for the talks largely in his own hands. Because it was necessary to operate under an American timetable and agenda, the risks for Canada were high.

The U.S. tried to increase the Canadians' potential disadvantage still further upon their arrival in Washington, when the Americans used their position as host to divide up the Canadian negotiators. Allan Gotlieb met the delegation at the airport, where the Canadian ambassador informed Reisman and Ritchie that the arrangements called for them to join their TNO staff at the USTR building on 17th Street, the cramped, nondescript quarters in which the Canadians had already spent too many long hours of frustration at Murphy's hands. Gotlieb then accompanied Burney, Wilson, and Carney, along with Wilson's deputy, Stanley Hartt, and Burney's aide, Donald Campbell, to the Treasury Department on 15th Street. Separated from their support staff by a stretch of Pennsylvania Avenue, Burney and the ministers would confront Baker and his team in the historic Treasury Building.

THE STAR CHAMBER

The U.S. Department of the Treasury is situated next door to the White House in a massive, Federal-style structure fronting on Pennsylvania Avenue. With its granite columns, endless marble corridors and high ceilings, the Treasury Building exudes the solidity that once characterized the fiscal policies of the department within. Late on Friday morning, the two political teams gathered in the treasury secretary's elegant conference room. It was here, in what was soon referred to by staffers as "the star chamber," that the elements of an agreement would be hammered out over the next two days. Burney, Wilson, and Carney, supported by Campbell, Hartt, and Gotlieb, were the principals on the Canadian side, while Baker, although he was supported by Yeutter and McPherson, dealt for the U.S. virtually single-handed.

Two blocks down Pennsylvania Avenue at USTR, the larger support staffs for each side were organized into working groups, responsible for the various issues under negotiation. As a particular issue arose in the main Baker-Burney forum during the next two days, the heads of that working group would be summoned to present status reports to the star chamber. There, they were put through an emotional wringer as Burney and Baker together grilled them on what they had been doing and why they had failed to come up with an agreement. Baker was especially tough on his own people as he delivered orders to them about how to proceed. The working groups were then dispatched to other rooms, or even frequently to the hallways, to carry out the orders of the political teams. When they had gone as far as they could on the basis of their instructions, group heads would pace the endless halls of the Treasury Building while waiting for another call to the star chamber to report progress and receive further direction. Their pacing would be uninterrupted by sustenance, since the Americans did not include the provision of anything beyond bad coffee in their defined responsibilities as host of the talks. Equality prevailed in the Republic, however, as both sides went hungry during the long hours of negotiation and waiting.

The numbers pacing the halls increased by one late on Friday morning when Simon Reisman appeared at the Treasury Building. The Americans had arranged things so that the TNO and USTR groups, including Reisman and Murphy, would be based at the Winder Building two blocks away. However, Reisman quickly realized that the real action would take place at Treasury, and he made his displeasure at being excluded from the main arena abundantly clear. A hasty invitation was issued to Reisman, and Ritchie, to come over to the Treasury Building, and protocol required the Americans to send Murphy along to accompany him. At Treasury, Reisman did not join the principals in the star chamber, however. Instead, he repaired to the small room next to Baker's office that had been provided to the Canadians as a caucus room, and there he and Ritchie were consulted by Burney on issues that were on the table in the star chamber. But while waiting for events to unfold, Reisman spent much of his time pacing the long corridors, and some of the USTR staffers who walked the halls with him were cheered by the sight. Embittered by Reisman's attacks on the competence of American negotiators, they took pleasure in the apparent exclusion of the chief Canadian negotiator from the main proceedings.

Baker's conference room provided the central arena for efforts to find a way around the impasse that blocked agreement. While the Gibbons proposal for a resolution to the subsidies–trade remedies issue provided the central topic for Burney and Baker, there were a number of other key issues that also had to be resolved directly by the political teams, principally investment and financial services. In addition, the working groups back at USTR were busy putting together the essential elements of agreement and disagreement on the other issues on the negotiating agenda, preparing these for presentation to the political teams for final decisions. For the next two days, the star chamber would be the vortex of whirlwind negotiations to rescue a free trade pact.

A FORTUITOUS MISUNDERSTANDING

When Baker and Burney had agreed on Thursday night that the Gibbons concept provided a basis upon which to resume talks, their agreement was based on differing interpretations of the meaning of the congressman's proposal. When Gibbons originally discussed the idea with Allan Gotlieb, he raised the possibility of applying *existing* trade remedy law on both sides of the border on an interim basis, that is until the subsidies–trade remedies issue could be satisfactorily resolved in extended negotiations. In addition, he suggested that some means be established by which to resolve disputes over appropriate applications of national trade remedy laws. In his memorandum to Burney setting out Gibbons's idea, Allan Gotlieb had addressed these two elements. First, he wrote that the proposal envisaged the creation of a binational tribunal to resolve differences over appropriate trade remedy applications. This would be a form of "court" to which Canada could appeal against the improper use of U.S. trade remedies for the harassment of Canadian exporters. Second, Gotlieb wrote that the proposal included a *freeze* on changes to existing trade remedy laws. This was important because it would prevent the U.S. from introducing new measures that were expressly designed to sidestep limits on the application of American anti-dumping and countervailing duties that resulted from decisions of the binational tribunal. Without a freeze, the U.S. might lose a tribunal decision, but then change its laws to avoid losing a similar case again.

In agreeing to discuss this proposal, the Canadians saw themselves making an important concession to the Americans. For months, Canada had insisted that the U.S. negotiate a subsidies code, that is, a set of rules to define acceptable subsidy practices and render countervailing duties unnecessary. This the Commerce Department negotiators had steadfastly refused to do, even if their refusal cost the U.S. a free trade agreement with Canada. But without some action on trade remedies, the Canadians were unwilling to enter into an agreement. The Gibbons proposal attempted to

sidestep this impasse by putting the subsidies issue aside for further negotiation, and focusing instead on settlement procedures for
disputes over the appropriate use of anti-dumping and countervailing duties. This shift required the Canadians to back off their
demand for an agreement on subsidies.

Having made this concession in agreeing to a resumption of talks
on the basis of the Gibbons proposal, the Canadians arrived in
Washington to discover that the Americans did not share their
understanding of the nature of that proposal. In the discussions on
Friday afternoon, it became clear that there was a profound misunderstanding over the implications of Gibbons's suggestion that the
two countries should continue to apply their *existing* trade remedy
laws on an interim basis while extending negotiations to find a
satisfactory resolution to the subsidies–trade remedies issue.
Gotlieb had interpreted this to Burney to mean that in the interim
period both countries would put a *freeze* on existing anti-dumping
and countervailing duty laws. A freeze would prohibit changes to
the laws intended to circumvent decisions of the binational agency
and would prevent the introduction of new measures to hamper
access to each other's market while negotiations proceeded. On
Friday, however, the Americans flatly rejected the proposal for a
freeze. Baker maintained that he simply could not do a deal that
would bind the Congress in this way, in effect limiting its constitutional authority to make or amend laws. In this position, the treasury secretary was strongly supported by the Commerce lawyers,
who opposed the Gibbons solution anyway, the Justice Department, where concerns about constitutional proprieties were para-
mount, and by soundings taken in the Congress.

There was also disagreement, though no misunderstanding,
over the structure and review powers of a binational tribunal.
Existing American law subjected the application of U.S. anti-dumping and countervailing duty laws by domestic agencies (the Department of Commerce and the U.S. International Trade Commission)
to judicial review by U.S. courts. Canada wanted to see a permanent
binational tribunal replace U.S. courts for purposes of judicial

review. In addition, the Canadians wanted the tribunal to operate on the basis of a fairly broad concept of judicial review. This concept would permit the tribunal to review whether domestic agencies had applied U.S. laws correctly, and to substitute its judgement for that of the agency in respect of both the law and the interpretation of the facts. The Americans disagreed with the Canadian position on both counts. Reluctant to consider the prospect of any judicial review in a binational forum, they were adamant that if such a system was to be created, it should operate through a system of panels with rotating membership, rather than a permanent tribunal. In addition, the U.S. wanted the agency to operate on the basis of a very narrow concept of judicial review, evaluating only the record of decision of the domestic agency to assess whether existing law had been properly applied in a particular case, but prohibited from considering the broader administrative record.

Baker and Burney had agreed to resume the negotiations on the basis of profoundly different interpretations of the nature of the Gibbons proposal. This misunderstanding allowed the two sides to get back to the table. By late Friday evening, however, it was clear that the only thing they could agree on with regard to the most contentious issue between them was that the subsidies issue had been removed from the table, perhaps for discussion in another set of negotiations. If Sam Gibbons's idea was still to provide a means to rescue an agreement, it would require creative solutions from the players. With only one more day to run on the fast-track clock, however, time was not on their side.

THE LONGEST DAY

The weather in Washington on Saturday, October 3, mirrored the downward turn in the talks, as rain enveloped the capital. Although the Gibbons proposal continued to occupy centre stage in the star chamber, there were significant gaps between the positions of the two countries on many of the other issues under negotiation, and these had to be addressed on this day as well. The issue-focused working groups continued to labour away at USTR, trying to find a basis for agreement or clear up outstanding matters on those issues that had been largely agreed upon before the suspension of the talks. All through the day, group heads were shuttled in and out of the star chamber, reporting progress and problems to the political teams before being sent off again with instructions about whether and how to proceed.

The looming deadline finally shook out the U.S. negotiating mandate, and there was a flurry of position-taking on most of the issues on which Murphy had stonewalled for so many months. On trade in services and government procurement, it finally became apparent that the Americans had no interest in negotiating anything beyond a minimalist agreement. While services might once have had a prominent place on the American agenda, in the crunch no significant deal was possible. As for procurement, when time constraints required the Americans to lay their cards on the table, they finally took the bulk of their procurement market off. Intellectual property, thought to be another high-priority item for the U.S., was also taken off the table, victim of a lack of time and a fit of pique. When the Americans scornfully dismissed the Canadian proposal on the issue as tantamount to doing nothing, the Canadians retorted that perhaps they should just agree to do nothing. With that, the intellectual property issue was removed from the negotiating table. But it was not off the free trade agenda. Separate from the agreement, Canada acceded to U.S. requests to resolve two long-standing complaints in the intellectual property area, concerning satellite retransmissions and compulsory licensing of pharmaceuticals. This side-deal was subsequently included in the American summary of the agreement issued on October 4 by USTR, but not in the summary distributed by Canada on that day.[2] And only the retransmission element was included in the preliminary transcript of the elements of the agreement issued by Canada, and in a revised summary produced by USTR on October 8. Despite the sleight of hand, this agreement was part of the free trade negotiations. But because it was a side-deal, Canada was able to claim, technically, that the FTA did not address the sensitive pharmaceuticals issue. However, the subsequent release of an early draft of the agreement, with the pharmaceuticals component included and initialed by a Canadian negotiator, caused some embarrassment in Ottawa.

Another key American issue was not so easily dealt with. If the Canadians needed some action on trade remedies to make a deal, the U.S. required investment. The link between these two issues had been acknowledged tacitly for some time in the negotiations, although little substantive progress had been made on investment because the Americans remained unwilling to move on trade remedies. On the day that Reisman suspended negotiations, the Canadian investment group had spent the morning at Treasury, where the two sides tentatively agreed to a number of principles that would be reflected in any agreement, plus some technical matters. Although the principles were important ones, including the grandfathering (keeping in place) of existing policies and recognition of Canada's right to screen foreign investment, progress on details had been halted by the Canadian walkout. Now that the Gibbons proposal had been substituted for the subsidies–trade remedies issue, it was time to talk turkey on investment.

The issue was seized on Friday when the investment working groups came together. The three-member Canadian team was immediately placed on the defensive when the Americans used their home turf advantage to field a group of 15 Treasury officials to engage Canada on the issue. The Americans pushed very hard on this top U.S. priority, which remained an issue of considerable political sensitivity in Canada. Deliberations were tense, and the outnumbered Canadians tired, but enough movement in positions occurred on that first day to permit the group heads to seek direction in the star chamber, where they received instructions to go off and do a deal.

Canada's luck took a turn for the better when the Americans put forward their proposals in writing. It was composed by a Treasury official with the department for 30 years, who tried to fit into one draft everything that he had ever wanted to achieve on the investment front. The proposal was an indigestible piece, incomprehensible even to other U.S. Treasury people. Always anxious to help, the Canadians volunteered to take a crack at redrafting the U.S. proposal. With the pen firmly in their hands, the group entirely rewrote the U.S. draft, and then offered it back to the Americans as a single negotiating text from which both parties could work.

Despite being outnumbered, the Canadians were able to persevere in the negotiations that followed. Although the U.S. was aiming at maximum access to Canada for American investors, they were forced to back off that position considerably as negotiations proceeded on Saturday. The Canadian group head, Andrei Sulzenko, adopted a very tough stance in the working group sessions. Instructions from the star chamber were reinterpreted, Sulzenko claiming that Burney, along with Wilson who was handling this "Finance" issue, had not agreed to elements the Americans thought had been nailed down with Baker at the main table. The U.S. working group head, Robert Cornell, would then have to go back to Baker seeking clarification. The effect was to whittle away at American demands. This tough stand in the working group sessions helped the political team in the star chamber as well, since Baker was relying on advice from Cornell on how hard to push the Canadians, rather than taking the lead on the issue himself. Cornell had already received a lesson in Canadian sensitivities on investment the previous spring, when Reisman became outraged over Cornell's opening position on investment, and handed it back to Murphy. The strong resistance to concessions that he encountered from the Canadians in the working group sessions throughout Saturday reinforced the lesson. Convinced that Canada could not be pushed too far on this sensitive issue, Cornell advised Baker that the U.S. would have to be prepared to compromise.

The earlier agreement in principle on the right to screen investment was incorporated into the Canadian version of the draft text, although the Americans waived their reciprocal right to screen on the grounds that it was a bad practice they did not wish to imitate. The principle of grandfathering powers to review and restrict investment in specific sectors was also incorporated into the text. Most important here was agreement that any limits on Canada's power to review takeovers would not extend to the oil, natural gas, and uranium sectors. The U.S. also agreed to a specific exemption for cultural industries from the investment provisions, as well as to the right of Canada to require divestiture to Canadians of cultural industries indirectly controlled by U.S. firms.

While the Canadians were successful in achieving significant exclusions from the investment provisions plus recognition of their review powers, some concessions to American demands for national treatment for U.S. investors were necessary to achieve the tradeoff between investment and trade remedies. The crucial issue here became the threshold levels for review of foreign takeovers. It was agreed that Canada would continue to review major direct takeovers, but not smaller ones. In addition, the review of indirect takeovers would be phased out over three years, with the threshold increasing from $100 million to $500 million before ending reviews altogether. The question, then, was what threshold would be used to distinguish between major and minor direct takeovers? Canada wanted the figure lower, the Americans higher.

The Canadians told Cornell that they would not negotiate this issue in the working groups, leaving it instead to the political teams to settle on a figure. In the star chamber, Baker put forward a threshold figure, and Michael Wilson, handling this issue for the Canadian team, countered with his own. There was a sizable gap between the two. Throughout the day, the two sides came back to the threshold question a number of times in the course of their continuing deliberations over trade remedies, making more explicit the tacit link between the two issues. Finally, in late afternoon the working groups were told to use a Canadian threshold review figure of $150 million in their draft text. Back in the working groups, the Canadians bought some additional room for review by insisting that the figure be phased in, with the review threshold moving in four annual stages from the then-current figure of $5 million to the agreed threshold of $150 million. They also persuaded the Americans to define the threshold in current dollars during the phase in period, so that over the four stages the threshold would effectively be reduced, permitting the review of slightly smaller takeovers. At the conclusion of the phase-in, however, the threshold would be defined in constant dollars.

Treasury officials would later come under heavy fire in Washington for conceding too much to the Canadians on investment. Senior officials in other agencies were very critical of the decision to accept the $150 million threshold for review, and the subsequent agreement to phase in the threshold incrementally. They felt that Cornell had folded on this issue, when he should have insisted on a threshold of no less than $500 million from the Canadians. The agreement to exclude the energy sector from the relaxation of restrictions on foreign investment was also criticized. The U.S. energy industry was particularly angry over the maintenance of review powers for indirect takeovers. And when the agreement was subsequently presented to the Congress, Treasury officials were grilled by members of the Senate Energy Committee who were not happy with the exemption, even though they agreed to go along with the deal. Although Cornell bore the brunt of the criticism, it was Baker who was running the U.S. side in the negotiations and, as treasury secretary, Baker had an advantage: investment was his special brief. The decisions on the exemption for energy, as well as review thresholds, and forced divestiture of cultural industries were all made by Baker at the main table. As for Cornell, the criticisms of his American colleagues are perhaps best explained by the TNO judgement that he was a fair negotiator, sensitive to Canadian needs, traits not highly prized in an American negotiator when dealing with Canada.

Treasury officials would later complain about being "nickel-and-dimed" on the investment issue by their Canadian adversaries. And since investment was a Treasury issue, and a high priority for the secretary, Baker was privately very unhappy over Canada's contentious behaviour. His opportunity to repay in kind came on the issue of culture. Canada's request to exempt cultural industries from the agreement had been matched by an American proposal to insert a notwithstanding clause on culture, permitting the U.S. to retaliate against Canadian actions to protect cultural industries with measures of equivalent commercial effect. Canadian negotiators were concerned because the clause would permit American retaliation in areas unrelated to culture, making intervention in the cultural sector more difficult for Canada. The cultural issue meant little to Baker. Nevertheless, when the Canadians pressed him to drop the retaliatory clause, he refused because he was angry over their recalcitrance on investment.

While those in the star chamber were preoccupied with the Gibbons proposal and, to a lesser extent, investment throughout Saturday, the working groups continued to grind away at the host of other sectoral issues that were still on the table. Although the Americans had lost their taste for a comprehensive deal on trade in services, an agreement on financial services remained possible. However, little progress had been made in the working group on this issue before the suspension of talks in September. Throughout the negotiations, financial services had proceeded on a separate track at the insistence of U.S. Treasury officials. There had even been some doubt about whether the financial services negotiators actually had to follow suit on September 23 and suspend their own negotiations, but they were sharply reminded that they were part of a larger process. When the crunch came on Saturday, the pieces of a deal quickly fell into place. Baker and Wilson were able to break away from the main table and wrap up the broad elements of an agreement on this Treasury-Finance issue between themselves, although the details were not finalized until the following day. On issues such as agriculture, automobiles, alcoholic beverages, and energy, working groups prepared brief summary statements of positions for presentation in the star chamber, where instructions for further movement were handed out. Throughout the day, final accommodations were reached on most of these elements. As night fell, the working group heads signed off on the agreed texts, until

only the issues raised by Gibbons's proposal remained to be resolved. But without this piece in the puzzle, the other elements
amounted to nothing.

HIGH NOON AT MIDNIGHT

The negotiations that had been launched with the prime
minister's request to the president two years earlier had finally
come down to what the U.S. was prepared to give, and Canada
prepared to accept, on the reformulated trade remedies issue.
The two sides were sharply divided over the question of a freeze
on existing trade laws and over the nature of the review powers
that would be granted to a dispute-settlement tribunal. Working
through Friday night and again on Saturday morning, the Canadians tried to craft a proposal that would address American
objections to the concept of a freeze, while still protecting Canada
from changes to U.S. trade remedy law. Allan Gotlieb argued that
the inclusion of a "good faith principle," requiring the parties to
act consistently with the spirit of the agreement, was all that was
required, but no one else in the group felt this offered sufficient
protection. Wilson's deputy, Stanley Hartt, proposed the adoption of a notwithstanding clause, requiring that Canada be explicitly named in any legislation to amend existing trade law or
introduce new laws. For TNO general counsel Konrad von
Finckenstein, this did not go far enough. Von Finckenstein and
Len Legault, the economic minister at the Canadian Embassy in
Washington, drafted a provision that would make any changes
in U.S. trade law that named Canada subject to review by a
binational panel. The panel would have watchdog powers to
determine whether the changes were consistent with the Free
Trade Agreement and the GATT, and whether their effect was to
overturn a previous decision of a binational dispute-settlement
panel. These watchdog provisions provided Canada with a facsimile of the freeze they considered essential to an agreement. On
the issue of review powers, the Canadians proposed to replace

existing national judicial review with a binational panel with very broad review powers and the power to make binding decisions.

The U.S. accepted the principle of review by a binational panel, and eventually they agreed that its decisions should be binding. But they insisted that the panel should operate on the basis of a very narrowly constructed procedural review. In addition, they rejected the Canadian facsimile of a freeze, arguing that it was too vague and unworkable. There the negotiations remained at an impasse throughout the day. The Americans insisted they could go no further and kept announcing newly discovered deadlines for a deal in an effort to push the Canadians to an agreement. Among the members of the Canadian team, Allan Gotlieb was most concerned that holding out for further American concessions on the trade remedies issue would endanger the prospects for agreement. He argued that the Canadians had achieved the essential elements of Gibbons's proposal. The U.S. had accepted the principle of binding judicial review, and the equivalent of a freeze could be achieved by securing an American commitment to respect the spirit of any agreement.

Burney was not persuaded by Gotlieb's arguments, however, and late on Saturday afternoon he decided that no further progress was possible. A telephone call was placed to the prime minister in Ottawa, and he was informed that the deadlock appeared to be beyond resolution. Mulroney spoke to Burney and the two ministers in turn, and each recommended against a deal on the U.S. terms. Two decisions were then taken. The first was to tell Baker that the Canadians were prepared to break off the talks over the issue, despite the impending expiry of the fast-track deadline. The second decision was to have Mulroney telephone Reagan directly to make certain that he was aware of the state of play, and its likely consequences.

At eight o'clock, Burney told Baker that no agreement was possible without further American movement on the Gibbons proposal. He also indicated that Mulroney intended to call Reagan at the president's Camp David retreat. After checking with the president's staff, Baker suggested to Burney that it might be better to delay the prime minister's call until closer to 10 o'clock, because the president was watching a movie that would not conclude until sometime after 9:30! At about the time the president's movie was due to end, however, Baker came to the Canadian caucus room to tell Burney to cancel the call. The Americans would try again to meet Canada's needs on the issue. Ordering his lawyers to be creative, Baker sent them off to find a way to get around the impasse. They looked again at the proposal the Canadians had put forward that morning, and apparently found it more to their liking. They rewrote the language of the Canadians' Saturday morning draft, but accepted its essential elements. Judicial review would be transferred to a binational panel. Instead of a freeze, each country would be required to explicitly name the other as subject to changes in trade laws, and the changes would be subject to review by a binational panel to determine their consistency with GATT codes and the object and purpose of the Free Trade Agreement, as well as their effects on prior panel decisions. Finally, negotiations would continue on a new timetable to establish a subsidies–trade remedies regime.

The Canadians went to the telephone again to brief the prime minister and others assembled in the Langevin Block on the contents of the American proposal. The litmus test for Mulroney was whether the proposed mechanism would have helped Canada deal with the softwood lumber issue that had caused such grief early in the negotiations. Assured that it would, Mulroney gave the go-ahead. Burney was not yet prepared to sign on, however. The Canadians had achieved much of what they wanted in their understanding of the Gibbons proposal package, but it was not enough. Baker's lawyers continued to insist on a very narrow procedural concept in the area of judicial review. With time running out, the temptation for the Canadians to bend to the pressure and take the gains already on the table was strong. Again it was Gotlieb who urged the others on the political team to take the U.S. offer, earning himself the sobriquet "run with it Gotlieb" with some of the Canadian negotiators. At this eleventh hour, Simon Reisman stepped firmly into the process to argue forcefully against Gotlieb's position, and he prevailed. Burney insisted to Baker that the U.S. position on the issue of judicial review was simply not good enough. The ball was back in the U.S. court.

Shortly past 10 o'clock, Baker returned the volley. Burney, Wilson, and Carney, along with other members of the Canadian group, were waiting for the next U.S. move, if there was to be one, when the treasury secretary walked alone into the room next to his office where the Canadians were headquartered. Baker had two things to say. First, he had a courier waiting downstairs to take his letter to the president informing Reagan that Canada and the United States had reached agreement. The letter had to be sent now to meet the fast-track deadline. "Should I send it?" he asked. Second, Baker said he had a "clarification" regarding the concept of judicial review. He stated the clarification, and then quickly left the Canadian room. The pressure was now back on the Canadians.

After Baker left, Burney turned to the others and asked whether the clarification was good enough; did it meet Canadian needs? While Allan Gotlieb once again urged acceptance, Stanley Hartt felt the clarification did not do the trick, and he attempted to compose alternative language to satisfy his objections. The result was judged to be too convoluted, however, given the time constraints under which the group was operating, and was rejected. Time was slipping away as the group deliberated. Von Finckenstein, the general counsel, advised Burney that Baker's clarification made a significant difference. It was much closer to the Canadian proposal for broad review powers. The previous U.S. position had tried to confine reviews to narrow procedural grounds. However, the clarification provided that the panel could look at all the documents that were before the lower tribunal, that is, the entire administrative record, including all documents filed by the applicant instead of merely the record of decision. On the basis of this evidence, the panel could tell the lower tribunal that its conclusion was wrong and ask it to redo the case. Von Finckenstein advised Burney that the U.S. clarification would give Canada the broadest judicial review possible, and he should accept it if it met his political requirements.

The Canadians now had only minutes to consider the political acceptability of the new U.S. position. When they put it together with the other elements that had been agreed to, including equal representation on the panels, deadlines for decisions, and the freeze facsimile, they agreed that the political test could be met by Baker's clarification. They could, in good conscience, advise the prime minister to sign an agreement with these provisions. As midnight approached, they rejoined Baker and his team in the star chamber to indicate their agreement to his clarification. When they attempted to agree to a proposal on paper, however, the U.S. lawyers tried to force the adoption of language that would again narrow the scope for review. The Canadians had finally had enough, and their pent-up frustration produced a 15-minute exchange that one senior official present described as the most extraordinary he had ever witnessed. This final disagreement resolved, the two sides finally came to terms. At five minutes before midnight, Burney and Baker shook hands, clinching a deal that had been a year and a half in the making. As negotiations go, the Washington weekend was not a long haul, but it was a very near thing.

NO REST FOR THE WEARY

Despite the formal handshake, the deal was not yet done. Even the most sure-footed were not exactly certain what had been rendered during the frantic Saturday hours. Throughout the day on Sunday, aides worked out the details of the agreement, while their political bosses demanded results to present to the media. Baker scheduled a press conference for two o'clock, delayed it for two hours at the Canadians' request, and then presented the agreement to the scribes, even as the staffs were trying to nail down the specifics of the deal. Much of their effort was devoted to the culture and softwood lumber issues, where there had been agreement in principle on Saturday, but no actual wording had been set down. Connected to the proceedings by telephone, Ottawa could only threaten in increasingly shrill tones that they must have something for the spin doctors to distribute. Finally, late on Sunday, and after Baker's press conference, Ottawa was able to announce the results of the Canadian weekend in Washington.

Still, only the broadest outlines of the deal were on paper. These elements of agreement would have to be translated into legal text, and this task was handed to Konrad von Finckenstein and his USTR counterpart, Charles "Chip" Roh. They began their meetings, accompanied by teams of lawyers, in late October. This normally complex undertaking was made even more difficult by the ambiguity that surrounded some of the elements agreed to in Washington. As the lawyers' labours stretched on toward winter, they isolated those issues in the agreement that would require further negotiation. And so, in late November Simon Reisman and Gordon Ritchie returned to Washington with some of the TNO staff to wrap up the final details with Peter Murphy. Plans called for the negotiations to be concluded in a single day, but Reisman and Murphy stayed true to their earlier form, and were unable to come to agreement. The two met again in Ottawa at the beginning of December, with the same inconclusive result.

To resolve the problem, Derek Burney was called on again to conduct talks at the political level, and he found himself at the centre of yet another marathon weekend of negotiations with the Americans, this time facing off against Treasury Deputy Peter McPherson, but in Ottawa rather than Washington. Throughout the first weekend in December, Burney and McPherson wrestled again with the panel review provisions of the trade remedies issue, and over an American effort to secure an upward revision in the content rule governing automobile trade. It was not until the early hours of the morning of December 7 that agreement was finally reached on these and a number of other issues. Still the deal was not wrapped up, however. It would take several more exchanges to resolve differences that remained over the retransmission of cable broadcasts. On December 10, 1987, the painful negotiations finally came to an end. And the anguish of a national decision in Canada was set to begin.

PART III:
APPROVING THE DEAL:
THE FREE TRADE ELECTION

9

TWO NATIONALIST VISIONS

In the aftermath of the free trade election of November 21, 1988, political columnist Richard Gwyn and economist Carl Beigie discussed their views of Canada on Gwyn's TVOntario public affairs program. Both men are Canadians by choice, Gwyn immigrating to Canada from Britain and Beigie from the United States. Although both favoured the FTA, much of their half-hour of reflection dwelt on a personal sense of loss for a Canada that could no longer be, and their feelings of sadness and anxiety over the bitter conflict their country had endured on the free trade issue. It seemed there was no stopping the growing globalization of the world, and Canada would have to adapt, but the process would exact a high price. Coming at the end of a two-year-long wrenching national debate, their views reflected those of many Canadians on both sides of the debate, and the majority caught in the middle.

There was an ironic twist to the outcomes of the two elections held in North America in November 1988. While Americans had elected a president who pledged to work towards a kinder, gentler America, Canadians had re-elected a prime minister who wanted Canada to become a tougher, more competitive nation. In this, Canadians had learned their lesson from Reagan's America, where the market had become the new mantra, even as the realities of international markets were denied. There was sad irony, as well, in the way the politics of free trade mirrored the bitter left-right divide that marked American politics in the Reagan era. The free trade decision was a wrenching experience for Canada because the significance of the FTA goes way beyond the economics of the agreement. Its consequences flow from the nature of the political debate that was conducted on the issue and the way the broad coalitions framed their supporting and opposing positions. Opponents of the FTA denied the legitimacy of the free trade decision, arguing that there was no electoral majority in support of the agreement. They also asserted that business had bought the election through their unprecedented and illegitimate financing of the campaign. Proponents of the deal were zealous in their insistence that free trade offered the only hope for Canada's salvation, denying the legitimacy of concerns expressed about the deal. It was the bipartisan middle that fell victim to the polarization between the two positions, and this could profoundly influence politics in the 1990s if the coalitions become the basis for a permanent realignment of Canadian politics into a more openly class-based system.

The free trade debate saw the emergence in stark form of two distinct brands of nationalism. One was centred in the anti-free trade forces, founded on a defence of the powers of the Canadian state as the crucial glue for Canada's unity and independence. The other brand was a nationalism based on the market in which the pro-free trade coalition asserted a new entrepreneurial confidence in the ability of Canadians to compete with the best in the world. The first brand of nationalists had always dismissed the second as continentalists, and it was true that the marketeers had looked to the continent in the past. The 1980s version of market nationalism was more entrepreneurial, however, and definitely more chauvinistic about Canada. It could not be written off easily using the slogans of the 1960s and 1970s.

These competing nationalisms took concrete form in the two coalition umbrella groups that were formed to conduct the battle over free trade. The anti-free trade forces gathered first in the Council of Canadians (COC), formed in March 1985, and then coalesced around the Pro Canada Network (PCN) which emerged out of the COC in April 1987. PCN was composed of an array of social organizations, from church groups to women's organizations, environmental lobbies, and native groups. The pro-free trade forces coalesced around the Canadian Alliance for Trade and Job Opportunities. The Alliance was formed by the major business associations in the country, although it described itself as a non-partisan, broadly based organization composed of citizens from all parts of Canada. A description of the protagonists in the conflict over free trade must also include the broader array of interests and institutional elements, such as the mass media and professional policy elites, that were either aligned with the formal coalitions or involved in the larger free trade debate.

THE GLADIATORS

In the final analysis, these coalitions were engaged in a battle for the hearts and minds of Canadians on the issue of free trade and their competing visions of Canada. The most notable gladiators in the conflict crossed partisan lines and included old names in new roles and no-names who achieved national status for the first time in the debate. The old names included Peter Lougheed and Donald Macdonald. Bitter enemies in the 1970s over energy policy, they became staunch allies on the speakers circuit, working tirelessly for the Alliance. They were joined by ardent pro-free traders like economist Richard Lipsey, who made the cool, cerebral case for the FTA, and business professor John Crispo, who added passion and energetic humour to Lipsey's rational advocacy. Thomas d'Aquino continued to make the case for free trade in his role as the head of BCNI. For someone accustomed to the privacy of the lobby, the behind-the-scenes power broker moved to an unaccustomed degree into the public spotlight in order to promote the agreement.

Combatants on the anti-free trade side included familiar nationalists from the 1960s, people like Mel Hurtig, the crusading Edmonton publisher who had been among the founders of the Committee for an Independent Canada, and University of Toronto academic

Mel Watkins, whose study for government in the 1960s ushered in Canadian policies to screen foreign investment. They were joined, and soon supplanted, by new blood on the anti-free trade side. These included: Maude Barlow, a feminist and strong social policy advocate; Duncan Cameron, a University of Ottawa political scientist who is an energetic and articulate critic of liberal economic theory and practice; and Tony Clarke, a priest who framed the economic critique by the Canadian Conference of Catholic Bishops that had enraged the Canadian business community during the 1982 recession.

In important respects, the free trade debate was carried by these extra-Parliamentary gladiators. Though they were not entirely immune to problems of partisanship, compared to the leaders of Canada's political parties they were free to propound their competing nationalisms, and the dangers associated with the alternative, in unrestrained ways. Indeed, both coalitions were angered by the apparent inability of the parties and their leaders to carry the free trade debate effectively. The PCN was worried that the Liberals and NDP seemed more concerned with the tactics of their own electoral machinations than with defeating the FTA. For its part, the Alliance was deeply concerned about the capacity of the Mulroney government to sell the deal effectively to Canadians.

THE OLD NATIONALISTS

To enter Mel Hurtig's Edmonton office is to immediately see the paradox of the man. The walls of the long narrow room are covered with newspaper clippings, chronicling Hurtig's political battles over two decades. An enormous political ego is clearly on display. But so too is a remarkable commitment to hard work for his political beliefs. The wall to the right of his desk contains several dozen file folders and boxes, each devoted to a different policy field, all in readiness for writing the next speech. Hurtig may be a paradox, but he is a committed and formidable Canadian nationalist. Late in 1984, barely four months into the Mulroney government's first term, Hurtig started to receive calls and letters from allies in the nationalist cause expressing concern about the direction of the Mulroney agenda, especially the open-door approach to foreign investment. Busy then with the launching of his most ambitious project, *The Canadian Encyclopedia*, Hurtig first tried to ignore the entreaties of his friends, but eventually he could not ignore the prospect of another battle. At a meeting in his office on January 11, 1985, he and 10 others conceived the Council of Canadians.

A larger group of like-minded Canadians, about 70 in total, was convened in Toronto in February 1985, and this meeting led to the founding meeting of the COC in October 1985. A key issue at that meeting concerned the lessons that could be taken from the mistakes of the earlier Committee for an Independent Canada (CIC), which Hurtig had helped found in the 1970s. The liabilities of the CIC were apparent with hindsight. It had been too elitist in its membership structure, with very little of its money coming from ordinary individual members. It was also composed of too many well-known Liberal partisans, undermining its claims to non-partisanship. Finally, the CIC was intellectually dominated by one man, the former Liberal finance minister Walter Gordon, the godfather of contemporary Canadian nationalism. It is ironic that Gordon's major work in the nationalist cause was done as the head of the last major royal commission on the economy prior to the one headed by Donald Macdonald, the Liberal who put an end to Gordon's design for an independent Canada.

From March 1985 until April 1987, Hurtig was able to increase COC membership from 1,500 to 3,000 persons. This was accomplished through speeches well timed to rally opposition to the government around events like the Shamrock Summits between Mulroney and Reagan, the *Polar Sea* incident, in which the U.S. icebreaker travelled through the Northwest Passage without prior Canadian agreement, and foreign corporate takeovers of Canadian companies. In April 1987, the COC held a "Maple Leaf Summit" parallel to the third Shamrock Summit, designed to counter the continental cosiness of the Reagan-Mulroney meetings. By the third

COC conference in October 1987, membership had grown to 7,000, and 5,000 people attended a November 1987 meeting to develop alternative policies to the Mulroney Conservative agenda, including free trade. By the time of its 1988 conference in the middle of the free trade election, COC membership stood at 14,000 people. Its chairman was now Ken Wardroper, a former External Affairs foreign service officer. Of the total COC membership, about 25 per cent had Liberal partisan affiliations and about 15 per cent aligned themselves with the NDP, leaving more than 50 per cent who were not partisans. At the height of the FTA conflict, however, it was clear that not many of these were leaning to the Conservatives.

It was at the COC's 1987 Maple Leaf Summit that the Pro Canada Network was formed. It became a more specific anti-free trade umbrella for 30 national organizations and 10 provincial coalitions. Its members included the COC, the Canadian Labour Congress, the National Action Committee on the Status of Women, cultural groups, environmental groups, aboriginal organizations, senior citizens' groups, and many Canadian churches. The Network claimed a total affiliated membership of about 10 million Canadians. The PCN saw itself as the popular counterweight to the Business Council on National Issues and to the Mulroney government's attempts to control and curb the debate on the FTA. It believed that a fundamental realignment of Canada's political and economic structure was occurring under the joint auspices of the Tories and the business community led by BCNI. This realignment was leading, in the PCN view, to the political disenfranchisement of ordinary Canadians, made worse by the weakness of the Liberal Party at the time.

The PCN was also created to keep its own members better informed about the FTA. As a "coalition of coalitions," united by opposition to free trade but not by any other clear alternative agenda, the PCN's organization was horizontal rather than hierarchical. It had no national bureaucracy. PCN national assemblies took place about every six months. Detailed proposals were worked out by three committees, on strategy and front-line matters, media and

communications, and research and analysis. Their work was debated at steering committee meetings composed of representatives
from each of the constituent national organizations and two from
the provincial coalitions, and Network positions were ratified at
national assemblies. It was under the banner of the PCN that a new
generation of Canadian nationalists fought their battle against free
trade.

THE NEW NATIONALISTS

Although the PCN originated with Hurtig's Council of Canadians,
its operations were most deeply influenced by elements of the
women's movement, church and union groups, and the activist
academic left. Front and centre was Maude Barlow, a feminist with
strong links to a network of women's groups. Barlow began her
public career in Ottawa as the high-profile director of the city's
office of equal opportunity for women. She regularly captured
headlines for her outspoken positions on issues, and gained a
reputation as an anti-pornography crusader. A Liberal partisan,
Barlow served as an adviser on women's issues in Pierre Trudeau's
PMO in 1983–84. An early activist in the formation of the Council of
Canadians, she deeply believed that the Tory agenda in general,
and free trade in particular, would hurt women and would widen
the gap between rich and poor in Canada. Barlow was instrumental
at the early COC meetings in promoting the need for a coalition of
groups who could unite around the twin themes of defending
Canadian sovereignty and preserving social democracy. She ran
hard, and early, for the Liberal nomination in the federal riding of
Ottawa Centre, starting her campaign late in 1986, long before an
election was even on the horizon. The head start backfired when
her high profile gave opponents in the riding a large target plus
time to take aim. Closely identified with Liberal leader John Turner,
Barlow unexpectedly lost her bid for the nomination to a local
candidate endorsed by Turner rival Jean Chrétien. However, that
loss freed her for a larger role in the anti-free trade coalition. In

October of 1988, in the midst of the election on free trade, Barlow became the whirlwind head of the PCN.

Tony Clarke was also a key member of the new nationalist coalition. Shocked and saddened by the human anguish caused by the 1982 recession, Clarke had mobilized the Conference of Catholic Bishops to protest against the needless suffering. He prepared an economic statement for the conference that espoused, among other things, the need for a commitment in Canada to full employment as a moral imperative. Though quiet and politically inexperienced, Clarke became the inspirational soul of the PCN. The coalition was later joined by other church groups as well, many of them in the front lines of the effort to deal with poverty in Canada by operating 1930s-style food banks. Another important element in the formation of the PCN came from the union movement, particularly younger union activists. They believed that unions had a responsibility to play a social and political role in Canadian society, and should not just focus on collective bargaining. These unionists too had learned from the 1982 recession and felt strongly that they needed to build a network of allies in the larger political community. This group included many public sector union members. In fact public sector unions made up the largest component within the Canadian Labour Congress and their members felt especially threatened by the Mulroney government's agenda.[1]

Academic activists played an important role in the formation of the PCN, as well, and none was more active than University of Ottawa political scientist Duncan Cameron. Although he had once worked in the Department of Finance, Cameron rejected the central tenets of liberal economics. He was not only intellectually suspicious of those who favoured unfettered markets, but he also came into close contact with individuals like Tony Clarke who added passion and commitment to his cerebral opposition. Cameron first came to some prominence when he put together a series of papers in 1985 under the title *The Other Macdonald Report*.[2] These were briefs from groups which Cameron believed were not heard by the Macdonald Commission in 1984–85. Many of these groups would later join the PCN, aided by another University of Ottawa political scientist, John Trent, who played an important role in promoting the need for the coalition of groups that would unite in the Network. In the heat of the FTA debate, Cameron headed a group of sympathetic academics and union research staff members who supplied instant critiques of the agreement and its possible effects.

Perhaps the most unexpected gladiator on the anti-free trade side was 72-year-old retired Edmonton family court judge, Marjorie Bowker. Prompted by concern over the effects of the FTA, Bowker conducted her own personal analysis of the free trade agreement, using materials in the law library at the University of Alberta. She initially circulated copies of the analysis to interested readers herself, asking them to photocopy the study and pass it on to others. After the highly critical pamphlet was reviewed by former Trudeau aide Jim Coutts in the *Toronto Star* and columnist Roy MacGregor in the *Ottawa Citizen*, it became a runaway bestseller in Canada, and Bowker became a media regular on the issue. Bowker's analysis enraged trade officials, but despite their vigorous rebuttals, for a while it became the focus of the free trade debate, stealing the show from the government's multi-million-dollar promotional effort. Neatly counterbalancing Bowker's intervention was that of another retired judge, former Supreme Court justice Emmett Hall. His statement at a critical juncture in the 1988 election campaign helped the pro-free trade side diffuse growing criticism that the deal would harm Canada's health care programs. Coming from the former head of the royal commission study that led to medicare in the 1960s, Hall's opinion carried special weight.

AN UPHILL BATTLE

PCN's leaders faced a formidable task in their effort to turn back free trade. There were genuine difficulties bringing this diverse set of interest groups together into a cohesive political force. Some of the social policy and women's groups feared that they might lose federal funding because of their open opposition to the Tories.[3]

Other groups simply were not accustomed to the kind of partisan politics that had developed over free trade. It took more than a year for some environmental groups to decide to join. There were also serious regional divisions in the coalition. A Saskatchewan group headed by David Orchard wanted to adopt far more radical tactics and positions than the larger coalition could tolerate. And there were limits on the way the sovereignty theme could be played in the Network's campaign, dictated by PCN relationships with groups in Quebec.

It was also difficult to sustain the two-year-long anti-free trade campaign, but not because the effort appeared hopeless. On the contrary, by mid-1987 the PCN leadership was convinced that the negotiations were going to founder. Tony Clarke's own visit to Washington in the summer of 1987 convinced him and others that there would be no deal. Duncan Cameron also came to this view because of his contacts with fellow academic John Crispo. Crispo, along with most officials in Ottawa, was convinced by the late summer of 1987 that free trade was dead, and he confided his views to Cameron. Satisfied that the free trade initiative would die a natural death at the negotiating table, the PCN temporarily relaxed its vigil on the issue. It was caught seriously off guard in October 1987 when a deal was salvaged on the Washington weekend.

With the announcement of the deal, the PCN leadership realized that the 1988 election would offer its only opportunity to influence the FTA decision process. As the election drew near, the coalition developed its political tactics more concretely. On May 30, 1988, just after Bill C-130, the FTA legislation, was tabled in Parliament, PCN representatives met Liberal leader John Turner and NDP leader Ed Broadbent to discuss strategies to fight the FTA. The two opposition leaders were handed a petition signed by 350,000 Canadians demanding an election on free trade. Late in August 1988, at a national assembly in Montreal, the PCN forged an election strategy. Its most visible tactic was the publication of more than two million copies of a cartoon-style booklet, *What's the Big Deal?* Distributed as newspaper inserts, the booklet succeeded in raising doubts among Ca-

nadians about the deal, and prompted an immediate counter-pub-
lication by the Canadian Alliance for Trade and Job Opportunities.
The PCN also pressed for televised debates, but with little success.
The national television networks would not allow a full-scale debate focused solely on free trade. The coalition leaders then lobbied
for the FTA to be the topic for one hour and 30 minutes of the two
hours scheduled for debate between the leaders, again without
success. PCN also challenged the Alliance to co-sponsor a full televised debate on the deal, but the Alliance refused to rise to the bait.
Finally, the coalition lobbied CBC's "The Journal" and "Le Point" to
hold debates, and both agreed.

The PCN strategy also included the development of an even-
handed working relationship with the Liberals and the NDP. Like
the Alliance, it was important for the PCN to try to achieve a
non-partisan stance, except concerning the Conservatives. Leaders
of the coalition met frequently with campaign chairpersons from
both parties, and they ensured a constant flow of materials and
volunteers to assist the two parties on the free trade issue. PCN aided
the two opposition parties by shadowing the prime minister and
senior Tory ministers, and planted anti-free traders to disrupt Conservative meetings and media occasions. It blitzed the "swing"
ridings that would be close in the election with anti-free trade
literature. As this strategy unfolded, however, PCN members did
not perceive an even-handed response by the two opposition political parties. Many concluded that the Liberals were more interested
in co-operating in the campaign to defeat free trade than the NDP.
There was some truth to this view, and after the election labour
leaders were highly critical of the NDP for its failure to give the FTA
its main strategic emphasis during the campaign.

In waging its battle against free trade, the coalition could not
even come close to matching the financial resources of its business-
sponsored opponents. A year after the 1988 election, the PCN was
still trying to pay off the cost of the free trade cartoon booklet. The
main assets of the coalition, as always for broad-based movements,
were its own activists. But when the election writs were issued, this

human resource dwindled because PCN members were also party activists and had to choose where to invest their time. As many left to work for their parties, the PCN lost some of its impact. At its core, the coalition strategy was an effort to rally Canadians around the PCN nationalist vision for Canada. It would represent Canadians who were more dependent on government for programs that benefited them, who felt intensely vulnerable to pro-market policies, and who disliked many features of American policy, especially in the Reagan era, which they feared might eventually be imposed on Canadians by the Mulroney Conservatives.

BUSINESS TO THE RESCUE

The founding organizations in the Canadian Alliance for Trade and Job Opportunities included the major business organizations in the country — BCNI, the Canadian Chamber of Commerce, the Canadian Exporters' Association, the Canadian Federation of Independent Business, and the Canadian Manufacturers' Association. The Consumers' Association of Canada also decided to join, allowing the Alliance to claim to represent interests beyond the business community. The consumer group made its decision only on the eve of the Alliance's first public press conference on March 19, 1987, based on the likelihood that free trade would contribute to lower prices for consumers. However, the decision caused sharp divisions within the consumer lobby's membership and later, during the election, it withdrew from the Alliance.

Eventually, the Alliance's membership grew to 35 associations, including such diverse groups as the Canadian Cattlemen's Association and the Western Canadian Wheat Growers. Some major associations, including the Canadian Bankers' Association and the Canadian Petroleum Association, joined only reluctantly. They would have preferred to keep a lower profile, the bankers because of divisions within the banking community over the FTA and the petroleum producers because of a desire to keep the energy issue entirely off the public agenda. There were also defections from the business common front. An umbrella group called the Business Council for Fair Trade was formed, and it aligned itself with the Pro Canada Network. This business crossover group included smaller associations such as the Canadian Independent Computer Services Association and the Petroleum Marketers' Association of Canada.

The Alliance was formed because of the view in key business circles early in 1987 that the free trade initiative was foundering. It was known that the negotiations were making little progress. In addition, U.S. trade actions on the shakes and shingles and softwood lumber cases, in addition to ambiguity about the status of such matters as culture and the Auto Pact at the bargaining table, were creating a field day for the opposition in Parliament. Question period was being used to put the government on the run. The Conservatives were also losing popular favour because of their various conflict of interest and patronage misadventures. As a result, growing criticism emerged in business circles that the government was not doing a good job of selling and defending this fundamentally important policy.

BCNI AGAIN

The precise origins of the Alliance are hard to pinpoint because of the interlocking memberships and affiliations of the key business players. Concerns about the Mulroney government's ability to carry the deal first surfaced in the International Trade Advisory Committee (ITAC). Philippe de Gaspé Beaubien, the head of Telemedia Ltd. and an ITAC member, was especially critical of the failure by the government to counter the aggressive claims of free trade critics. At the same time, John Crispo was actively pushing for a coalition to be called unabashedly "Canadians for Free Trade." It was evident, however, that ITAC itself could not be the vehicle for a new alliance, and eventually the initiative fell to the BCNI and its president, Thomas d'Aquino.

D'Aquino's office at 90 Sparks Street in downtown Ottawa stands in stark contrast to the humbler quarters of the Pro Canada Network. With its Italian-crafted African hardwoods, it exudes the elegant, but unmistakable, power of the boardroom. Here there are no wall-to-wall newspaper clippings bearing testimony to past conflicts, only the opulent evidence of battles won, along with the discreetly placed picture of a prime minister or a president. D'Aquino had become in the 1980s one of Canada's most influential unelected power brokers. His political influence is based on the corporate clout of BCNI, but it is more than that. An engaging personality who speaks three languages, plays the violin, and entertains with charm and élan, the native of British Columbia had a personal network of contacts in Ottawa that was unsurpassed. A specialist in international law, including trade law, d'Aquino had transformed the BCNI into Canada's most formidable business lobby. His approach was that of policy advice proffered quietly and privately, backed by the authority of thorough research. This was the recipe d'Aquino had followed in the early stages of the free trade initiative when he established the BCNI trade policy committee, and he was ready in 1986 with BCNI's own framework document on free trade, which he delivered to Simon Reisman.

But in 1987, d'Aquino, along with BCNI member and chairman of Alcan Aluminum David Culver, became players in the free trade saga in a much more public way. The first members of the Alliance for Trade and Job Opportunities were recruited by d'Aquino and Culver in the space of a few days. For its first three months of existence the Alliance was run out of the BCNI offices, and later its headquarters were shifted to Alcan's offices in Montreal. After the Alliance was formed, d'Aquino adopted a lower profile while the public campaign was carried by the two co-chairmen, Peter Lougheed and Donald Macdonald. The former Conservative premier of Alberta and the former Liberal Finance minister and chairman of the royal commission on the Canadian economy were chosen to symbolize the non-partisanship of the Alliance. When Macdonald subsequently stepped down, he was replaced by Gerald Regan, the Liberal Trade minister who had given the free trade initiative its unexpected start in 1983.

In 1987, before the free trade deal was struck, the Alliance ran a series of full-page advertisements in major newspapers that made the general case for free trade, arguing that Canada must look confidently outward to a highly competitive world. When the FTA was announced, speakers' bureaus were mobilized, as were writers of op-ed editorial pieces supporting free trade. Alliance members were active in more than 500 free trade conferences, meetings and press conferences that were held across the country, with Lougheed, Macdonald and John Crispo easily the busiest on the speaking circuit. During the period from March 1987 to April 1988, the Alliance spent almost $3 million on its free trade crusade, with the bulk of the funds raised through BCNI's member companies. Over two-thirds of this total was spent on advertising and consultants. At the start of the 1988 election campaign, the key strategists in the Alliance were confident that the Conservatives would win a majority, making Canada safe for free trade. After the televised debates, however, they were stunned by the Liberal gains, and a second wave of pro-free trade advertising began. A further $2.3 million was spent in an effort to rescue the agreement, mainly on a large four-page newspaper insert designed to counter the anti-free trade cartoon booklet distributed by the Pro Canada Network. The four-page ads ran on several occasions during the last weeks of the campaign. During the campaign, as well, business mobilization ceased to be strictly a top-down process led by the Alliance. As the heated claims of John Turner and Ed Broadbent escalated, a genuine surge of populist pressure in support of the FTA emerged bottom-up from the business community. Local chambers of commerce and individual businesses advertised their views, held public meetings, and lobbied company employees. The funds spent on this activity are difficult to estimate, but they probably exceeded the total monies spent by the Alliance during the election.

THE MEDIA AND THE MANDARINS

Other interests were loosely affiliated with the broad coalitions that formed during the debate. There were charges by both sides that the mass media were unbalanced in their coverage of free trade. A study by Alan Frizzell and Anthony Westell of television and print media coverage of the issue during the election campaign examined this question.[4] They investigated whether more than 585 national network television items and almost 7,000 print items in seven major daily newspapers would strike a viewer or reader as favourable towards the free trade subject, unfavourable, or neutral. They reported that for television more than 90 per cent were assessed as neutral.

For the print media, Frizzell and Westell probed even further, in part because of the controversy that arose over the coverage by the *Toronto Star* and the *Globe and Mail* of the free trade issue. Pro-free traders, not the least of them Simon Reisman himself, were especially critical of the *Star*, as were anti-free traders of the *Globe and Mail*. The editor of the *Star*, John Honderich, did not deny his newspaper's crusading tradition, but he did argue that the *Star's* coverage included all points of view. Frizzell and Westell showed that the *Star* gave more coverage to free trade than any other paper, and went on to compare the balance of the *Star's* coverage against six other papers. They found that the proportion of items judged to convey an unfavourable view of the subject was almost twice that of any other paper. However, Frizzell and Westell also concluded that, given the selective reading habits of most readers, it was unlikely that the *Star's* coverage determined many votes. They could easily have added that in the context of the battle in Toronto over free trade, the *Star's* coverage provided a counterweight to the pro-free trade position of the *Globe and Mail's* editorial writers.

In other cities, some major papers took editorial positions against free trade. These included the *Gazette* in Montreal and the *Edmonton Journal*. But the majority of papers editorially supported the FTA. In general, the media gave free trade "extensive, even excessive, coverage, the great majority of which was thought to be neutral in its impact."[5] In the final analysis, the televised debates between the party leaders had more influence on voters than did general media reporting on the free trade issue.

Of equal interest were the evolving views of the public sector policy elite. Survey data from a study by Compas Inc. tracked the views of nearly four hundred key individuals in the Canadian policy-making process from early 1988, before the election, to early 1989 when the free trade deal was in place.[6] The policy elite included senior public servants in the federal and provincial governments, policy advisers to senior politicians at federal and provincial levels, scholars with professional involvement in public policy, and respected journalists in the field. The study concluded that the policy elite as a whole was evenly divided in its evaluation of the impact of the FTA. About 23 per cent saw economic harm, 22 per cent saw economic benefit, 31 per cent saw no net impact, and the remainder had no opinion. One interesting finding of the survey was that journalists were alone among the four in being anti-free trade, and their position became even more opposed as the debate progressed in 1988–89.

Significantly, the survey found that very few respondents saw sovereignty as a major issue. However, when asked if they felt that the FTA would seriously limit the ability of federal and provincial governments to assist specific sectors of the economy, in the summer of 1988 54 per cent believed governments would be so restricted. By early 1989, this figure was reduced to 45 per cent. Among public servants, the study found stronger pro-free trade views among mandarins trained in economics and among younger senior officials. For political advisers to ministers, opinion divided along party lines, as could be expected. Indeed, these divisions became even more intense after the 1988 election, with Liberal and NDP advisers believing that the FTA was harmful to the Canadian economy. The Compas study also brought out the expected regional divisions among both public servants and policy advisers, with those from Quebec and the West strongly in favour of the FTA, and those from Ontario opposed. The Quebec elite's favourable view was, however, much reduced in magnitude following the election.

These data do not show how dramatically the views of the policy elite had changed from the early stages of the free trade story. Before the initiative was adopted by Mulroney and his key ministers, most of the deputy ministers in Ottawa were opposed to free trade. Most were products of the basic post-war consensus that supported the multilateral trade regime, and they defended it instinctively. It was only after the public commitment by the prime minister, when the free trade juggernaut rolled through Ottawa, that they shifted over to the new bilateral orthodoxy, although frequently with reservations. As for the more general mass of public servants and government employees, both polling and voting data showed that they were unrepentant and remained opposed to free trade.

VISIONS OF CANADA

The public debate over free trade was a maddening mixture of competing facts and values that produced alternative visions of Canada. It was a battle over attitudes, involving intense efforts to define powerful images and visions of the nation in order to force Canadians off the middle ground. The free trade debate could not be based on the simplistic nationalist-versus-continentalist lines that had been drawn in the 1960s and 1970s, because now there were two brands of nationalism. Pro-free traders portrayed themselves and the Canada they wanted to create as worldly and outward looking, confident, and competitive. They described their opponents as timid and protectionist, defenders of the status quo of a "little Canada." The anti-free traders accused their opponents of selling out the country, charging that they wanted to make Canada the fifty-first state and dismantle its social programs in the bargain. Opponents of the deal asserted their support for liberalized trade, but insisted it should be achieved through the internationalist path of the GATT. They did not want to join Fortress North America, but instead stood for policies that would move Canada into a wider world.

In the heat of the debate there was little room for the middle ground. A siege mentality gripped both sides where everyone was counted for or against, and free trade became a test of commitment to a vision of Canada. The 1988 election marked a turning point in the development of the Canadian nation from which there would be no turning back. Both sides sensed this, and facts, values, and visions blended into mutually exclusive tests of political loyalty. In the realm of facts the debate was uneven. Most of those on the pro-free trade side believed their case was more factual and objective than that of their opponents, who were seen to lack facts to support their opposition, appealing excessively to emotion, especially fear, instead. By facts, pro-free traders meant both the benefits that had already been derived from post-war trade liberalization, and the evidence to be found in several macroeconomic and general equilibrium studies showing how the Canadian economy would benefit from the adoption of free trade. Initially these studies were based on hypothetical free trade scenarios, and then eventually on the actual provisions of the FTA. Although the projected gains were reduced as assumptions became more realistic, in general the studies confirmed the lessons of the past, associating trade liberalization with economic gains. Thus, the authority of institutions like the Macdonald Commission, the Economic Council of Canada, and the C.D. Howe Institute, and economists like Richard Lipsey, provided factual armour for the pro-free trade coalition.

These studies could factor in the normal variables that the science of economics said would produce gains from trade. These included gains from Canada's inherent comparative advantage in certain products, the effects of lower prices, third-country effects, and greater economies of scale from secure access to the huge American market. Beyond these variables were others that could not be modelled, including entrepreneurial dynamism, reduced uncertainty, and improved real income effects that would result from free trade. Dynamism and reduced uncertainty were the areas where pro-free traders resorted to their own visionary metaphors, including the "leap of faith" and a "cold shower." These were used to support the belief, or hope, that the results of free trade would be even better than the models predicted.

The political facts at the heart of the anti-free trade case were much harder to model because they were not quantitative, but qualitative. But this did not mean that the distinction between the two sides in the debate lay in their use of fact as against fiction. Instead it centred on opposing judgements, the one side's case based on numerical evidence, the other's on narrative evidence. Anti-free traders were concerned less about aggregate economic benefits than they were with sovereignty and independence, and about the qualities that distinguish Canada and Canadians in North America and the world. These concerns were impossible to quantify, however. Opponents of the deal relied instead on the development of scenarios to describe how free trade would touch off a chain of events that would diminish Canada politically. Combining precedents, anecdotal evidence, and causal assertions, these narratives derived credibility from the coherent description they offered about how a free trade future could unfold for Canada.[7] But their weakness was the absence of evidence for many of the crucial causal assertions that linked events in the chain. The arguments of anti-free trade forces were also undermined to a degree by trade policy ignorance. Many simply did not know the extent to which Canada already had international obligations under the GATT. There was often an unthinking embrace of GATT by those who opposed free trade, even though sovereignty can as easily be lost to international regimes as to giant neighbours.

Facts of both kinds, numerical and narrative, can easily slide into values and visions in order to appeal more strongly to emotions. Although the advocates of free trade did not perceive themselves in such terms, the most ardent pro-free traders did display an emotional, as well as intellectual, attachment to markets and trade liberalization, and this required them to squash all but confirmatory arguments. And while proponents of free trade charged anti-free traders with being consumed by the emotion of nationalism to the exclusion of facts, in fact most pro-free traders were no less committed to Canada than were their adversaries. In the final analysis, there were two nationalisms and two sets of passions at work in a free trade debate that centred on competing visions of

Canada, and involved both leaps of faith and fear of change. The pro-free trade side presented the FTA as an economic vision, to which its opponents were forced to react defensively. But when the debate shifted to political ground, it was the government and business community that became defensive. This political defensiveness was revealed starkly in the document leaked in 1986 that set out the Tory communications strategy to sell the deal.[8] It was based on the tactical assumption that the higher the profile of the issue, the less public approval there would be. The government also insisted that the FTA was only a trade deal, even though it went far beyond traditional trade matters. The wider the recognition that the deal was about issues beyond trade, perhaps including the powers of the state to act on behalf of its citizens, the more it worried the government.

The free trade debate broke new ground in Canadian history in the extent to which the two coalitions formed around competing visions of the future. Both deserve to be called nationalistic, but with significant differences over the roles that markets and government should play in expressing that nationalist vision. Each side in the debate had a vision that was a mixture of faith and fear. For one, the faith in markets and a new Canadian entrepreneurial spirit was combined with fear of a new age of American protectionism and Canada's declining competitiveness. For the other, faith in the capacity of the state to ensure a more humane Canadian community was coupled with a fear of closer integration into the American empire. The great debate was hardly elegant. Its incendiary mixture of facts and values brought out the worst and best in Canadian politics. But it cannot be said that the FTA was not debated in Canada, or that it was foisted on an uninformed Canadian public. Indeed, the enduring impact of the FTA may lie in the fact that in the debate, Canadians were forced to confront themselves and the kind of economic and social world they were entering as the 1980s came to a close.

10

THE GREAT
FREE TRADE ELECTION

The 1988 election offered Canadians their only chance at a referendum-like choice on free trade. Even as a single-issue election, it was not a true referendum, however. Canadians were choosing a government under parliamentary norms in a first-past-the-post, single-member, simple-majority electoral system in which there were three contending parties. Under these conditions, a rational outcome would be the exception rather than the rule. Nevertheless, it was the opposition Liberals and New Democrats that insisted the FTA be decided by the Canadian people in an election. Still, it was no surprise when many opponents of free trade denied that the electoral decision conferred democratic legitimacy on the agreement since more than 50 per cent of Canadians supported the Liberals and New Democrats, both opposed to the FTA. They argued that free trade had to be treated as a constitutional issue, and Canada should not proceed unless there was majority support for it. Still others argued that Canadian business had bought the election with its last-minute blitz of pro-free trade and pro-Tory advertising.

Even accounting for the vagaries of the electoral system and the influence of big business, there was nothing inevitable about the outcome of the 1988 election. The Tory victory, and the legitimacy it conferred on the FTA, was the product of intensely political forces, and the effects of their combination could only be known with hindsight. The strategic manoeuvring along the partisan dimensions of the free trade issue by Brian Mulroney and his party turned out to be adroit, but only with substantial assistance from the tribulations and tactics of Liberal Party leader John Turner and NDP leader Ed Broadbent. The electoral political tables were also turned on the Liberals and the NDP in 1988 when these normally progressive parties found themselves on the defensive in institutional and policy terms, arguing against change without politically compelling trade policy alternatives to offer voters.

THE POLITICS OF FREE TRADE

Brian Mulroney's free trade initiative was a policy choice deeply rooted in a partisan strategy. Mulroney and his advisers wanted to differentiate themselves from the centralizing and state-led policies of the Trudeau government. They were also determined to build a strong Tory base in Quebec and to practise national reconciliation, especially regarding Western Canada. Finally, the Conservatives wanted to build a closer and more co-operative relationship with the United States. Free trade offered the means to accomplish all four goals simultaneously. The pursuit of a strategic Quebec-Western Canada alliance also implied the prospect of a counterpart "bash Ontario" strategy. This became even more probable when Ontario elected its first provincial Liberal Government in over 40 years, headed by a premier who opposed the FTA from the outset.

Of course, the Conservatives could not afford to write off Ontario entirely in this strategy. But they could, and did, argue that if prosperous Ontario, enjoying an export-led economic boom, was opposed to free trade, then it must be good for Western Canada and Quebec. These were also the two regions of the country where the commercial nationalist vision evoked the most support. As for Atlantic Canada, the Conservatives hoped they could hold their own in an election, but were emboldened by electoral arithmetic to risk the prospect of serious losses in the region. While the Quebec–Western Canada strategy was based on the results of polls on regional support for free trade, it was also a natural alliance that was reinforced by partisan ties between federal and provincial governing parties and by the composition of Mulroney's cabinet. In an election, these links took on special importance.

The Conservative government received strong support, both publicly and behind the scenes, from Robert Bourassa, the Quebec Liberal premier, not only on free trade but also on the Meech Lake constitutional package. Mulroney also had the support of the Western premiers, three of them Tory in fact and the other, British Columbia's Bill Vander Zalm, a Tory by faith. Even Ontario's David Peterson offered some comfort to the Conservatives in the election battle because, despite his opposition to the FTA, the Ontario premier did not wage a vigorous campaign against the deal during the election. The Western premiers had warned Peterson that national unity would suffer irrevocably if Ontario succeeded in defeating a policy that Western Canadians saw as essential to the economic health of their region. He was also under intense pressure from Ontario business not to undermine the deal.

The Quebec–Western Canada alliance was reinforced within the Conservative cabinet as well. The power of Quebec ministers in cabinet was self-evident. It began with Mulroney himself, and his personal determination to make history as the first Tory prime minister in this century to win two elections from an entrenched Quebec power base. Key positions were also held by other Quebec ministers, including individuals with strong Quebec nationalist sentiments like Marcel Masse, Benoît Bouchard, and Lucien Bouchard. On the other side of the alliance, Western Canadian ministers enjoyed more influence in the Mulroney cabinet than any national government since the 1930s. Ministers such as Don Mazankowski, Joe Clark, and Patricia Carney held key portfolios. And it was Mazankowski, Mulroney's own Mr. Fixit, who persuaded Michael Wilson to go against his own budget-cutting instincts, as well as pressures from Bay Street, and announce several spending programs, primarily for Western Canada, in the run-up to the 1988 election. All in all, the alliance between Quebec and Western Canada was a marriage made in Conservative heaven.

BACKING INTO THE FUTURE

The course of the 1988 election was also fundamentally influenced by the inability of the Liberals and New Democrats to turn their gaze from the more congenial past. The two opposition parties backed into the free trade future, unprepared for a contest that centred on trade policy and unable to adapt to the new agenda in national politics. For both, this was an uncomfortable and disorienting political posture. For all of Canada's political parties, the post–World War II consensus on a multilateral GATT-based approach to trade had removed trade policy from the arena of conventional politics. The trade policy field was left to a small band of trade professionals in the bureaucracy who spun out their policies in relative obscurity. Sheltered by the GATT consensus, both government and opposition parties became increasingly illiterate about trade developments. As a result, when the national agenda was seized by the free trade issue, the two opposition parties in particular were left scrambling, trying to learn trade policy on the run, and without the bureaucratic expertise available to the Mulroney government. Neither was able to successfully develop politically credible trade alternatives, harking back instead to the conventional, and comfortable, doctrines of multilateralism.

The Liberals and New Democrats were also on the defensive in the free trade battle because control of the political agenda had slipped from their hands in the 1980s. For most of the post-war era it had been their broadly left-of-centre agenda that dominated Canadian politics, and both parties were accustomed to being on the leading edge of progressive change. When a mildly neo-conservative agenda was imported to Canada in the Reagan-Thatcher era, the Liberals and the NDP were constantly forced to defend the seemingly irrelevant policies of a by-gone era.[1] For the Liberals, in particular, this defensiveness was difficult. As the permanent governing party of Canada, the Liberals had spent decades secure in the knowledge that the federal Tories did not know how to govern, could not hold Quebec, and could never be the party of national unity. When it was faced with the realities of the Mulroney Conservatives, the shock to the party and its leaders was immense. When the Liberals' trade policy illiteracy was added to this fundamentally defensive posture, the result was a formula for political defeat. But of course the loss of the 1988 election and the defeat of the Liberal-NDP free trade position was due to other factors as well, chief among them the leadership difficulties of John Turner and the tactics adopted in the election by Turner and New Democrat Ed Broadbent.

THE TURNER DILEMMA

During its two and a half months in office in 1984, John Turner's Liberal government flirted with sectoral free trade with the United States. Despite this flirtation, it is unlikely that a re-elected Turner government would, or could, have adopted a comprehensive free trade policy. Although it was the party of Laurier and source of earlier free trade initiatives, by the mid-1980s the Liberal Party was more a creature of its Trudeau-Pearson mixed-market heritage. With proponents of an activist role for the state firmly ensconced in the party establishment, a Liberal state was simply less likely than the Conservatives to withdraw in favour of the market. More important, the Liberal position and strategy on free trade were integrally tied up with the leadership ordeal of John Napier Turner.[2] Badly beaten in the 1984 election and bewildered by their unfamiliar role in opposition, the Liberals floundered in the House of Commons during 1984–86. Turner got out of the House and concentrated his efforts on party reorganization, seeking to rebuild a grass-roots structure based in the provinces.[3] In doing so, he was trying to erase his image as a Bay Street Liberal. But his reorganizing efforts left little time to develop credible policy alternatives. On the one issue where Turner had taken a clear stand, in support of the Meech Lake constitutional accord, his party was badly and openly divided.

In the summer of 1987, when free trade was still only a concept, with no actual agreement to debate, the Liberal position on the issue was a compromise between the party's anti-free trade wing, led by Lloyd Axworthy, and a smaller wing sympathetic to free trade led by Donald Johnston. After Johnston resigned from the House of Commons over Turner's stand on Meech Lake, there was no one left in the Liberal caucus of any stature to argue for free trade. When Turner appointed Lloyd Axworthy as the Liberal trade critic, he gave an early signal of the position he would take on the trade issue. Later in 1987, Turner's office took steps to beef up its policy capabilities. Critics inside and outside the party had rightly accused Liberal policies of being driven almost entirely by the tactical warfare of question period. Greater policy cohesion was to be supplied by the appointment of Robert Jackson, a Carleton University political scientist, as a senior adviser to Turner. However, Jackson's labours produced a massive and unwieldy 40-point policy agenda, which the Liberals used to launch the 1988 election, and from which their campaign never recovered.

In any case, Turner's personal preoccupations were with political survival rather than policy. And this hobbled the party, because on major policy issues — like the FTA and Meech Lake — policy is usually leader driven. But if the leader is too preoccupied to deal with key policy issues, they will fall to whoever is driving the leader. Very early in his leadership, Turner was dragged reluctantly by the Axworthy wing into strong opposition to the FTA. Although this position probably conformed to his instinct to oppose the deal, any doubts on this score were resolved by Turner's decision to support Meech Lake. It would have been tactically and politically disastrous for the opposition leader to offer support for both free trade and Meech, the two major items on the Tory policy agenda. While his decision to oppose free trade was made early, Turner's opposition was fairly muted until the actual deal was in place. At that point, his emotional and well-crafted free trade speeches easily became the best of his House of Commons performances. Yet little of the intensity of his opposition was communicated to the country until the leadership debates in the 1988 election. By that time, however, the strength of his commitment could not overcome the damage caused by the image of a party and its leader in disarray.

Turner's dilemma centred on the question of how intense his opposition to the FTA should be. In October 1987, NDP leader Ed Broadbent was riding high in the opinion polls, and he pressed Turner, unwisely as it turned out, to say forthrightly that he would tear up the free trade deal. Many of Turner's advisers had been urging him to take a softer, less inflammatory line. He could say that he would "abrogate" the agreement, but at the same time indicate what alternative approach he would take on the trade issue. This, they argued, would be the more responsible, and politically prudent, position. The business community was also pressing Turner hard to get on side on free trade, and he was sending out signals that the party might back off its strong anti-FTA position. Eventually, however, the pressure of his own caucus hawks, combined with a fear that the Liberals would lose the initiative on the issue to the NDP, led Turner to say in the House of Commons, following the release of the elements of the agreement, that he would "tear it up." Although the Liberals did have an alternative trade policy position ready, it got lost in the dust produced by the tear-it-up rhetoric and the media coverage of quarrels within the Liberal Party over Turner's leadership.

The Liberal dilemma also resulted from the fact that there was considerable support for free trade in the provincial wings of the party. In Quebec, Alberta, and New Brunswick, provincial Liberals leaned more toward free trade than against it. And in Western Canada, where Turner hoped to rebuild support for the party, a strident anti-free trade position did not go over well. Despite this provincial party support for free trade, it is no doubt true that a majority of the party's constituent elements were opposed to the FTA, and John Turner's position in the election campaign accurately reflected majority Liberal opinion. This rank-and-file opposition to free trade was intense and reflected a collective pride in the party's post-war policy legacy. At the same time, because of this strong sense of the past, the party was incapable of creating a politically viable alternative trade policy for the future, one that did not simply look like a replay of the past.

Despite these handicaps, the Liberals might still have won the election. They struck many of the right emotional chords among Canadians. Had there not been a CBC report in the second week of the election campaign on yet another plot to challenge Turner's leadership, anything might have been possible. But their ultimate inability to present a persuasive alternative position to free trade was a fundamental failure by the Liberals to fulfil their obligation to develop new approaches to Canada's economic future. The outcome of the free trade election confirmed this failure.

THE TEMPTATIONS OF POWER

In 1987–88, the New Democratic Party found itself in an unaccustomed position, ahead in the opinion polls.[4] The self-styled party of principle now also had to behave like a party that might actually attain power, and this inherent contradiction drove both its position on free trade and its choice of electoral tactics. In principle, of course, the NDP was against free trade in general, and the FTA in particular. But in practice it wavered on the issue, alienating many of its supporters in the labour movement and its allies in the Pro Canada Network.

NDP opposition to the FTA was instinctive and automatic. Along with the rest of the Mulroney pro-market agenda, free trade was the antithesis of the New Democratic view of the proper policy direction for Canada. Since the early 1960s, the NDP had called for increased controls on foreign investment, an aggressive industrial strategy, and nationalist energy policies. And with free trade, the Conservatives were cementing an alliance with the neo-conservative Reagan administration, held in contempt by most New Democrats. In the election battle, however, NDP strategists saw real problems with a frontal attack on the FTA. The party was polling to an unprecedented extent in the campaign, and its pollsters advised that the NDP's best issue remained the integrity of Mulroney and his government. The New Democrats wanted to base the campaign on their competence to govern with integrity and with concern for all Canadians, and not just the wealthy. Focusing too much on free trade would deflect attention from the integrity issue. The pollsters also advised that free trade was seen as an "economic management" issue, where the Tories generally scored well with voters. This was another reason to play down the issue in the NDP campaign. Ultimately, however, the New Democrats' strategy on free trade was driven by simple electoral arithmetic. Polls showed that Canadians were split 50-50 on the issue. This meant that the anti-free trade vote would split between the two opposition parties, so the NDP needed other issues to attract additional votes. This calculation was basic to the strategy adopted by the party. With the prospect of power at hand, the strategists were determined to appeal to as broad a range of opinion as possible. And it was this determination that brought the party into conflict with organized labour.

The unions were worried concretely about their members' jobs as a result of free trade.[5] Organized labour had declined the government's invitation to join the consultative process during the free trade negotiations, and was unalterably opposed to the deal that had been negotiated. While the NDP was worried about workers in the abstract, the prospect of political power offered a powerful inducement to play down the free trade issue. The split between the party and the unions surfaced immediately after the election when both Bob White of the Canadian Auto Workers and Gerald Docquier of the United Steelworkers released letters criticizing the NDP for abandoning the free trade issue. They also blasted party strategists for their excessive reliance on polls, and for using an American pollster, to boot![6] When Turner's campaign succeeded with its assault on free trade, the NDP scrambled to recapture the lost ground, charging that the trade deal would directly and adversely affect health care, social programs and the environment. The party did not target energy, however, because of its strong base in Western Canada where the energy provisions of the agreement enjoyed wide support. The social policy attack was blunted when Emmett Hall, the architect of Canada's health care system, publicly rejected the NDP claim that free trade would undermine medicare.

The party's strategy was also based on the high regard voters had for Ed Broadbent, in comparison with both Turner and Mulroney. As a result, the NDP campaign devoted far more attention to profiling the leader than had ever been done before. Even this was undermined by the Liberals' free trade campaign, however, since the image of sober competence projected for Broadbent stood in sharp contrast to Turner's self-portrait as passionate nationalist. The New Democrats accepted too quickly the conventional wisdom that the Liberal Party, fractious and divided, was in permanent decline. Broadbent even mused publicly, and carelessly, that a two-party system of Tories and New Democrats would be a good thing for Canada. A final important factor in the NDP political calculus was their desire to build a base in Quebec. The party was investing significant resources and time in a province that had never elected an NDP member to Parliament. Although in the past Quebeckers had been sympathetic to mildly social-democratic policies, they were increasingly pro-market in their political orientation. The children of Quebec's Quiet Revolution were now entrepreneurs on the make, and free trade did not seem threatening to them. For all of these reasons, the New Democrats chose to play down the free trade issue in the campaign. Although the goal of winning power had never dominated the party's political agenda, it was the prospect of power at last that tempted NDP strategists to play it safe.

No Credible Alternatives

In the final analysis, neither the Liberals nor the New Democrats were able to come up with politically viable policy alternatives to free trade. Perhaps this is no surprise since the politics of opposition in Canada's parliamentary system are overwhelmingly about tactics, not policy. The effects of mass media coverage of question period reinforce this bias. And both opposition parties were thrown on the defensive by Mulroney's success in capturing the political agenda with his pro-market stance. Still, each tried without success to find a workable alternative to the Conservative challenge to past orthodoxy. Trade policy for the Liberals was largely the preserve of Lloyd Axworthy, assisted by Turner's policy adviser, Robert Jackson. They also received periodic advice from others knowledgeable about trade, including Mitchell Sharp, the former minister of Finance in the Pearson government and External Affairs minister in the Trudeau government, and Mel Clark, a former trade and industry official in the federal Department of Regional Industrial Expansion. Their five-point alternative trade policy was formally announced by the Liberals in June 1988.

For the NDP, trade alternatives were developed by MPs Steven Langdon and Bill Blaikie, with considerable input from the Canadian Labour Congress and individual unions. The Pro Canada Network was also lobbying both the NDP and Liberal trade policy groups, and while the NDP trade policy position was influenced more by the Network, PCN tactics received a warmer welcome in the Liberal camp. The NDP trade document was released in January 1988. For both parties, their trade policy positions were not developed by people with extensive trade experience and knowledge. Most of Canada's existing expertise was at the disposal of the Conservative government, including independent trade experts who were largely in the free trade camp. This deficiency was apparent when the opposition parties called for sectoral free trade agreements with the U.S., at a time when expert trade opinion had concluded that sectoral deals were politically impossible, and in most cases, contrary to the GATT. The two opposition parties were also adept at supporting the GATT as an abstract alternative to free trade, but they were not prepared to accept GATT decisions when they went against Canada.

In their five-point trade program, the Liberals highlighted the need for export expansion and increased competitiveness, and placed primary emphasis on the GATT to achieve these goals.[7] They would press in the multilateral organization for new rights and obligations and a better dispute-settlement process. The Liberal program also called for a revival of their 1983 sectoral free trade option, which had died in 1984. They proposed to create a new department of trade and development, reversing the 1982 decision of the Trudeau government to integrate Trade and External Affairs, as well as a national trading corporation with a special mandate for the growing markets of the Pacific. The program promised a well-funded Canadian adjustment board to deal with adjustment problems, and it identified a research and development spending target of 2.5 per cent of gross domestic product. This Liberal alternative to the FTA was internationalist and mildly interventionist, with new state institutions to promote and manage trade. Notably absent were any 1970s-style initiatives to strengthen Canadian ownership. In general, the alternative was pretty tepid when compared to either the Tories' package or the Liberals' own rhetoric on the evils of the Mulroney agenda. In the final analysis, Liberal trade policy got lost in the complexities of their larger 40-point election program and in the morass of Turner's leadership problems.

The New Democrats' alternative trade policy was a more familiar recitation of its basic economic agenda. But the party's standing in the polls clearly prompted some recasting of priorities and language. For example, the policy asserted that the "alternative to the surrender of Canadian sovereignty is to exercise it," but also acknowledged that Canada's full potential requires using both the "energy and enterprise of the private sector and the ingenuity and vision of the public sector."[8] The statement also omitted the usual references to nationalizing sectors such as oil and banking. The NDP called for a national approach to "upgrading our industrial national potential," proposing to double research and development spending over five years, promote labour market policy and skill development, encourage domestic investment and support for small business, and to ensure "that foreign investment works for Canada."

With respect to Canada-U.S trade, the NDP promised to improve the bilateral relationship through the establishment of a joint institution to anticipate and conciliate emerging trade problems. Finally, the policy document reaffirmed NDP support for the GATT and for global monetary and financial management, and the need for codes of conduct for multinational corporations. In the language and order of presentation of the elements of its trade program, the NDP was careful not to jeopardize its high ranking in the opinion polls with inflammatory rhetoric. Although it would not abandon the essential interventionist elements of the agenda favoured by its supporters, the party was determined to demonstrate its competence to govern. As a result, the NDP trade policy was left without distinguishing character, and Turner stole the anti-free trade show with passion, but not policy.

A QUESTION OF LEGITIMACY

On November 21, 1988, the Mulroney Conservatives won 170 of the 295 seats in Parliament. The Liberals won 82 and the NDP 43. The shares of the popular vote were 43 per cent for the Conservatives, 31.9 per cent for the Liberals, and 20.4 per cent for the NDP, with the Reform Party and others garnering the remainder. In parliamentary terms, the Conservatives had secured their mandate on free trade by winning 58 per cent of the seats in the House, but with the support of only 43 per cent of the electorate. The first-past-the-post, single-member simple-majority system had again worked its magic in a three-party race, rendering a decision where deadlock might otherwise result. Nevertheless, the Liberals and NDP quickly accepted the result, since they had pushed for an election on the issue. But opponents of the deal continued to question the legitimacy of the decision, pointing to the fact that more than 50 per cent of the vote had gone to the two anti-free trade parties, and claiming that a majority of Canadians had opposed the FTA in the election. As usual, the truth was much more complicated than either side would care to admit. As subsequent studies of the election would show, while it was true that more than 50 per cent of Canadians supported the Liberals and NDP, it does not follow that a majority of Canadians used their votes to oppose free trade.

Jon Pammett's analysis of the vote for the Carleton University election study confirms that 1988 was unique because "free trade was not only an unusually dominant issue, it was an unusually specific one."[9] In comparison with other elections in which a single issue dominated, the 1988 election was extraordinarily focused. In pre-election surveys, free trade was mentioned as the most important issue by 82 per cent of the electorate. However, the Carleton study also revealed that only about half of voters claimed to be making up their minds on which party to support mainly on the basis of the free trade issue. Furthermore, only 21.5 per cent of those who cited free trade as the most important issue intended to vote Conservative, while 16.9 per cent intended to vote for the Liberals and 10.2 per cent for the NDP. In a strict sense, then, these findings indicate that only slightly more than 20 per cent of Canadians had supported free trade in the election, while 27 per cent had opposed it, hardly a majority for either side![10] Pammett, with more than the usual academic penchant for understatement, concludes that "strictly speaking . . . the public judgement on free trade was not clear-cut, supporting yet again the position that elections are a very poor mechanism for genuine public consultation on specific policy issues."[11]

Another Carleton election study was based on exit poll data, soundings taken as people left the polling stations after actually casting their votes. Its findings cast even more doubt on the conventional wisdom that the election was a vote on free trade. The exit poll revealed that only 40 per cent of the electorate had actually voted on the basis of the free trade issue, and of these, 40 per cent voted Conservative, 42 per cent Liberal, and 17 per cent NDP. This means that only 16 per cent of the electorate voted on the basis of issues, saw free trade as the major issue, *and* voted Conservative;

and only 24 per cent of the electorate voted on the basis of issues, saw free trade as the major issue, *and* voted for parties opposing free trade.[12] The Carleton studies show that while a majority of *free trade* voters opposed the FTA, a majority of the Canadian electorate voted neither for nor against free trade.

A somewhat different look at the legitimacy question is provided in a study of the election by Richard Johnson and his associates.[13] During the campaign they asked roughly 80 Canadians each day (3,600 in total) about their views on several issues, including free trade. But the question was posed in two different ways. Half the respondents were asked to say whether they supported or opposed the deal "negotiated by Canada," and the other half the deal "negotiated by the Mulroney government." Following the televised leaders debates, use of the Mulroney version reduced support for free trade by 14 points, compared to the Canada version. But thereafter, support for the FTA grew, almost all of it among respondents given the Mulroney form of the question. In other words, patterns of support and opposition on the free trade issue were strongly related to attitudes towards Mulroney and his government.

The results also revealed that in neither version of the question were supporters or opponents ever a majority. This was because the undecided vote, about one in six, split among the three parties roughly in proportion to the rest of the electorate. One person in six who intended to vote Conservative was actually uncommitted on the free trade deal, and one person in 12 was in outright opposition. For Liberal and NDP supporters, one in six was uncommitted about the deal, and one in 10 actually favoured free trade. In general, the study concludes that "a majority for or against the agreement simply could not be found because a significant minority could not make up its mind."[14]

Attacks on the legitimacy of the deal were not based solely on the electoral outcome. Opponents also pointed to the efforts of the Mulroney government to avoid public debate on the issue. The Conservative communication strategy was to limit discussion of the deal as much as possible, since they assumed that the more people heard and knew about the agreement, the more likely they were to oppose it. This approach was hardly designed to enhance the credibility, or legitimacy, of the FTA. Despite the Tories' fancy footwork, however, free trade was fully, if not always elegantly, debated. It received unprecedented attention over a three-year period in a wide variety of public venues, including Parliament and provincial legislatures, the mass media, and federal-provincial and business-government arenas. Only Canada's labour unions officially declined to be involved in the formal consultative process, although they were certainly active in the Pro Canada Network.

A more serious challenge to the legitimacy of the electoral decision came from the charge that business bought the election with the extraordinary advertising binge it mounted as part of the rescue operation for the FTA. There is no doubt that business has a privileged position of influence in the Canadian liberal democracy. This is partly because government is heavily dependent upon business to generate jobs, goods, and services. But business influence also flows from the resources at its command to lobby government, in sectoral policy fields and on general issues vital to business, and to finance the two main free enterprise parties, the Progressive Conservatives and the Liberals.

In any ordinary election, which the 1988 election clearly was not, business financing of the two parties would probably not exceed the amounts spent in the free trade election. The difference in 1988 was that the total sum of normal business donations plus the advertising dollars contributed by the Alliance and local business, was targeted on the single issue of free trade. And that issue was supported only by the Mulroney Conservatives. Normally, business will try to cover its bets by dividing its financial support between the two parties that it trusts.[15] In this election, however, it trusted only one, and financial support flowed to the Conservatives. If business truly buys elections with its financing activities, then the 1988 election was not different because it was bought, but because it was bought differently.

There are important democratic issues at stake in the challenges raised to the legitimacy of the outcome of the free trade election, and these must not be dismissed lightly. But when the entire three-year period of decision, from the initiation of negotiations in September 1985 to the election in November 1988, is taken into account, it is hard to argue persuasively that large numbers of Canadians were not involved in the free trade debate. Not only were they engaged in a discussion of the specific content of the FTA, but they were also drawn into a profoundly important debate over the competing values and visions of two brands of Canadian nationalism.

As for the electoral decision, the fact is that the results of the 1988 election were too complex for the question they were intended to answer. The plainest truth may be simply that the 1988 election supplied a mandate for the FTA congruent with the norms of parliamentary democracy in a multi-party system. While the electorate cannot be said to have chosen free trade, neither can the legitimacy of the FTA be denied on the grounds that a majority of the electorate supported the opponents of free trade. Despite an unprecedented propaganda blitz by both sides, less than half the electorate actually voted on the basis of the free trade issue. And despite the extraordinary concentration of the campaign on this single issue, in the end the election produced no majorities because a large number of people simply remained undecided. As it turned out, the 1988 ballot was not the great free trade election.

PART IV:
THE POLITICAL EFFECTS
OF FREE TRADE

11

SOVEREIGNTY VERSUS POLICY CAPACITY

The path to North American free trade originated in the depths of the 1982 recession. Its implementation began in 1989, the year when change in the Soviet Union and Eastern Europe transformed the entire architecture of the post-war international system. The FTA will cross paths in 1992 with Western Europe's mammoth efforts to become an even more complete and vast common market in excess of 300 million people, a crossing that will be even more significant if the United States, Mexico, and Canada negotiate freer trade for North America as a whole. Against the backdrop of these events, unanticipated as the free trade story began to unfold, the FTA decision seems almost inevitable. Everywhere, sovereign states are forging closer economic links, and globalization has become the watchword for the 1990s.

But the FTA was not inevitable. It was the object of genuine political struggle and debate. For many, especially those opposed to free trade, the political core of the debate centred on the potential loss of Canadian sovereignty and fears about North American policy harmonization that would result from free trade. Opponents also argued that the powers of the state had been weakened or unnecessarily bargained away as a result of the free trade agreement, and raised specific concerns about Canada's future ability to make trade, industrial, energy, and social policy in the interest of Canadians.

With respect to the broader political impact of free trade, a consideration of the agreement in the context of more general global trends suggests that the concepts of sovereignty and harmonization, while obviously important, are not especially useful as litmus tests for the FTA. It is often more important to ask whether Canada's policy capacity is eroded, remains unaffected, or is enhanced as a result of the agreement. Policy capacity refers to a combination of attributes that a country needs to possess in order to solve many of the economic, political, and social problems that confront it. One of these attributes is the availability of policy instruments, including the power to spend, tax, and regulate. Another is a knowledge of how to use such devices, and not to use them when experience suggests that past policy is failing. And a third aspect of policy capacity is the degree and nature of political mobilization and consensus that is needed for the effective use of policy instruments.

When the effects of the FTA are assessed against this notion of policy capacity, it appears that Canada's capacity to make trade policy has been reduced in certain anticipated ways and enhanced in other important respects; its capacity to make industrial policy has been weakened; its capacity to make energy policy has been marginally reduced; and its social policy capacity has not been harmed, and may even have been strengthened as a result of the agreement. In each policy field, and in the relationships among them, care must be taken to distinguish those effects that can be directly and unambiguously attributed to the FTA from those that result from combinations of other institutional conditions and concurrent decisions in such areas as interest rate or exchange rate policy.

SOVEREIGNTY AND HARMONIZATION

Sovereignty is a legal concept that refers to the legal capacities of the nation state to make independent decisions.[1] Harmonization, on the other hand, is a non-legal concept describing the process by which one country's basic policies, rules, and regulations affecting commerce or public policy tend to become virtually indistinguishable from those of other countries. For anti-free trade nationalists, losses of sovereignty and trends towards harmonization with American policies, rules, and regulations are potent negative developments that are expected to result from the agreement. Whatever the legal and rhetorical significance of the terms, however, the twinned notions of sovereignty and harmonization need to be examined for their applied meaning. They cannot be used as if they have uniform meanings in all circumstances and policy areas. In addition, they have several contradictory characteristics that must be kept in mind in any assessment of the FTA in terms of its effects on sovereignty-harmonization.

Our central reference point is that in the post–World War II era, there has been a world-wide trend towards the declining sovereignty of most countries.[2] The evidence for this is overwhelming, and ranges from the growth of multinational enterprises, the emergence of the GATT itself, the development of trading blocs, often involving the surrender of considerable sovereignty by countries, as in the European Community, and numerous international treaties and obligations in dozens of policy fields. Beyond these legal obligations are an array of daily pressures from international policy communities — networks of professional policy experts and interest groups — that contribute to and give further evidence of an extraordinarily interdependent world.

But one can quickly become trapped by a perverse logic if this trend is seen only as a loss of sovereignty or increasing harmonization. This is because many of the new interdependencies and obligations in fact enhance, rather than detract from, Canada's underlying policy capacity. If capacity is understood to mean the actual ability to solve problems and achieve results, then many solutions and achievements are possible only through such international and bilateral rules and obligations. In this sense, another country's loss of legal sovereignty may contribute to the enhancement of Canada's policy capacity.

Another way to consider the difficulty in applying the sovereignty-harmonization criteria is to think of Canada in capsule historical terms. Few would claim that Canada was more sovereign 50 years ago that it is now. Yet, five decades ago Canadian governments possessed a full policy tool kit, with a virtually total array of policy powers at their disposal, in theory at least. Gradually since then, the inventory of available policy tools has been reduced in some respects, and increased in others, by the constraints of international obligations, but the country's policy capacity has been enhanced. For example, tariffs as a policy instrument have been reduced but trade policy capacity has been enhanced by GATT rules, along with economic prosperity. Environmental policy capacity has been enhanced through international agreements and protocols even though each signatory country's sovereignty was reduced in the process.

For these reasons, sovereignty and harmonization are not always useful concepts for a test of the effects of free trade. But there is one vital aspect to Canadian sovereignty that accounts for their widespread use for testing purposes, and this is its historical definition with primary reference to the United States. In Canada, it is one thing to experience losses of legal sovereignty to international institutions and regimes such as the GATT, but it is quite another, psychologically at least, for Canadians to lose sovereignty to the United States.[3] Canadians admire and emulate many features of American life. For example, Canada's adoption of a Charter of Rights and Freedoms is arguably more Americanizing in its impact than the FTA. At the same time, however, Canadians feel suffocated by the American presence and intensely dislike some features of American life, such as its violence. Thus, losses of sovereignty bilaterally take on a special significance for Canada.

While the special importance of the U.S. cannot be denied, it does not eliminate the need for more careful thinking about the effects of the FTA on actual or probable Canadian policy capacities. If some policy powers are partly or entirely closed off from further use, what new ones, or variations on existing powers, are likely to be used, and to what effect? What losses of U.S. powers may Canada be able to exploit? Are there any "Mack Truck" clauses in the FTA, wide enough to drive a truck through, loaded with a new generation of non-tariff barriers? The FTA certainly constrains some powers, but it will also stimulate governments and interest groups to look for other policies and devices to respond to national needs as they evolve. The history of the political economy of trade and economic policy reveals quite clearly that waves of pro-market policy will yield both winners and losers and, as a result, nation-states will have to find new ways to keep these conflicting claims in some kind of political equilibrium.[4] The reduction of tariffs brought in its wake an array of non-tariff barriers, and the removal of these non-tariff barriers will probably produce another generation of new ways to protect vulnerable and sometimes powerful interests. Western democratic governments have alternately leaned towards free markets and then protection, but over the entire post–World War II period, the tilt to liberalized markets has been the stronger impulse.

TRADE POLICY CAPACITY: GAINS AND LOSSES

National trade policies accordingly are Janus faced, looking both inward and outward, seeking to protect domestic markets and penetrate foreign ones. Canada's trade policy capacity to protect its domestic market has been significantly, and intentionally, reduced by the FTA as a result of the agreement to remove tariffs and other barriers to bilateral trade. These instruments of protection may be retrieved, but only by withdrawing from the entire agreement. However, Canadian trade policy capacity is also enhanced by the FTA in three specific ways: through enhanced access to the American market, through improved dispute-settlement procedures, and, paradoxically, by the absence of an agreement on subsidies.

Enhanced access: Substantial improvement in access for Canadian producers to the U.S. market has been achieved through the numerous specific provisions of the FTA, from tariff reduction to easier movement of business persons across the border, to name only two.[5] No guaranteed access has been achieved, but this was an impossible goal in any case. Given the protectionist U.S. political environment of the early and mid-1980s, this improvement in access is no small achievement. The choices for Canada were not between a stable status quo and an absolute guarantee of unfettered entry, but rather between a badly deteriorating status quo and improved access. And improved access is especially important for the smaller country in a trading relationship. Improved access does not, of course, guarantee that the economic benefits of free trade will accrue to Canada. This potential effect of trade policy will depend far more on the thousands of decisions by business firms throughout Canada and elsewhere, as well as on the proper conduct of public policy in several related policy fields in the coming years.

It is unlikely that many of the features of improved access could have been achieved through multilateral negotiations. Indeed, Canada's actual trade history shows that the multilateral versus bilateral options do not pose nearly as clear a choice for Canada as was presented during the free trade debate. During the various rounds of GATT negotiations, Canada was always required to focus the bulk of its attention on its trade relationship with the U.S. So even if Canada had rejected the bilateral approach in favour of multilateral negotiations, its principal negotiating partner would have been the United States.

The FTA should give Canada more latitude in future multilateral trade negotiations, however. Canadian negotiators would normally devote the bulk of their energies in any multilateral round to dealing with Canada's most important trading partner, the U.S. But with the FTA in place, that relationship is largely taken care of, permitting a greater Canadian focus on Europe and Japan. In addition, whereas Canada's other trading partners used to benefit from Canadian agreements with the U.S. in multilateral rounds, because they were entitled to the same arrangements with Canada under the most favoured nation principle, they will now have to pay directly to deal with Canada in multilateral negotiations.

Dispute settlement: Canada's trade policy capacity has also been enhanced by the dispute-settlement provisions of the FTA. Although no binding "supreme court of trade" was obtained to resolve bilateral disputes, the dispute-settlement provisions of the agreement offer improvement in the procedures for the application of trade remedy laws. Paradoxically, had a super court been established, it would have involved an even greater loss of sovereignty for Canada, as well as for the U.S. This again illustrates how the sovereignty criterion can cut both ways. The case for improved capacity through the dispute-settlement provisions lies in the fact that before the FTA was concluded, U.S. institutions and players on matters of countervail were, to a far greater degree than now, prosecutor, judge, and jury. Even though, on countervail matters, only judicial review power has been achieved, with the FTA in place Canadians are now involved in decisions that were previously handled only by Americans, and often with a suspected bias.

The potential importance of the dispute-settlement elements of the agreement is indicated by the fact that Canadian firms were quick to take advantage of the Chapter 19 provisions to challenge a number of American countervail rulings. Of course their enthusiasm for the process will depend on the outcome of individual cases.[6] But Canadians cannot expect to win all future disputes. The real test of this key element of the FTA will be in its effects on U.S. behaviour. In the case of American producers, the question is whether the existence of a review process in which other nationals are involved will reduce the number of countervail actions that are even attempted. And in the case of U.S. government agencies, the test of the effectiveness of the provisions will be whether the potential for review will produce more carefully rendered decisions, without the capriciousness that Canadians charged had marked the process before the agreement. These questions will be answered only after several years, as experience is accumulated. The evidence to answer them will come not only from the nature of actual disputes resolved, but also in the form of "non-events," namely countervail actions not attempted or disputes avoided through prior consultation. If changes occur in the behaviour of both firms and agencies, then Canadian interests can be expected to prevail more often than would have been the case without the FTA provisions.

Subsidies: Certain features of the subsidies issue are essential background to the examination below of Canada's future industrial and social policy capacities. Perhaps most important is the basic problem of defining a subsidy.[7] Over a 40-year period, GATT members have tried to agree on a definition of subsidies, and whether they cause "material injury" to others. Early efforts were directed at restraining direct export subsidies or government assistance contingent upon export performance. From the mid-1970s on, the business of defining a subsidy was dominated by the United States. As directed at Canada, the American preoccupation took the form of 16 countervail cases against Canadian producers between 1980 and 1989.[8] In these cases, subsidies came to mean any Canadian government practice that American trade authorities said provided a subsidy.

In principle, any government support in the form of grants, tax breaks, regulations, concessionary loans, or direct investment could directly or indirectly assist a firm or industry. Much turns on how general or specific the intent, and the effect, of such policy instruments is, including their combined use. The first question that has to be posed in determining when a subsidy is present concerns whether the government's actions are intended to affect particular companies, an industrial sector, a region, all industries generally, or the population as a whole. Logic suggests that progression along this continuum, from company-specific to general support, should make actions less likely to be defined as a subsidy. This notion is important for our discussion of Canada's future industrial and social policy capacity, below.

But even this general question is only the first step in defining a subsidy. This is because the real concern of governments and firms is with subsidies that *distort* trade away from some natural state of comparative advantage. Distortion occurs when subsidies help increase exports or displace imports. But this is precisely where the asymmetry between the Canadian and American economies is vitally important. Canada is the more trade-dependent country, and most of Canada's trade is with the United States. The U.S., in contrast, is far less dependent on trade, and trades extensively with Europe and Japan, as well as with Canada. It follows that any particular Canadian practice has a greater chance of being alleged by the U.S. to be trade distorting than does any specific American practice by Canada, simply because Canadian production affected by the practice is more likely to be exported, probably to the U.S.

Given the ambiguities in the meaning of a subsidy practice, and Canada's greater vulnerability to charges of subsidization from the U.S., it is clear why Simon Reisman decided to try to get agreement on what practices would be allowed, and therefore not subject to countervail. As a result, it may seem perverse to claim that the failure to achieve a subsidies agreement in fact enhances Canadian trade policy capacity. However, our argument centres on the fact that had there been a subsidies agreement, it is likely that there would not have been an FTA. Because, despite the fact that a subsidies deal was central to Reisman's approach to the negotiations, it is probable that no domestic Canadian political coalition in support of the FTA could have been held together if subsidies had been eliminated or even severely reduced. Even partial restraints on regional subsidies would probably have proved fatal to the FTA. There were simply too many provinces, regions, or interests that would have gone public against the deal. The probability that the pro-free trade coalition would come apart at the seams in the face of the reduction or elimination of politically sensitive subsidies would likely have doomed the agreement.

The subsidies issue was left for a later date, to be negotiated between the two countries over a five-to-seven-year period. This postponement is also good for Canada, because it permits the FTA to become fully operational and both countries to gain experience with the dispute-settlement machinery created under Chapter 19. There is a widespread belief in the U.S. that other countries subsidize and Americans do not. This fiction has been sustained in part by the virtual American monopoly in the subsidy definition business, and by the fact that few trade remedy actions have been launched against them. As the 1990s began, however, it was clear that Europe, Japan, Pacific Rim countries, and Canada were determined to break the U.S. definitional monopoly. Discussion of the subsidy question in the Uruguay GATT round gave these countries an opportunity to push the U.S. further to test the definitional issue against a world standard. Buying time in this process is vital both for trade and other policy reasons, since the subsidies question goes to the core of defining what the proper role of the state is or can be under different democratic regimes. It is not simply a narrow trade matter.

In view of the obvious political sensitivity of subsidies in Canada, it is ironic that the issue was carried over for another round of negotiations with the U.S. The U.S. Department of Commerce strenuously resisted Reisman's efforts to construct a subsidies regime as part of the FTA. In the end, however, Commerce officials were convinced that there might be something to the idea as a way of getting at Canadian subsidy practices, and the commitment to continue negotiations was inserted in Chapter 19. However, outside the context of the larger negotiation, where the Americans might have had to pay on other issues for Canadian concessions on subsidies, Canada is dangerously exposed in a negotiation that focuses exclusively on the subsidy issue. The exposure is to both American demands and to Canadian domestic political sensitivities. As a result, whereas Canadians had pushed the issue to the top of the agenda throughout 15 months of free trade negotiations, they might now be just as happy to have it go away. This is unlikely, however. While the U.S. is probably willing to let the issue slide in the short term, at least as long as it is being addressed in the Uruguay Round, and perhaps in the trilateral North American negotiations as well, the Americans will be determined in the longer run to pursue the subsidies issue.

INDUSTRIAL POLICY CAPACITY: A CLEAR LOSS

Industrial policy consists of co-ordinated government actions targeted at key firms or sectors, and designed to enhance their international competitiveness in product development in the economic interests of Canada.[9] In practice, this would mean the capacity of Canadian governments to assist firms such as Bombardier or Northern Telecom, or perhaps consortia of firms in an active industrial policy sense. Or it could refer to reactive or defensive industrial policy to prevent or influence foreign takeovers of key Canadian firms.

This narrowing of the definition of industrial policy to the range of actions set out above is necessary for any reasonable discussion to occur. If it is defined loosely as being virtually any action taken by government that directly or indirectly affects industry, then debate will be hopelessly muddied. Industrial policy, therefore, is not used here to refer to a range of other so-called framework policies, e.g., general policies on research and development (R&D) incentives, taxation, and education and training, that are pursued by governments to help business compete in a general sense. Such framework policies are indeed vital to Canadian prosperity, as we will stress in Chapter 12, but they do not constitute industrial policy for our purposes.

There are two provisions of the FTA, national treatment and investment screening, that significantly reduce Canada's capacity to make industrial policy as defined above. National treatment is a GATT principle intended to ensure that once goods have been imported into any country, they will not be the object of discrimination. The application of the principle to services and investment was deemed necessary in the FTA because of the increasingly co-mingled nature of trade in goods and services, and their links to investment. The principle of national treatment makes the conduct of industrial policy more difficult. It does not make it impossible, however, because in the service sector, for example, existing discriminatory policies are grandfathered. Only future policies cannot be discriminatory.

As for Canada's capacity to screen foreign investment, it is also clear that the FTA reduces to some extent this element of industrial policy capacity. The Agreement eliminates the right to screen smaller companies that are taken over by foreign interests, but it permits screening for takeovers of large companies. Overall, about 80 per cent of assets can still, in principle, be screened. Although it is doubtful that screening was ever a good instrument for an active industrial policy, the FTA provisions also constrain reactive industrial policy capacity. Moreover, if screening is to continue, and larger takeovers are to be judged as to whether they provide a net benefit to Canada, then the federal government must develop some criteria for interventions among sectors or types of firms. For this, Investment Canada requires far more guidance from the politicians than it has been receiving so far.

Many will question whether a diminished industrial policy capacity is a loss at all. This was precisely the view of bodies like the Macdonald Commission, the Economic Council of Canada, and numerous economists knowledgeable about Canada's past attempts to practise industrial policy. Conventional liberal economic approaches to this issue argue that governments should restrict themselves to the establishment of good framework policies.[10] In this sense, free trade is Canada's best policy for industrial development. Or, to illustrate the potential for confusion in the language of the debate, it led many to argue that free trade was Canada's best industrial policy.

More specifically, many studies pointed in practice not only to Canada's uneven record in this sphere, but also to the fact that it has seriously harmed, rather than helped, Canada's economic performance because it slowed Canada's capacity to adjust to international competitive forces.[11] Still others point to the absence of the appropriate political institutions and political consensus required to support such actions.[12] They also cite the absence of the necessary technical and organizational capacity within government to mount the kind of coherent industrial policy that Japan and other countries have practised successfully.[13]

Although much of this judgement of Canada's past efforts is quite accurate, it still does not deal adequately with the situation Canada is going to face in the 1990s and beyond. The Canadian economy does need free trade, with expanded access to the American and world markets, as the foundation of its economic policy, but as a small trade-dependent economy in an increasingly technological and global product market, Canada will also need a more concerted industrial policy to complement free trade. This is because comparative advantage in international trade is to *some* extent engineered.[14] The economic case for firm- or sector-specific activities — in short, for a real industrial policy — resides in the notion that some product development cycles are characterized by imperfect competition, or quasi-monopoly situations. Thus, a case can be made for government to assume a role in helping Canadians garner some of the greater economic gains available in such situations or, alternatively, to prevent Canada from losing out entirely. The FTA does not completely prevent this possibility, but it makes it more difficult.

If future industrial policies are needed as a complement to free trade, then Canadian political leaders will have to be far more sophisticated, and honest, about how they go about constructing the right political institutions within which better industrial policies can be devised. They will certainly not be able to subsidize everything in sight. At the same time, devising industrial policies is truly a difficult task, even if intended as a complementary capstone to an approach based on free trade. It is clear that during their term in power, the Mulroney Conservatives, while they have embraced the need to reduce subsidies and develop a more technologically based economic policy, have been unprepared, both ideologically and practically, to even contemplate an industrial policy. It is doubtful, however, that free trade, crucial though it is, will be enough in the decade ahead.

ENERGY POLICY CAPACITY: MARGINAL LOSSES

Some critics of the FTA have argued that the agreement amounts to a virtual sell-out of Canada's resources, including not only oil and natural gas, but also water.[15] Compared to the Canadian energy wars of 1979–80, however, rhetoric over the energy issue was fairly subdued in the free trade debate. In terms of policy powers, there is little doubt that the federal government has given up some of its future policy-making flexibility in the energy field. The loss of capacity to set export taxes and discriminatory export prices, and the need to carry out the proportionality provisions does reduce the range of options available to any future government that might face an energy crisis or other energy shortage. The government of Canada could still set domestic prices and intervene significantly, but a combination of actions like those that constituted the NEP could not be repeated in the future. As we have seen, this is precisely what the Western oil- and gas-producing provinces wanted from the FTA. And they were not alone in regarding the array of NEP provisions as being badly mistaken energy policy, and hence their removal a desirable loss of sovereignty.

Despite the loss of powers inherent in the FTA, the provisions represent only a marginal loss in Canada's energy policy capacity because of the realities of continental decision-making in the area of energy. This judgement depends upon a particular reading of the probability and nature of future events, including future energy crises, the pace of instituting conservation measures, and security of supply. In each case, it is our view that the likely range of future choice for Canada is not between nationalist white and continental-ist black, but rather between a number of extremely fine shades of grey.

If a future energy crisis were triggered by, or were reflected in, sudden price increases and shortages as in 1973 and 1979, it would be primarily a crisis of oil, and it would be a world crisis, not just a continental one. Events like those in the Persian Gulf in 1990–91 could produce such a crisis next time around. In that kind of situation, the FTA would give way to Canada's previous obligations under international energy agreements to share supply. Such a sharing mechanism would be implemented through the International Energy Agency, involving demands on Canada that would likely be greater than those imposed by any FTA conservation measures that would apply to oil, gas, and electricity. So with respect to oil crises specifically, the FTA effects are extremely limited. Canada's primary obligations actually pre-date the FTA, and were then supported by many who are now energy nationalists.

What, then, might happen if there were a more gradual, less crisis-like realization that Canada must declare shortages for other conservation purposes, triggering the proportionality provisions of the FTA? These provisions deal with contracted supplies and are in the FTA to ensure that good customers are treated fairly. Even without an FTA, if there were a North American supply problem, especially for natural gas, Canada would still have to treat the American buyers fairly. In fact, negotiations would probably occur over how to reduce supply proportionately. This is why the pre- and post-FTA situations are grey zones, rather than the black and white of continentalist and nationalist options.

However, well before any such slowly developing shortages actually came to pass, other events and actions would probably occur. For example, since there is no longer a 25-year surplus test for gas exports, the main first line of determination for ensuring adequate future supply is the challenge process that is available before the National Energy Board. Canadian firms (and presumably the government of Canada itself) could bid for gas exports at the prevailing market prices. This would, in fact, be a more open process for putting a price on how much security of supply Canadians really wanted, and what they would pay for it. The old surplus test ensured some security of supply, but it was basically paid for by Western producers to help Eastern consumers and industries. Now Eastern interests must pay and show openly how much security they are willing to buy, as opposed to having it submerged in a subsidy conferred by regulation. This process will require, however, more public monitoring, through hearings by the National Energy Board, than is currently being done. Estimates of Canada's future reserves must be openly scrutinized through frequent general hearings, as well as through the challenge process that now applies to individual export licence applications. But this extra monitoring activity can easily be done within the terms of the FTA.

Beyond these kinds of scenarios, the concept of proportionality has been left deliberately vague in the FTA because no one can totally foresee the exact circumstances of a future supply problem. Given the well-established energy and economic interdependence of the two countries, almost any scenario that might occur under the FTA, or that might have occurred without an FTA, would have involved intense Canada-U.S. bargaining. Such scenarios are really only surrogates for the continuing debate over how Canada should ensure its energy security, and whether it should be done through the powers of the state or reliance on markets.

A relatively greater reliance on the state, through surplus tests and export taxes, for example, can be referred to as a "hoarding" approach. It ultimately implies the existence of an all-knowing (presumably federal) decision-making body that, figuratively speaking, sits on Canada's energy reserves and releases them for sale (domestically and for export) at just the right time and at just the right price. But energy markets, and certainly Canada's political system, have never allowed the existence of such a single purposeful decision-maker. Instead, there exists a mix of public and private decision-makers on both sides of the border, coaxing, cajoling, bargaining with, buying from, and brow-beating one another into numerous energy deals. Moreover, the energy markets of the 1990s are not like the energy markets of the 1960s. There is far more energy substitution among fuels and hence a much more mature market structure.

The past record and plausible future scenarios suggest that the overall impact of the FTA is to weaken, but only marginally, Canada's energy policy capacity. Some policy powers are certainly diminished, but, in any case, the reality of the extensive interdependence of the North American energy political economy is simply at odds with much of the normal rhetoric of an autonomous energy policy.

SOCIAL POLICY CAPACITY: NEUTRAL EFFECTS OR POSSIBLE GAINS

Social policy embraces the main elements of the modern social welfare state — health, education, and welfare — but for our purposes it also includes areas such as unemployment insurance, training and, in many respects, regional policy. In the 1990s, the field should also be considered to include environmental policy and related areas of social regulation. In these areas, we conclude that the effects of the FTA on social policy capacity will be, at worst, neutral and that conceivably gains in policy capacity could occur. The possibility of gains will depend upon how the subsidy issue evolves, and on how the mobilization of political interests occurs in the 1990s, both in Canada and the U.S. To understand the rationale for this conclusion we need to review the FTA social policy debate, looking at the specific provisions of the Agreement, and reintroduce the social policy agenda that was presented in the Macdonald Commission report. We also have to consider briefly the fact that social policy in the 1990s will be very different from what it was in the 1960s, when the Canadian image of its social policy achievements was formed.

It was over social policy that the sharpest divisions occurred among pro- and anti-free trade forces.[16] Supporters of the deal saw the FTA as an economic arrangement with no adverse social policy consequences. Indeed, the more optimistic among them argued that the economic benefits from free trade would make better social programs possible in the future. In effect, they were arguing that economic development comes first and social policy, especially the redistribution of income from rich to poor, is the result.

Opponents of the deal saw the FTA having severe negative consequences at two levels. The first was a fear that the pro-market ethos of the FTA, as well as the rest of the Mulroney Conservative agenda, was undermining the social values that anchored the Canadian social welfare state.[17] This welfare state was in fact a dual one. One axis was formed by an array of universal, insurance-based, and demi-grant programs that produced a modest redistribution of income but that also supplied a safety net against the recurrence of a more catastrophic 1930s-style depression. Often this array of programs was quite inaccurately summed up in the battle cry of "universality," where all programs were classified as rights and entitlements even where they manifestly were not. The second axis of the welfare state was an interregional one, and consisted of both equalization grants to have-not provinces and numerous regional incentive programs. The latter regional programs consisted of many activities that pro-free traders and pro-market advocates regarded as increasingly wasteful industrial policy. They argued that Canada could no longer afford to bring "jobs to people," meaning have-not regions, but instead had to bring "people to jobs."

The second negative effect feared by anti-free traders stemmed from a belief that over the long term there would be inexorable pressure from business interests to harmonize social policy downward to U.S. standards, thus reducing Canada's capacity to continue building a different kind of society from that of the United States. In many ways, the opponents of free trade were economic determinists in their view of how social policies are achieved and changed. Social policy concerns also entered the debate regarding the kinds of adjustment policy measures for workers and communities that might be required in the event of industrial job losses or dislocation created by free trade, or by other international competitive forces. Both the Macdonald Commission and, later, the International Trade Advisory Committee argued that there could not be an adjustment assistance program that was specifically earmarked to help adjust to a free trade agreement. This was because, at any given time, people's economic misfortune could be due to any number of factors, and hence it would be both unfair and impractical to assist only those harmed by trade, as opposed to those harmed by new technologies or high interest rates. But the Macdonald Commission did recommend a major, broad-based adjustment program and a guaranteed annual income, policies we refer to again below.

Underlying all of these elements of the social policy aspects of the free trade debate was a crazy-quilt of myth and fact regarding Canada-U.S. social policy comparisons. In some areas, such as health care, family allowances, and unemployment insurance, the alleged inferiority of U.S. social policy practice was true and self-evident. It is also true that Canada spends a percentage point or two more of its gross national product on social policy expenditures, as a whole. In other areas, however, such as pensions and in several aspects of environmental standards, the U.S. has a superior record. In addition, U.S. unemployment rates are routinely two or three percentage points lower than Canadian rates, in itself a successful social policy indicator.

Thus the social policy aspect of the free trade debate was partly factual, but was also based at times on some exaggerated self-images of Canadian superiority in social policy. The quality of the debate was intensified by the very real dislike many Canadians had for the hard edge of Ronald Reagan's conservative version of America, and all that it implied. This became, not surprisingly, the focal point in the free trade debate for the way many Canadians defined themselves, in practice, as being different from Americans. But the climate of the social policy debate must be contrasted with the actual provisions of the FTA that dealt with social policy.[18] The three provisions of the deal that warrant special attention are those dealing with services and national treatment, technical standards, and, once again, subsidies.

The FTA chapter on services allows trade in the *management* of health and social services. It exempts the direct provision of health, educational, and social services but an annex lists commercial management services. The national treatment provision also applies, meaning that future rules governing such management services cannot discriminate between Canadian and American firms.

The concern of social policy advocates here is that it may open the door to greater pressure to privatize social services, beginning with their management, and then, it is feared, extending to the provision of the services themselves. The FTA does not require Canadian governments to procure commercial management services, but the argument of the social policy community is that future trade negotiations will widen the list of services, and the ethos of private management firms is such that they themselves will create pressure for the privatization of service delivery. Furthermore, the private ethos will produce an emphasis on the bottom line of profitability and reduce the sensitivity and compassion of social service delivery practices.

While this provision of the FTA is a cause for concern for some, the probable cause-and-effect relationships are really very indirect. Although an opening exists for further privatization, the intervening factors that could block such an outcome are numerous. Not the least of these is the strong underlying body of support in the Canadian electorate for the public provision of core social services.

The FTA provisions on technical standards include rules regarding labelling and packaging, but they also include norms to encourage the simplification of product standards. At the same time, the national treatment provisions make clear that health and safety laws are perfectly justifiable provided that they do not discriminate between Canadian and American producers. Citing this part of the FTA, environmentalists expressed alarm that continental economic pressures would eventually force Canadians to adopt lower environmental standards. This argument was exactly parallel to the more general social policy argument, but it was not accompanied by much evidence that U.S. practices are in fact of a lower standard. The failure to support the claim with evidence is partly a result of the difficulty of obtaining and interpreting comparative environmental data. There are virtually no such general data and, accordingly, cases must be examined on a "hazard-by-hazard" basis in order to reach any conclusion. The many claims about Canada's alleged environmental superiority are just not credible in any general sense, however. In addition, these claims ignore the fact that for many environmental issues truly effective regulatory capacity ultimately depends upon international and continental co-operation and joint agreement, with or without free trade.

It is possible, however, that the technical standards area of the FTA may become the device through which new protectionist barriers to trade will emerge. Tougher or new environmental and safety standards may be pressed on governments by environmentalists, supported by economically vulnerable domestic producers. For example, Canadian wood products such as cedar shakes and shingles have come under attack by U.S. interests who assert that they are unsafe for housing construction because they lack acceptable fire retardant qualities. It does not require much political imagination to envisage certain coalitions of convenience arising in other health, safety, and environmental areas.

At this point, we would argue that the FTA is probably neutral with respect to social policy. But this leaves unexplored the possible links between social policy and the subsidy issue. The majority of social policy advocates recognize that generally available programs, such as those for health, post-secondary education, and old age security, are precisely those that are not defined as subsidies, unlikely to be touched by any future agreement. These programs differ fundamentally from government actions that are specifically intended to benefit individual firms and perhaps sectors, measures that stand a good chance of being defined as subsidies.

Between these two poles is a considerable range that is more uncertain. Regional programs fall in this range and may have to be judged on a case-by-case basis. The status of income maintenance programs for the so-called working poor, either in their current form or as the guaranteed annual income recommended by the Macdonald Commission, is also uncertain. Canadians will argue that such programs are, in principle, broadly based efforts to alleviate poverty and to redistribute income. But the U.S. could argue that they provide a trade distorting subsidy because labour is the largest cost component for many sectors. If this argument is made, however, many American social programs could be similarly attacked.

Thus, in any future subsidy agreement, the odds are that general social programs will not be defined as subsidies. All other things being equal, this means that universal or general programs, including a guaranteed annual income, will be the best ones to have. There may, in short, be a new avenue of opportunity for social policy interests to rescue the notion of universality. For most of the 1980s, universal programs have been under attack, and have been augmented by targeted programs. But targeted programs may be somewhat more vulnerable in any subsidies agreement, or failing an agreement may simply be much more vulnerable to countervail.

The subsidies issue forces us back to a reconsideration of the kind of social policy agenda that was advanced by the Macdonald Commission. Although the Commission was best known for its free trade recommendation, it also saw its social policy proposals as a necessary complement to an FTA in order for Canadians to realize the potential economic benefits of free trade. These social policy measures centred on two major changes. The first was a generous adjustment program for labour and communities, linked to reforms in unemployment insurance and in training. The second was a guaranteed annual income to ensure that the working poor were not caught by the existing traps of Canada's hodge-podge welfare system, in which they were frequently penalized for seeking work. While the Macdonald Commission's social policy recommendations can be criticized for not going far enough, they nonetheless contain a direction for social policy that is still both sensible and necessary as a complement to free trade. Indeed, another reason for our conclusion that the FTA contains the seeds of potentially better social policy in Canada is that it should now force Canadian attention to the important social policy issues that Macdonald identified. It should also force a more considered discussion of the fact that social policy is not just a residual outcome of economic development, but is instead a contributing factor to economic efficiency.[19]

This link is more likely to be made as the 1990s progress and as the social policy constituencies mobilize after a decade of being on the political defensive. For example, it is likely in our view that in some social policy areas in both the United States and Canada, new programs will be advocated not only for equity purposes, but also as economic necessities, to retrain workers or to compete with other countries. Canadian-style medicare is already being advocated for these reasons in the U.S. by auto industry interests and others. Day care programs are another candidate in both countries for this social-economic merger of interests.

THE FUTURE MOBILIZATION OF POLITICAL INTERESTS

As we stressed earlier, the notion of policy capacity refers to three attributes — the existence of policy instruments, the national ability to learn intelligently from past successes and failures in their use, and the mobilization of interests. Mobilization refers to future ways in which business and social coalitions seek and obtain political representation and leverage in the Canadian political process in the 1990s and beyond. In this regard political interests, including governments, political parties, and industrial and social interest groups must mobilize themselves in far more effective ways than they have done in the past. This includes not only using knowledge about domestic and international product markets and opportunities, but also using the state to devise a more coherent consensus around the vital role that both markets and governments must play.[20]

We are in no position to predict the way that political interests will in fact be mobilized. We suspect that the strong pro-market ethos of the 1980s will elicit a counter-reaction in the 1990s, but not one resembling the form that prevailed in the 1960s or earlier. Both the nature of modern technologies and of social movements in the 1990s will produce a new kind of partnership between market and state, because there will be new issues, such as an aging population, to deal with. But it will not happen easily, or without sustained political action and debate. Consider again the future conduct of industrial policy. We have argued that the FTA reduces Canada's industrial policy capacity and suggested that Canada will need industrial policy as a necessary complement to free trade, either for active or defensive economic reasons. But as the 1990s begin, this is clearly not the majority view. Nor will it likely materialize unless Canadian governments and business leaders make a far more concerted effort, thinking and acting systematically, to forge the necessary interest group networks and coalitions. It will also require a detailed level of industrial knowledge, including ways of working with key firms, as other competitor countries have learned to do. One of the paradoxes of the FTA is that because it helped exorcise the ghosts of free trade and pushed Canadians psychologically into a more concrete awareness of the global trading world, it may now help promote the first truly serious and concerted debate on the complementary need for, and practical limits of, an industrial policy.

As for Canada's social policy future, much depends on whether there will be a renewed mobilization of political interests in support of broad Canadian social policy traditions and values. This is ultimately a domestic Canadian political issue. The election of an NDP government in Ontario, Canada's industrial heartland, is indicative of the remaining strength of Canada's social policy concerns. But the outcome of these and other events will also be influenced by developments in the U.S., particularly if, as seems possible, the American political system in the 1990s loses the hard edge of the Reagan era.[21] Politics in the U.S. will always manifest more suspicion of state-led social policy intervention. However, a revival of Democratic Party fortunes is likely to propel social policy issues to a higher place on the American agenda.

Nevertheless, it is primarily within Canada that political mobilization in support of social policy must be increased. This brings us full circle to a consideration of the political staying power of the interests encompassed by the Pro Canada Network and the Canadian Alliance for Job and Trade Opportunities. It was the PCN that was most gloomy about the destructive impact of the FTA, as well as other elements of the Mulroney policy agenda, on the values that underpin the welfare state. This was because the coalition was on the run over the main thrust of the agenda, and because it had grown lazy in its understanding of the way the economic world had changed. It had too easily succumbed to ideological short-hand thinking, labelling all critics of government or supporters of markets as ideologues. Rocked back on its heels in the 1980s, the social coalition in the 1990s has the task of learning how to work around these forces without abandoning the broad thrust of its belief in equality and in Canadian human and community values.

It is unlikely that a coalition like the PCN will itself survive in the 1990s as an institution. Its glue was the free trade battle. Moreover, it came together because of a particular point of weakness in the Liberal Party. As the FTA recedes as a focal point for the political battle over "markets versus the state," the components of the coalition will likely dissolve back into the political arenas where they had previously resided, some as independent people's movements and interest group lobbies, many of them within the NDP, some elements within the Liberal Party and the Conservative Party. Other pressure points will be established in various provincial governments. Despite the likely dissolution of the coalition, there is no law of social or political relations that points to the inexorable decline of social-democratic values or the disappearance of Canadians who understand and will fight for good social policies. If social policy interests and organizations fold their tents in the wake of the FTA, then social values and programs probably will be reduced in Canada. This seems as unlikely to us as it would be undesirable.

In a similar vein, the pro-free trade business coalition centred in the Alliance will likely resume its more pragmatic stance of support for the two free-enterprise parties. The glue holding it together also vanished when it won its battle in the 1980s for free trade. But business is unlikely to be able to deliver in the 1990s on the full benefits of the FTA unless it rethinks its views on just how important good economic and social policy is for Canada's economic and political survival.

12

FAITH, FEAR, AND
CONSEQUENCES

By any standard, Canada's free trade initiative deserves to be viewed as a landmark decision in Canadian political history, one that defies easy explanation. Our account of the free trade story through all of its stages — from the emergence of free trade on the policy agenda to the three-ring circus of the negotiations, and from the battle of the two nationalist coalitions to the 1988 election — has shown that the decision was the product of both faith and fear for almost all Canadians who were involved in or touched by it.

This is evident especially at the level of values and symbolic politics. After all, as the FTA evolved and lurched through its political stages, it was mainly a battle over feared or promised future consequences. Actual effects could only be guessed at, would take a decade to materialize, and would, in any case, become inextricably linked with a host of other factors as the 1990s stretched into a new century. There is little doubt that the FTA will produce significant change in the Canadian political economy, but it is unlikely that the change will match the extremes of either the fears or the promises that surfaced during the election.

What, then, can reasonably be concluded about the free trade story? To answer this, we look to the central questions that were posed at the beginning of the book. What made Brian Mulroney undertake a politically risky initiative less than two years after he had publicly opposed free trade? In the negotiations themselves, was Canada politically out-negotiated or did Canadian negotiators manage the politics of a large and complex negotiation reasonably well? Does the deal make economic sense for Canada, given the alternatives that were available in the mid-1980s and given the competitive situation that is probably in store for the 1990s? Did the election that climaxed the free trade initiative provide the legitimacy that many argued was required for a policy decision of such fundamental importance to Canadians? And finally, how have the events surrounding the free trade saga, and the agreement itself, affected the basic elements of Canadian political life, including Canada's future policy capacity, the extent of regional decentralization in the country, and the balance of national versus continental integration?

THE FREE TRADE CHOICE

It was the prime minister alone who ultimately decided that the risks of pursuing the free trade initiative were worth the political candle. Although he consulted his colleagues, there was no serious discussion of the issue in cabinet prior to the meeting of the Priorities and Planning Committee in Vancouver in August 1985, when Mulroney had already made his decision to leap. Much like the Liberals' National Energy Program in 1980, the Conservative cabinet received the FTA decision as a *fait accompli*, already judged and decided to be worth the risk by the prime minister and his advisers. To be sure, ministers such as Michael Wilson, James Kelleher, Don Mazankowski, and Joe Clark had taken part in discussions of the issue, but these were informal and restricted to a very small group.

Once the decision to negotiate had been made, a more active, albeit formal, role for cabinet did emerge. Five sessions of the whole cabinet, plus others of its trade executive committee, were held to discuss and approve negotiating mandates. However, because

Reisman's strategy was to keep the mandates as general as possible, and because of the lack of progress at the negotiating table, these sessions typically consisted of TNO slide shows, followed by efforts on the part of worried ministers to find out what was actually happening in the negotiations. By far the most detailed and extensive cabinet discussions took place over the mandate for investment provisions, although concerns about culture and agricultural protection were aired as well. Joe Clark, Flora Macdonald, and Marcel Masse were the cabinet's leading worriers, but the questions they raised certainly never threatened the negotiations. Ministers knew without any doubt that this was Brian Mulroney's show, and that the life of their government could depend on the successful conclusion of a deal. Too much political capital had been invested in the initiative for doubting souls in cabinet to rock the free trade boat.

It should be clear from our account of the dynamics of the agenda-setting phase in Part I, however, that Mulroney's free trade decision was no ideological outburst by a Canadian Reagan-Thatcher clone. Mulroney is a political conservative who undoubtedly favours liberalized markets, but this alone would not have produced a leap of faith. Nor was it the power of the economic arguments favouring free trade, put forward by the Macdonald Commission, the Economic Council of Canada, and others, that persuaded Mulroney, because he never received a comprehensive briefing from his trade officials on the economics of Canada-U.S. free trade. Instead, the prime minister made an intuitive political judgement that this was a policy whose time had come.

That judgement was reinforced by an assessment that the initiative could meet several intensely political tests that suggested free trade would be a difficult issue to handle, but not as risky as the historical mythology of 1911 made it out to be. First, Mulroney saw free trade primarily as a means to secure access to the U.S. market in the face of growing American protectionism. This was a view that mirrored the concerns of the Canadian business community, and pursuing free trade would serve the dominant interests of that community. It would also further Mulroney's goal of establishing a new, more collaborative, and less combative era in Canadian-American relations. His apparent confidence that he could achieve these goals stemmed in large measure from the personal rapport that he had established with Ronald Reagan.

The second key factor in Mulroney's conversion to free trade was his desire to promote national reconciliation. Here, the role of Peter Lougheed was particularly important. Lougheed was the dean of Western Canadian politics and a senior Tory political leader, and his voice in favour of free trade counted for a great deal in Mulroney's political calculus. It convinced Mulroney that free trade would help heal the deep regional wounds produced by the National Energy Program. As well, strong support from Lougheed helped reduce the risks associated with the venture by balancing the opposition it attracted from many other quarters. The fact that the four Western premiers also endorsed the free trade initiative buttressed Mulroney's view that the political risks were manageable.

In the light of the vital role usually played by the bureaucracy in policy formation, one of the surprising features of the agenda-setting phase of the free trade story is that the initiative was kept on the agenda despite opposition from most of Ottawa's senior mandarins. And here the role of Derek Burney is pivotal. As we have seen, Burney was virtually the lone ranger of free trade in the External Affairs bureaucracy. He kept nudging the issue forward, ensuring that it was not pushed aside, insisting that ministers be presented with a full array of alternatives, including comprehensive free trade, over the opposition of other senior External Affairs officials. Some opponents in External, and other government departments, resisted Burney's free trade crusade because they had genuine doubts about the wisdom of putting all of Canada's economic eggs in the American basket. Others were simply playing the Ottawa game of winners and losers. They made a judgement that the free trade balloon would not fly politically, and set out to block a losing cause. Burney would not be turned, however.

Burney's role must also be seen in the context of the tension that existed between the senior bureaucracy and Tory ministers, particularly the prime minister. Mulroney is a partisan to the core and was all the more so in the early days in power when his legendary back-room distrust of anything that smacked of entrenched Liberal institutions was much in evidence. In 1984–85, most deputy ministers in Ottawa were being kept at arm's length by the new Conservative government because of their suspected Liberal sympathies. Burney, however, had access to Mulroney because he had organized the prime minister's first Washington visit, and did it well. A personal rapport and trust developed between Mulroney and Burney, serving Tory desires to reach below the top level of official Ottawa to find sympathetic allies in the bureaucracy. Burney was like Mulroney in that he was not an ideologue for free markets, but saw the free trade issue in terms of securing market access and getting the U.S. relationship right.

The next step in Mulroney's conversion came from the Macdonald Commission. Initially suspicious because it was a Liberal creation, Mulroney came to see the value of the commission to his own purposes. He was impressed by the extent of its work, which eased any remaining doubts he may have had about the desirability of going for a big trade deal. This did not mean that he was personally persuaded by the economic rationale for free trade that was offered by the commission as an answer to Canada's productivity crisis. Instead Mulroney was impressed by Macdonald's argument that free trade would simultaneously address two pressing national problems: it would secure market access in the face of U.S. protectionism, and it would promote national unity, especially regarding Western Canada, both of which were themes central to the agenda of the prime minister. But it was the intense partisan in Mulroney who, upon receiving Macdonald's report in the summer of 1985, relished the prospect of using a former Liberal cabinet minister to give bipartisan legitimacy to his initiative. And to make sure that free trade was tied to Macdonald, the launch of the initiative was announced within days of the official publication of the commission's report.

These were the key influences in Mulroney's embrace of free

trade. That the embrace was gradual, and not an ideologically driven decision to pursue free trade made at the start of the new government's term, is reinforced by the incremental adjustments that were made in relations with the United States throughout the year preceding the announcement of the initiative. Policies like the dismantling of FIRA and the NEP, and changes in banking policy, would have been held back for bargaining purposes, rather than given up freely, had the decision to negotiate a free trade agreement already been made. In fact they were not, and the government can be faulted for its failure to put these policies on hold until the bilateral trade question had been settled. Instead, important cards in the Canadian hand were dealt away during that year.

In general, Mulroney's decision was the product of a confluence of political reasoning, fortuitous events, and personal influences. The damaging recession early in the decade and the spectre of U.S. protectionism that haunted important segments of the Canadian business community created the necessary preconditions for the free trade decision, but these were not in themselves sufficient to ensure its eventual emergence on the Conservative policy agenda. Free trade could easily have been knocked off that agenda had there been no Peter Lougheed to act as political godfather to the initiative, no Derek Burney to run bureaucratic interference, no Donald Mac-donald to offer the security of bipartisan legitimacy, and, above all, no Brian Mulroney.

WAS CANADA POLITICALLY OUT-NEGOTIATED?

The FTA negotiation must be assessed both in relation to political criteria, as an exercise in political power, and in relation to economic criteria. In the politics of negotiation, as in other spectator sports, armchair quarterbacks abound. With hindsight, vision is even more acute for spectators of the negotiation process because there is often an outcome to judge, the deal itself. Critics are quick to seize on what they see as excessive, or unnecessary, concessions, as well as unacceptable shortfalls in gains when evaluating outcomes. The problem with this approach is basic: to understand the product of a negotiation, you must understand the process. Negotiation is a joint decision-making process in which both sides can exercise a veto to prevent the joint decision, by walking away. That process centres on efforts to influence the location of a settlement point in a potential zone of agreement that neither party can identify, because each has only imperfect information about the preferences of the other.[1] In short, a negotiation is a supremely political event, and it must be assessed against political criteria, in the first instance. We offer conclusions about the economics of the bargain later.

In a situation of high uncertainty, the parties to a negotiation offer and demand concessions in an effort to locate the zone of agreement, or bargaining range, and then to maximize their gains within it, without provoking the other party to exercise its veto over a joint settlement by walking away from the table. Whether concessions are excessive, or demands too modest, is difficult for the negotiating parties themselves to gauge until a deal is struck, and even then uncertainties remain about how far one could, or should, have gone. The art of the deal lies in pushing the other party close to the edge of its acceptance range, but not over, since that would produce a veto and no agreement. The problem lies in knowing the location of that edge, knowledge that can only come, in part, from the learning that occurs during the negotiation process itself. Judgements about what is excessive, and what modest, are deeply coloured by that process, and second-guessing is difficult without being there.

A judgement about whether Canada was out-negotiated is made difficult as well because it must take into account factors other than negotiating conduct that affect outcomes. In the free trade negotiations, there were a number of these conditioning factors that must be kept in mind when judging the agreement. In the first place, negotiating a comprehensive Canadian-American free trade agreement was an unprecedented task of tremendous complexity. Even the chief negotiators were learning on the job. The Mulroney government committed significant resources to the task and its management, and it is unlikely that more could have been done on this score. In fact, the elaborate facilities and large TNO bureaucracy may have worked to Canada's disadvantage, leaving little doubt in American minds that free trade was the biggest deal going in Canada. This encouraged the U.S. to play out the string as long as it did, knowing the Canadians would be reluctant to put the negotiations at risk by digging in their heels and refusing to make further concessions. The relative imbalance in the power of the two countries was another factor that fundamentally affected the outcome of the negotiations, and about which skilful Canadian conduct could only do so much. Finally, and related to the asymmetry in power between the two countries, was the plain fact that Canada was the *demandeur* in the negotiations, the party most anxious for an agreement, and both sides knew it. Complexity, asymmetry, and its role as *demandeur* were characteristics of the negotiating situation over which Canada had limited control. Their influence on the outcome, independent of the skill of Canada's negotiators, is difficult to determine, making a judgement about whether Canada was out-negotiated, or was simply a victim of circumstance, equally difficult.

Nevertheless, our task demands a political assessment of Canada's conduct of the negotiations and the outcome that was achieved. Keeping in mind the limits to judgement outlined above, we can set out a number of political criteria for making such an assessment. First, we can look to the negotiating *process* itself, essentially asking who had to move, most frequently and furthest, to reach agreement. A second criterion for assessment focuses on the *agenda* of issues under negotiation, asking which party, on balance, secured more of its own agenda in the agreement. Finally, we can look to the *goals* with which the parties began the negotiations and ask which came closer to securing its goals.

Process: Peter Murphy's strategy in the negotiations, whether by necessity or design, was to keep Simon Reisman coming, making Reisman lay out his positions on the issues of interest to the U.S., while denying the Canadian any movement at all on those on which

Murphy did not want to deal. While Murphy's approach was partly a result of a slow start-up and meagre resources, it was more a reflection of deliberate strategic planning, especially his determination to preserve bargaining room in order to keep important domestic interests on side. But Reisman had never negotiated with anyone like Murphy, and he was deeply frustrated by the experience. Reisman gave vent to his frustration, repeatedly, and Canadian contempt for the chief U.S. negotiator became all too apparent, and was deeply resented by other members of the U.S. negotiating team. But through it all, the Canadians did not fundamentally alter their approach to the negotiations. They continued to lay all of the elements of a big deal on the table, convinced that they could bring the Americans on side.

Was Murphy's strategy successful? It is a fact that the negotiations very nearly ran out of time on the fast-track clock because he kept playing out the string on Reisman; a non-agreement was narrowly avoided. It is also a fact that Murphy had conceded very little to Reisman by the time of the Canadian walkout, while he had on the table the essential elements of a continental energy agreement plus some principles that would govern an investment regime. Canada, on the other hand, had little to show for its elaborate preparations and 15 long months of negotiation. In terms of the task he had set himself, Murphy's strategy had been successful: few important concessions had been made to the Canadians. From his own point of view, Murphy had done his job. When Baker faced Burney in the star chamber on that weekend in October, the concessions were still there for the treasury secretary to make. Reisman had received little in return for his willingness to deal with the Americans on their issues.

On the other hand, Canada recovered on the process following the suspension of talks and during the October weekend. Burney, fully backed by Reisman, finally insisted on American movement before Canada would strike a deal, and he stubbornly held to that position. Baker tried repeatedly to persuade the Canadians to continue to come along, both in the talks leading up to the resumption of negotiations and in the star chamber itself. There were some in the Canadian group, Allan Gotlieb in particular, who wanted to take what the U.S. was offering and run with it, happy to get an agreement. Burney refused to be played by Baker, however, and he succeeded in convincing the Americans that Canada preferred no deal to the one the U.S. was offering. But the Canadians were already behind in the process by this time, and Burney was holding out to achieve a minimally acceptable outcome on the trade remedies issue, the key Canadian demand.

Agenda: Chapter 4 demonstrated the difficulties in applying a strict balance sheet to the agreement, assessing whether the internal trade-offs within the deal were good for Canada. And as we pointed out, this type of assessment is flawed by the deficiencies of armchair quarterbacking, because the trade-offs are a reflection of the dynamics of the negotiation process itself, and are difficult to judge independent of the process. Instead of trying to add up a balance sheet, we can look at the agenda of issues under negotiation, and compare the relative success of the two countries in securing the inclusion of their respective issues in the agreement, or in excluding issues where this was the intent, and whether over the opposition of the other country. We can also note respective gains and losses associated with the inclusions or exclusions, but we make no judgement, at this stage, of the economics of these items, deferring this consideration to our assessment of the economics of the bargain.

This evaluation can begin with those issues that both Canada and the U.S. wanted to include. The tariff provides the foundation for any free trade agreement, and both countries had the removal of tariffs on their agenda. They successfully negotiated their elimination according to a phased schedule, which requires both countries to move to zero at the same rate. Since Canadian tariffs were, on average, 50 per cent higher, Canada has to reduce its rates at a faster pace than the U.S. While many saw energy as an American issue, it was actually a shared agenda item as well, with Canada seeking secure access for provincial energy exports, and the U.S. protection against any repeat of the National Energy Program. The FTA gives the U.S. more energy security under the proportionality clause and prohibits differential pricing for domestic supplies and exports, providing effective guarantees against any more NEPs. Canada delivered on its promises to the Western producing provinces, and to Quebec for exports of hydro-electricity.

The negotiating agenda also included a second set of issues that the U.S. brought to the table, but Canada was not opposed to their inclusion. Provisions concerning the general service sector, which the U.S. had carried on the agenda, were included in the final agreement, but changes to the status quo were modest. In the related area of financial services, the Canadians were prepared to negotiate the issue, but they objected to its treatment as a separate agenda item. The U.S. prevailed, however, and the Canadians agreed to give up their greater edge of protection in this sector. Finally, the agenda included the Americans' issue of intellectual property, but it was excluded from the final agreement.

Also on the negotiating agenda were a number of disputed issues, which one country wanted to negotiate and the other wanted to exclude. On the American agenda were the issues of wine and distilled spirits, the Auto Pact, and investment. The U.S. had long been exercised about Canadian barriers to the import of American wines, and the free trade negotiations gave them an opportunity to press on this agenda item. They were successful in negotiating the removal of measures related to the internal sale and distribution of the products of U.S. wineries. However, Canada was able to limit American gains on the issue by grandfathering existing measures that protected the Canadian beer industry. The U.S. also insisted from the start of negotiations that the Auto Pact was on the table, and, over initial Canadian opposition, that is where it ended up. Although the agreement entrenches the pact, it does so without mention of investment guarantees in the Canadian industry and without the Canadian duty remission schemes that gave Canada some policy leverage. Investment was another American item that the Canadians attempted to keep off the agenda, at least until the U.S. was ready to deal on trade remedies. In the agreement, Canada conceded some of its powers to regulate foreign investment, but secured recognition of those that it retained.

On the counterpart Canadian agenda were the issues of government procurement and trade remedies, as well as the desire to exclude culture and agricultural supply management issues. Procurement was an important issue for Canada because of the size of the American procurement market. Although the U.S. agreed to discuss the issue, in fact they did not want an agreement. The Canadians were successful in their efforts to include procurement in the final agreement, although it was only the smallest of deals, one that gave Canada only modest gains in access to the American procurement market. The U.S. strongly opposed the inclusion of the second key Canadian agenda item of trade remedies. The issue was not included in the final agreement. Instead, the two agreed to postpone the subsidies–trade remedies issue to further negotiations, and to institute a temporary system of binational panels to review the application of national trade remedy laws. This outcome was not what the Canadians had been after, but it was deemed to be enough. Canada was basically successful, on the other hand, in keeping supply management and cultural issues out of the agreement.

On the two shared agenda items, the Canadians agreed to move faster on tariffs and further on energy. On those issues that the U.S. brought to the table unopposed by Canada, it achieved its agenda on financial services but got only small changes in general services, and no agreement at all on intellectual property. On disputed issues, however, the U.S. succeeded in carrying its agenda. On wine, automobiles, and investment, the Americans prevailed, securing an agreement with Canada on each issue. Canada did not enjoy the same consistency on its agenda. Agreement was reached on government procurement, but the trade remedies issue was put off for further negotiation, and the Canadians agreed to a temporary dispute-settlement procedure instead. Culture and supply management were on the plus side of the Canadian agenda scorecard. On balance, the U.S. was more successful than Canada at securing agreement on the agenda items that it brought to the table and preventing agreement on those brought by Canada. In the battle of agendas, advantage goes to the Americans, though the decision is less clear cut than for the negotiation process.

Goals: At the conclusion of the negotiations, Simon Reisman claimed that the Canadians had "snookered" the U.S. While Reisman's hyperbole was in character, and probably the result of the frustration he had suffered for so long in dealing with Peter Murphy, it was also intended to counteract criticism of the deal by anti-free traders. And the claims by opponents of free trade that the Canadians had sold the farm were certainly equally exaggerated. For their part, the Americans, wisely, were quiet about the outcome, except for Clayton Yeutter's remark that the deal could have been done six months sooner had it not been for Reisman. To get beyond exaggerated claims, we need to base an assessment of the outcome on the goals that the two countries were seeking to achieve through the negotiations, and ask which one came closer to attaining its goals.

Throughout the extended negotiating period, Canada and the U.S. were pursuing a myriad of objectives, related to the individual issues under discussion. Our interest here, however, lies in the more fundamental goals that each was attempting to reach through the free trade negotiations. The principal Canadian goal was to achieve secure and enhanced access to the American market for Canada's exports. Enhancement meant improving the entry of Canadian producers to the U.S. market, and this would be done by removing barriers to trade. Canada also went into the negotiations looking for relief from harassment from U.S. trade remedy actions. To obtain this relief, they wanted to establish limits on American use of anti-dumping and countervailing duties. As stated by the prime minister in the House of Commons in March 1987:

Our highest priority is to have an agreement that ends the threat to Canadian industry from U.S. protectionists who harass and restrict our exports through the misuse of trade remedy laws. Let me leave no doubt that first, a new regime on trade remedy laws must be part of the agreement.[2]

The key American goal in the negotiations related directly to Canadian energy and investment policies. The U.S. was determined to use the negotiations to ensure that they would never again be a target of discriminatory actions like those embodied in the NEP and FIRA. In the final agreement, the U.S. achieved its goal. The FTA creates a continental energy market, eliminating discriminatory pricing and supply practices. The Americans also achieved significant reductions in the regulation of foreign investment, although they had to acknowledge Canada's right to regulate investment in certain respects.

Canada, for its part, achieved increased access to the U.S. market for its exporters through the elimination of many tariff and non-tariff barriers to trade between the two countries. However, for the goal of secure access, the Canadians were left to decide if the Chapter 19 solution to the trade remedies issue, the temporary system of binational panels to review the application of national trade remedy laws, provided sufficient grounds for agreement. The decision was truly a difficult one for the Canadians, and their hesitation was not a negotiating ploy to disparage the U.S. offer, because it was so far from what Canada had been seeking to achieve originally. This difficulty suggests that it was the minimally acceptable outcome for Canada on its top priority issue. In negotiating parlance, the Canadians had arrived at their reservation outcome or bottom line, the least they could take on the issue politically and still make a deal. It appears, therefore, that Canada had dropped to its bottom line on trade remedies, and had been forced to concede quite a bit to get there. In terms of the achievement of key goals, advantage goes to the Americans again.

Despite Canada's commitment of significant resources to the task, and the elaborate preparations that were undertaken, the Americans appear to have come out on top in these free trade negotiations, at least according to the political criteria we set out — who had to move most to reach agreement, who secured more of their agenda, and who came closer to achieving their key goals. An important reason for this is that at the end of the day, Canada simply wanted a deal more than the U.S. In part this was because the decision to seek the negotiations was more difficult for the Canadians, and the government was subject to intense scrutiny, and criticism, during the negotiation process. It was hard to contemplate going through that ordeal without getting an agreement in the end. Conceivably, the very existence of a second term for the Mulroney government was at stake as well. The U.S. also had an incentive to get a deal, of course, particularly concerning its future capacity to strike agreements with other trading blocs. But U.S. incentives were not as great as those for Canada. And, even more important, neither was the cost of failure as great. As a result of this difference, Canada was more disposed to take risks, primarily in the form of making concessions, to achieve an agreement, while the U.S. had less incentive to take similar risks, and therefore was more willing to withhold concessions.[3]

The way the Canadians structured their brief worked against them as well. Because the free trade initiative was seen in Canada primarily as a means to secure market access and deal with the problem of American protectionism, U.S. trade remedy law had to be the key issue for Canada. Reisman attempted to approach it first through national treatment, then through the concept of a subsidies regime. The U.S. insisted from the beginning that its trade remedy laws were not on the table, but the Canadians kept pressing, convinced that the U.S. would eventually see the light. The Americans remained obdurate, however, and as a result Canada's negotiating energies were concentrated on an issue on which there appeared to be very little room for American movement. Any concessions that could be wrung from the U.S. on trade remedies would come at a very high price. There had been some assessment by the Canadian negotiators of whether a change in the application of American trade remedies to Canada was possible, and of what it would cost Canada to achieve such a change. But as the string was played out, a stubborn single-mindedness set in, and the Canadians stuck to the same game plan until the final walkout.

Reisman's role: After the free trade battle was over, the TNO split into two camps, divided in their view of whether Simon Reisman or Derek Burney should receive the lion's share of credit for the FTA. One group sided with Burney, largely on the grounds that Reisman's belligerent and stubborn one-track approach to the negotiations had helped to create the impasse and that Burney, more than anyone else, had picked up the pieces and assembled a deal. But Reisman's supporters will have none of this. Not only do they argue that the main contours of the agreement took shape in the months of hard slogging that preceded the breakdown in negotiations, but they insist that Reisman was side by side with Burney as they held out against American pressure late on the Saturday of the Washington weekend. Reisman's supporters bridle at the portrait of him as a forlorn figure, pacing the corridors at Treasury while others did the deal.

Anyone who has worked for, or with, Simon Reisman has inevitably encountered both bombast and charm. He is that seemingly rare thing, an unabashedly passionate Canadian. Reisman is the same man in private and in public. He has no compunction about browbeating those who disagree with his views, whether it is a cowering TNO staffer in front of colleagues, a *Toronto Star* reporter in the midst of a media scrum, a Trade minister in the presence of staff members, or Peter Murphy in a formal negotiating session. What you see is what you get, and this can be more than a little wearing. But he also generates a fierce loyalty, even among those who have been on the receiving end of his sharp tongue.

It must also be said that the Reisman persona was exactly suited, although perhaps too exactly, to the intense competitiveness of the politics of the free trade issue. In this three-ring circus, Reisman knew from the outset that he would be locked in combat, not just with the Americans, but with other players in the Ottawa policy arena as well. Those he could not out-muscle, he would have to negotiate with. As a result, there quickly developed in TNO an aggressive confidence that frequently made relations with other departments tense, especially when the lack of progress in bilateral negotiations produced a siege mentality in TNO, a feeling that its positions must be defended at any cost. Even within TNO, Reisman was often forced to negotiate with members of his own staff to resolve conflicts. In this high-conflict Ottawa environment, the pressures towards compromise to keep the peace, with ministers, the provinces, or other departments, were intense, and Reisman undoubtedly had to be hard-headed to prevent excessive compromise in his (Canada's) position. A less combative person might not have survived politically.

It should also be clear that Reisman was not the only fighter in this arena, and some of the others had personalities almost as prickly. For example, the relationship between Reisman and Trade Minister Patricia Carney was, in a word, poisonous. Their aides anticipated meetings between the two with dread, because of the almost certain prospect of high-decibel conflict. Sylvia Ostry was another thorn in Reisman's side, this time pricking from inside TNO. They were longtime colleagues in the Ottawa mandarinate, and Ostry had been moved into the TNO from External Affairs to take charge of Canadian participation in the GATT round of multilateral trade negotiations, but reporting to Reisman. Predictably, turf battles erupted between the two, often with genuine differences over policy at stake. The most contentious involved Canada's agricultural marketing boards, which Ostry wanted to offer up for elimination in the multilateral talks. Pressing Reisman to be consistent and do the same in the bilateral negotiations, Ostry found herself in a fierce confrontation. Reisman knew that the marketing boards were untouchable if the political coalition in support of free trade was to be preserved, and he dealt a knockout blow to Ostry. Marketing boards would be off limits in both sets of negotiations.

Reisman's deputy at TNO, Gordon Ritchie, was also a good match for his combative boss. Ritchie's own no-nonsense reputation around Ottawa was one reason why he was recruited by Reisman, and the deputy quickly became the chief negotiator's right-hand man. Throughout the negotiations, Ritchie probably had the best handle on the FTA, with a detailed knowledge of both the individual issues and the connections between them, and afterwards he became one of its most articulate and thoughtful advocates. Ritchie and Reisman saw eye to eye on many things, but where they disagreed their strong personalities often produced intense conflict. This was particularly true over issues related to who ought to have access to Reisman himself, with Ritchie preferring a vertical structure that required all communications to pass through him on the way to Reisman. When the two disagreed, Reisman usually prevailed, but frequently not without a fight with his strong-willed deputy.

While Simon Reisman's personal style and the strategy he chose to pursue contributed to Canada's problems at the negotiating table, there is no doubt that he was a pivotal player in the free trade story, and his role was critical to the success of the venture. From the beginning, he saw free trade as a deal made for Canada, and he came out of retirement to make it his personal mission. Reisman supplied the original breadth of vision for the conduct of the negotiations, and he managed them for almost two years under intense political pressure and public scrutiny. In the end he was forced to step aside so that others could do the deal, but in doing so, and admitting that he could not bring it off, he put an agreement above his own vanity.

Could Canada have conducted the negotiations differently in order to avoid being politically out-negotiated? In important respects, the Canadian room for manoeuvre was limited. The relative power of the two countries and the fact that Canada was the *demandeur* in the negotiations meant that the U.S. could hold out longer than Canada to force a deal on American terms. Could the Canadians have done things differently to counter this advantage? The answer is yes, but only if they were prepared to undertake some basic alterations in their approach to the negotiations, such as the following: 1) refrain from laying all of the elements of a big deal on the table for the Americans to look over, instead holding back issues and deliberately matching the U.S. pace of non-negotiation; 2) make a very hard-headed assessment of the likelihood of U.S. movement on the trade remedies issue, and the probable cost of that movement in the form of Canadian concessions, and continuously reassess as a means to structure and engineer the trade-offs that would eventually have to be made; and 3) most important, accept the increased risk of non-agreement by matching the U.S. refusal to negotiate, and take the risk sooner rather than later.[4]

Why did Canada play the hand it did? To a large extent, the approach resulted from the extremely difficult task the Canadians had set themselves. The Mulroney government went into the negotiations looking for relief from American trade remedy actions. When the softwood lumber issue blew up in the middle of the negotiations, the effect was to make the trade remedy issue even more central to Canada's approach to the negotiations. Secure access was the mandate given Reisman and his team by the government. It was their job to persuade the Americans to deal with an issue the U.S. insisted was non-negotiable, and they tried to do this the best way they knew how, under the circumstances. If the Canadians can be faulted, it is for refusing to give up their belief that the Americans would see the light and come around on trade remedies. By continuing to negotiate up to the eleventh hour, Reisman had put Canada in a very difficult position. If the Americans could be persuaded to deal, there would be little time left on the fast-track clock to move them along very far or to put together the elements of the kind of big deal favoured by the Canadians, improving the prospects for the limited agreement preferred by the U.S. It was late in the summer of 1987 before Canada confronted the non-agreement alternative head-on, and this was very late in the day. But when Burney finally made it clear that there was no prospect of an agreement without some American movement on trade remedies, Baker told his people to be creative. This demonstrated that the Americans could be moved. The Canadian stand had come very late, however, and there was time to secure only a little movement from the U.S. In the final analysis, Canada ended up paying a high price to achieve a minimally acceptable outcome on the issue.

THE ECONOMICS OF THE NEGOTIATION

It is important to assess the politics of the FTA negotiation because it can provide important lessons for Canada as it faces further negotiations, both domestic and international, in the 1990s. But the FTA bargain must be judged against its economic rationale as well.[5] Here, the assessment is not of how the negotiators fared in terms of process, agenda, and goals. Instead, we want to assess whether the agreement is likely to produce net gains, improving the economies of both countries. We should also ask how the deal stacks up against the alternative economic policies that were available to meet the situation that faced Canada in the mid-1980s. Finally, an economic assessment must ask how well the agreement positions Canada to meet the economic challenges of the 1990s?

On the question of mutual economic gain, most economists have judged the agreement to be a good one, in which both sides are winners and the distribution of gains and losses is secondary to the overall benefits that will accrue to both countries. The fact that Canada and the U.S. have agreed to commit themselves to the removal of mutually harmful barriers to trade is viewed as the most positive aspect of the agreement. This judgement rests on the argument that benefits have in the past flowed from the liberalization of trade, through both bilateral and multilateral agreements. Still lacking evidence drawn from the actual operation of the FTA, Canadians must rely heavily on mainstream economic thought to provide an assessment of its probable outcome for their country. In this sense, what was true of the decision to negotiate free trade remains the case in assessing the outcome of those negotiations. And mainstream economics maintains that liberalized trade is basically a sound policy, that free trade represents a continuation of past policy, not its abrogation, and that it was necessary because Canada faced a crisis in economic productivity. This productivity crisis was not just in relation to the United States, but also to other trading blocs and newly industrializing countries, especially the aggressive Asian economies.

As indicated in earlier chapters, several economic studies had shown that Canada would gain, in terms of both economic growth and competitiveness, from free trade with the U.S. These studies differed on the magnitude of the gains, but they all pointed in the same positive direction. The Finance Department was also persuaded to support the free trade initiative because the traditional levers of fiscal and monetary policy were, in a practical sense, less readily available for use than they had been in previous decades. This was especially true for fiscal policy, where the huge federal deficit had persuaded Michael Wilson in 1984 that he could not spend his way to renewed prosperity.

While most economists are instinctive supporters of free trade, some did argue from the outset that although free trade is desirable, the country that pursues it should pave the way by ensuring first that its various strong and weak industries are ready for it.[6] This means that some kind of industrial policy ought to either precede or accompany free trade. But this presented a real dilemma for policy makers, because another significant body of influential economic opinion in the mid-1980s argued that such prior "getting ready to get ready" industrial policies were just not feasible for Canada. There was no consensus for them politically, and the experience with industrial policy initiatives in the 1960s and 1970s did not leave a credible trail of achievements on which to build an alternative "faith" to that of the free trade option. The GATT multilateral option was also rejected, for the reasons set out in Chapter 3. Only the unavoidable cold shower of free trade would sufficiently change economic behaviour, it was argued.

We also conclude from our examination of the free trade saga that Canada should, on balance, benefit economically from the FTA even though it was politically out-pointed. The numerous improvements in access to the U.S. market will help Canada's economy. But these gains, by their nature, will only emerge over the medium to long term. They deal with changing the basic production structure of the economy, and this effect clearly cannot be properly gauged in the first two years of the implementation of the agreement.[7] The serious job losses that occurred in 1990–91 must be viewed in this context. While some loss had to be expected as a result of economic adjustment in the wake of free trade, and while losses of that magnitude were clearly a cause for concern, it would be wrong to attribute most of the problem to the FTA, or even to the psychology of a new era of free trade. In the first place, the largest losses occurred in sectors, such as transportation and the public service, that were excluded from the FTA. Second, Canadian losses did not represent American gains in any overall sense. The United States also experienced increased unemployment during the same period. By far the largest proportion of the job losses in Canada were caused by the 1990–91 recession, by high interest rates, and by the increase in the value of the Canadian dollar.

The effects of the two-year marginal reduction in tariff protection under the FTA are simply dwarfed by the consequences of these economic and policy conditions for Canada's most vulnerable industries. However, the sharp rise in interest rates and the dollar following the conclusion of the agreement does inevitably raise the question of whether any side deal was made, as part of the free trade bargain, by which Canada agreed to increase the value of its dollar, through interest rate hikes. Some American politicians had urged that this be a condition of the deal, and some in Canada have speculated that this might be the case, but our research does not indicate that such a bargain was struck. Canadian trade negotiators deny that any such arrangement was officially suggested, or agreed to, and we have no evidence to dispute that position. There is no disputing the fact, however, that high Canadian interest rates, and the related appreciation in the value of the dollar, account for the largest part of the jobs lost in the wake of the FTA.

For the longer term, the potential for Canadian gains from free trade is critically dependent on four factors, and these have only a very uncertain status in the early 1990s. The most important condition influencing any future economic gains from the FTA resides in the Canadian business community itself, where literally thousands of astute business decisions will have to be made regarding investment, product development and marketing. However, these decisions will depend, in part, on the presence of the remaining factors, which are largely the responsibility of governments. For it is governments that must create supportive macroeconomic and industrial policies to encourage economic growth through gains from trade. If appropriate interest rates or adequate levels of research and development expenditure by governments as well as firms, to name but two examples, are not ensured, then much of the potential for gain from the FTA will be lost. Another important area of responsibility lies in the critical sphere of social and labour market policy. Labour, the working poor, and threatened communities will have little confidence in their ability to adjust to a more competitive world unless more generous human investment is provided, and delivered through institutions they trust.[8] And finally there is a basic need to ensure national unity, partly by taking deliberate steps to heal the scars of the free trade battle. It is the last of these factors to which we give special attention, and which, in turn, is bound up in several political aspects of the FTA event as a whole.

THE POLITICAL EFFECTS OF THE FREE TRADE EVENT

For Canadians, free trade was much more than a trade agreement with the United States. It was a major political event in Canada, involving the decision to seek free trade, the negotiation of the agreement, the battle of the two nationalist visions, and the 1988 election. The political effects of the FTA event are manifold. They include perceptions about the legitimacy of the process of the FTA decision itself, as well as its possible effects on the capacity of future governments in Canada to make policy. The effects also reside at the psychological level for every Canadian, in terms of what we have learned about the current and future role of government, the place of the federal government in the Canadian Confederation, and the integration of Canada into the continental North American market.

Nor can the effects of the FTA event be viewed in isolation. They must be gauged in combination with subsequent developments on other policy fronts, especially the Meech Lake constitutional crisis that began in 1987 and reached a peak in the summer of 1990. For many, the effect of these two events, free trade and Meech Lake, is to substantially alter national political life in Canada. The net mix of gains and losses in policy capacity inherent in the FTA will probably result in a transfer of power to influence the course of the nation from government to the market, and the national or commonly shared character of the Canadian political experience will be diminished as a result. This is because Canadians to a significant extent see themselves as a political community primarily through what the state does, and how they are represented in it. This reduction in federal authority is reinforced by the national disarray attending the failure to ratify the Meech Lake Accord, placing sharply increased strains on the fabric of an integrated Canada. Whatever other developments may flow from the Meech Lake imbroglio, it has made the federal government's task of nation building much more difficult. This will, without a doubt, offset some of the beneficial effects that were hoped for from the FTA.

Legitimacy: With respect to the legitimacy of the free trade decision, we concluded that among Canadian voters there was neither a majority for nor against the FTA. The 1988 election did, however, produce a mandate for the FTA in the parliamentary majoritarian sense. Moreover, Canadians cannot be said to have avoided debate on the issue, if not on all the details of the deal, then certainly on the competing values and visions involved. In this general sense, the FTA decision can be said to have been democratically legitimate. But it was much more divisive than it had to be. There is also the related issue of whether business interests "bought" the 1988 election through extravagant financing of the pro-free trade side. On this we conclude that while business certainly had a disproportionate influence in the election, it would exaggerate that influence to conclude that big business had purchased the electoral outcome.

In the past, business interests have always spread their financial support to the two free enterprise parties. What was different this time was that business trusted only one, partly as a result of John Turner's leadership of the Liberal Party. And it is paradoxical that Turner, who was known for most of his later political career as a "Bay Street boy," should preside over the party's loss of most of its core business financial support. A more responsive Liberal party position on free trade, perhaps supporting some aspects of the deal while rejecting others, that better reflected the overall opinion that actually prevailed among Liberal rank and file, federally and pro-vincially, might have allowed the Liberals to fare better politically. But the Turner Liberals rejected this course, and instead took a desperate no-holds-barred anti-free trade position. And while a more moderate Liberal position could have reduced some of the divisiveness of the debate, the bitterness was also clearly a result of the strategy adopted by the Mulroney government.[9]

Policy capacity: A broader array of political effects of the FTA can be seen in its impact on policy capacity. We concluded in Chapter 11 that the effects on policy capacity are likely to vary across policy fields. This is one reason why people can reach different judge-ments about the overall value, or cost, of the FTA. Broadly speaking, we see gains in policy capacity in the fields of trade and, potentially, in social policy, and losses in industrial and energy policy capacity. These judgements can only be made by looking at specific elements of the FTA, gauging the lessons to be learned from past successes and failures in using policy instruments, and forecasting how political interests might be mobilized in the future. This mobiliza-tion will be based, in turn, on the kinds of political lessons that are drawn from the FTA experience by the two coalitions that battled over the free trade issue, as well as by other important institutions in Canadian political life.

Political learning: The FTA event was beneficial for Canadians' basic political understanding of themselves, because it compelled them to confront their past and future in ways that might not have been possible otherwise. Even without the free trade negotiation,

however, Canada eventually would have been forced to face growing continentalism and globalization, and the need for trade liberalization. The FTA event forced the collective Canadian psyche to
begin to deal more concretely with some of the realities of the
modern global marketplace, particularly Canada's absolute dependence on trade and its vulnerability if it does not wean itself from
its historical, and even psychological, dependence on natural resources. It also showed Canadians how much they value their social
policy differences with the U.S. as a defining national characteristic.
All of these realities had been stated before, but it is doubtful that
they had ever been brought home to Canadians quite so forcefully.
In this sense, the FTA provided an important, and beneficial, political learning event for Canada. Whether this will translate into a
Canadian decision to do something about economic competitiveness or continental drift remains to be seen.

This is not to argue that the political lessons about integrated
markets have been uniformly learned, or are fully understood
among various segments of Canadian political opinion. As Richard
Gwyn has recently suggested, Canadians, probably for the first
time in the post–World War II period, do feel themselves to be
psychologically "at risk."[10] The inherent comfortableness of
Canada's post-war position as a prosperous, socially progressive
country hitched to the world's most dynamic economic superpower is now jigsawed out of all recognition. Entire countries of
course do not "learn" about new realities in any conventional sense,
because the nation is not an aggregated version of the classroom. If
learning occurs, it is often uneven, and frequently jarring and
divisive. It is in this sense that the FTA event, or something like it,
may have been inevitable. The Macdonald Commission argued
that the country needed to do something to deal with its declining
international competitiveness, and suggested that free trade would
do the job. Had the FTA not been instituted, some alternative would
have had to be invented to force Canada to face the economic and
social future.

If some change was necessary, then we must ask whether an

alternative approach to free trade could have been devised, one that would have been less divisive, but still salutary for learning about the economic realities facing Canada. The answer is a qualified yes. We have already concluded that the FTA was democratically legitimate in a majoritarian parliamentary sense. There was also a considerable consultative exercise launched with interest groups and provinces that is to the credit of the Mulroney Conservatives, certainly when compared to the closed shop of previous GATT negotiations. But it cannot be said that the Conservatives were as open in their approach to the Canadian people as they could have been. Despite the fact that trade policy is certainly no more complex than tax policy, there was no effort to sketch out for the Canadian public, in a white paper or similar process, what the basic problems, issues and trade negotiation options were. Adopting a process similar to the one the government followed on the reform of tax policy obviously offered no guarantee against divisiveness over the FTA. But a similar process might well have made a difference in overall public understanding of free trade, had the government been willing to take Canadians, rather than just Canadian interest groups and provinces, into their confidence. The usual counterargument to such exercises during international negotiations is that a process that is too public will only give advantage to the other country. But in the end, the costs of a relatively open consultative process would probably have been less than the price that was paid in the loss of national unity as a result of the acrimonious debate over the government's *fait accompli*.

DIVIDED NATIONALISMS

In our account of the key political dimensions of the FTA event, we placed special emphasis on the division between two nationalist visions, one state-led and the other imbued with a confident entrepreneurial competitive spirit. In the immediate wake of the FTA battle, the differences remain strong and continue to divide Canada. These divisions will remain until both sides learn some lessons about the validity of the other's claims and values. One nationalist vision, centred in the Pro Canada Network, the NDP and major elements of the Liberal Party, sees Canadian nationalism in terms of strong powers for the state, especially for the federal government. This coalition of opinion views the FTA as a danger to Canada, even if some concede that certain economic benefits will occur. In the FTA debate, we portrayed this coalition as being politically on the run. Accustomed to being at the leading edge of progressive change, they found themselves on the defensive in the 1980s, trapped by a rhetoric and an understanding of markets that was significantly, but not totally, out of date.

Their rhetorical emphasis on sovereignty and fears of harmonization has only limited validity, because in important respects they do not fit easily into a world of growing interdependence where a country's policy capacity varies by policy field. But their instincts were quite right when they criticized the Mulroney government for failing to think in a more concerted way about what the proper role of the state ought to be in the 1990s and beyond. As a regional coalition, with its power base in Quebec and Western Canada, and as a group of political conservatives suspicious of government, the Mulroney Conservatives were not equipped to think carefully about the role of government in general, and the federal government in particular. By this we mean that their core political urge was to favour markets and reduce the role of government, especially the federal government. This in itself is a legitimate view to hold, and many of the Conservative instincts led to sensible policies for Canada. But this is not the same as trying to sort out, systematically, what powers and capacities a federal government ought to retain even in a more market-driven world. There is little evidence that enough of such thought occurred in Tory Ottawa, where the urge to dismantle and deal away has often been too palpable and ingrained. A similar view prevailed in the government's approach to Meech Lake, and on the combined effects of Meech Lake and the FTA.[11] It simply was not in the Tory mentality to worry about such things.

The second nationalist vision was anchored in the business-led pro-free trade coalition, which was centred in the Canadian Alliance for Trade and Job Opportunities and led by the Business Council on National Issues and the Canadian Manufacturers' Association. We have described this as a new form of entrepreneurial nationalism, to contrast it with the older, 1960s-style of continentalism. While greater continental integration is undoubtedly one of the consequences of the FTA, there was a key difference from the 1960s in the degree to which the business community expressed their own brand of confident Canadian capacity to compete. While some of this newly expressed nationalism was doubtless bravado that disguised fear about how to compete in a rapidly changing world, a larger part represented a genuine conviction of confidence, especially by Western Canadian and Quebec business leaders, but also by small business in Ontario. This confidence was due to the fact that in the post–Tokyo Round period, the number of Canadian firms, especially within the membership of the CMA, engaged in international trade had increased significantly, and they were eager to move into expanded markets, knowing full well that it meant more competition.

The question in the post-FTA era is whether this new-found competitive nationalism is solid enough to deliver the promised economic benefits of free trade, or whether it was mainly rhetorical. Although the FTA represented the agenda of the business community, actual political leadership on the issue was confined to a narrower base within the established corporate sector and among major business interest groups. And the need to maintain a strong united front required that doubts about the ability of Canadian business to meet the challenge posed by free trade be suppressed. Nonetheless, the reality is that the primary responsibility for implementing the free trade agreement will fall to Canadian business firms, through the thousands of separate investment and product development choices they will make.

If the blind spot of the anti-free trade coalition was its failure to understand markets, then pro-free traders in the business community failed to appreciate the role of government and social policy in modern economic prosperity. Caught up in the rhetorical virtues of liberalized trade, deregulation, and privatization, business, with support from the Mulroney Conservatives, has engaged in the fine art of government-bashing to a point where their own interests may be in jeopardy. Canada's future competitive capacity depends on a role for government, both in establishing overall economic framework policies and in providing supportive industrial, social, and adjustment policies. But there has not been much subtlety in the business critique of government; nor has there been much foresight in attempting to identify what constitutes an appropriate realignment of functions between state powers and market forces. As a result, less room has been left for government to play its required role.

We have already argued that Canada, as a smaller, open trading country, will need some form of enhanced industrial policy as a complement to liberalized trade. We also suggested that better and more generous social and labour-market policies will be essential for continued economic prosperity. Development of these policies will require government to mobilize consensus under far more difficult circumstances than it has faced in the past. This is due partly to the attacks on the role of government that were mounted during the free trade debate, and partly to the antagonisms between pro- and anti-free trade forces that were generated by the debate. To adapt to free trade, Canadian business will need to reconcile itself to some of the forms of government partnership it opposed so vigorously in the past. And opponents of free trade will have to be persuaded to re-engage in the policy process from which they were so sharply alienated by the alliance between business and government, and by the free trade decision itself. Successful policy adaptation will require both sides of the divided nationalisms to step back from the inflated rhetoric that was fashioned to fight the free trade debate. Pro-free trade forces are going to have to learn to live with a role for government, and anti-free trade forces will have to learn how to help make free trade work.

THE FUTURE SHAPE OF THE
CANADIAN POLITICAL COMMUNITY

There are many who doubt, either from despair or resignation, whether the two brands of nationalism can be forged in the 1990s into a newly energized Canadian political community. Those who despair see the battle as having been essentially lost. Canada will be submerged in a sea of continental pressures, subject to a harsh array of market values. Those who are resigned simply paint a picture of a world in which the centralist and sovereign nation-state is everywhere under pressure, from both international interdependence globally and regional decentralization nationally. What is happening in Europe, and in Asia, is also occurring in North America. These pressures could cut two different ways on Canada, depending upon whether the country's past is viewed as a weakness or a strength. As the former, Canada's weak national identity, at least relative to the United States, makes it especially vulnerable to forces promoting political disintegration and absorption. Or, alternatively, because the country has been so decentralized and interdependent internationally, Canadians are somehow ahead of their time, already adept at coping with the pressures to which others must now learn to respond.

We can certainly conclude that Ottawa's role in the 1990s and beyond will be different as a consequence of free trade. Whether this role is stronger or weaker, better or worse, depends on how the future policy agenda unfolds, and how we rank political values. Proponents of a strong role for government may take comfort from the aphorism that "the small state is a strong state, but the big weak." If government is a large and ungainly entity, involved in too many activities, as many believe it was in the 1970s and early 1980s, then it may become immobilized, incapable of responding effectively to truly national pan-Canadian concerns. On the other hand, the small state may be a strong state because it retains its nimbleness and its inherent capacity to adapt. It takes on only those functions that it can, and ought to, do well. So a reduced role for government need not be a bad thing, even for supporters of an activist state. However, free trade requires Ottawa to consider its role in deliberate fashion, because the federal government will wither unless it sorts out those roles it ought to play, and can play well, in the face of the internationalist and decentralist pressures that will be unleashed by the FTA and other international trade and political forces.

We can agree with both critics and supporters of the FTA who assert that, on balance, it will result in the decentralization of authority away from the federal government, in favour of the provinces. As we have seen, the deal was essentially the product of a Western Canada–Quebec alliance that was central to Mulroney's political calculus. This coalition sought, and obtained in the FTA, a more decentralized Canada. The impact of the agreement on the distribution of powers favours the provinces in the short term, since it is federal powers that have been most constrained by the key provisions of the deal. In addition, even though the provinces had no seat at the negotiating table, the consultation process created for the negotiations opened the door for a larger provincial role in trade policy in the future.

These decentralizing pressures may, however, be countered in the longer run by other developments, the shape of which cannot be seen clearly at present. First, the FTA itself, coupled with GATT decisions, will probably increase pressures to remove interprovincial trade barriers within Canada. Since these barriers mainly involve provincial powers, their elimination or reduction will help to offset decentralist tendencies. A second counter-pressure may flow from the application of the provisions of the FTA. If practices based on provincial powers are found to be appropriately subject to U.S. countervail actions, the utility of the practices, and the powers on which they are based, will be reduced. Provinces may also learn from the experience, and avoid initiatives that they fear will be countervailed.

Finally, 1960s-style initiatives, like medicare, frequently serve as the baseline for judgements that the FTA will limit Ottawa's capacity to undertake national social programs or other unifying projects.

However, limitations will depend on the policy concerns that are likely to dominate national politics in the 1990s and beyond. Each policy field is different, and the physical and political characteristics of future national projects cannot be anticipated using the simple medicare metaphor, nor can it accurately forecast the constraints that the FTA will impose. A national day care initiative, or a major role for Ottawa on environmental policy or technology training, would not be some simple equivalent of past national projects, even without the FTA. In fact, the federal role in social policy may be enhanced if general social programs are determined to be not subject to countervail in future negotiations. The fate of social policy progress is also critically dependent upon the coalitions that form on both sides of the 49th parallel in support of new initiatives in the 1990s.

The final political effect of the FTA event is undoubtedly that of greater continental, and global, integration. The consultation processes and the dispute settlement mechanisms built into the FTA will institutionalize Canada-U.S. relations to a greater degree than in the past. And in the early 1990s Canada is engaged in two concurrent negotiations to extend the integration of the continent still further — the North American free trade talks with Mexico and the United States, and the bilateral negotiations with the U.S. over subsidies and trade remedies.[12] What lessons does the free trade story offer for these sequels to the FTA? The first is that Canada probably has very little choice but to negotiate. After all, on subsidies it was Canada that pushed the issue forward throughout the FTA negotiations, and although the sequel has been put on hold while multilateral and trilateral talks are under way, it will be difficult to decline should the Americans decide at some point to press ahead with a bilateral subsidies negotiation. As for the North American talks, at a minimum Canada has to be at the table to prevent a bilateral Mexican-American agreement that might be harmful to its position in the all-important U.S. market.

A second lesson suggests that Canada may be more vulnerable in one important respect in both these negotiations than it was in the FTA, and less vulnerable in another respect. In the bilateral negotiations over subsidies, Canada is probably the greater sinner, directly subsidizing more than the U.S., and it will be difficult for Canadian negotiators to trade off a loss of powers here against gains on other issues, as they were able to do in the FTA negotiations. In the trilateral negotiations, Canada will be under pressure to come to terms with the other two, and to do so quickly, in order to avoid a separate bilateral Mexican-American deal and reach agreement in time for elections in the autumn of 1992 in Mexico and the U.S., and possibly in Canada as well. Balanced against these vulnerabilities is the fact that the Mulroney government probably does not need an agreement on either subsidies or North American free trade as much as it needed the FTA. This should mitigate some of the worst effects of the intense pressure to make a deal that marked the FTA experience, and provide negotiators with a much firmer bottom line.

This reduction in pressure may also permit the government to act on another FTA lesson. It is imperative that a Canadian consensus be fashioned for national policies on the order of magnitude of free trade. It is not sufficient to simply force a policy through in the face of intense opposition, because the damage done to the national fabric by the intensity of the conflict may, in the end, exceed the benefits of the policy, and undermine its legitimacy in the bargain. The country must be persuaded, again if necessary, of the benefits of more integrated North American markets, and mechanisms must be devised to enable the government to take Canadians into its confidence to a far greater extent than it did for the FTA. The search for acceptable and workable solutions to Canada's economic problems cannot be divorced from the requirements of national unity and political legitimacy, for all will be necessary if economic and social progress is to occur in the wake of these sequel negotiations as the century ends.

Canadians, and their government, are going to have to come to terms with these issues, because the pressures for greater continental economic integration are not likely to abate. Additional pressure to move towards a North American trading bloc will probably come from the drive to gain collective access to the new super Europe of the 1990s. The development of a North American bloc will doubtless involve a further loss of sovereignty, and it will reinforce Canada's position in the American sphere of influence. But there may be little choice in a world of regional economic blocs, where joining is the price to be paid for continued prosperity. And further North American integration may or may not result in a loss of policy capacity. As we have seen, outcomes will vary greatly across policy fields, and will offer opportunities as well as constraints.

What, in the final analysis, has the free trade decision meant to Canada? Its underlying economic rationale of extending and reinforcing trade liberalization should continue to serve Canada well in a world where risk abounds, and where the old certainties of Canada's status in the post-war world no longer exist to give economic or political comfort. Indeed, they have not existed for some time, and free trade is simply confirmation of the inescapable realities that Canadians should now understand better, even if they cannot agree on appropriate solutions. But further economic gains from the FTA, and from its sequel agreements, depend fundamentally upon getting Canada's policies right in the industrial and social-labour market areas. And these, in turn, must be based on a commitment to national unity and workable political institutions with leaders and political parties at the helm that trust all of their people, rather than just some of them.

Whether viewed narrowly as a trade deal, broadly as an economic constitution for North America, or as a political event of enormous psychological importance to Canadians, free trade leaves Canada forever changed. Fear and faith propelled it, and will be its uncertain legacy as the two Canadian nationalisms try to learn to deal with a changing world that offers both promise and risk for Canada.

NOTES

2: LIBERAL LEGACY
FOR A CONSERVATIVE AGENDA

1. A. Gotlieb and J. Kinsman, "Reviving the Third Option," *International Perspectives* January/February 1981.

2. For a description of the various stages in the decision, see B. Tomlin, "The Stages of Prenegotiation: The Decision to Negotiate North American Free Trade," *International Journal*, Vol. 44 (Spring 1989), pp. 254-279.

3. G.B. Doern, "Liberal Priorities 1982: The Limits of Scheming Virtuously," in G.B. Doern (ed.), *How Ottawa Spends Your Tax Dollars* (Toronto: James Lorimer and Company, 1982).

4. See S. Clarkson, *Canada and the Reagan Challenge* (Toronto: James Lorimer and Company, 1982).

5. See I. Gillespie and A. Maslove, "Volatility and Visibility: The Federal Revenue and Expenditure Plan," in G.B. Doern (ed.), *How Ottawa Spends Your Tax Dollars* (Toronto: James Lorimer and Company, 1982).

6. Government of Canada, *Canadian Trade Policy for the 1980s: A Discussion Paper* (Ottawa: Department of External Affairs, 1983).

7. See the article by Deputy U.S. Trade Representative Michael Smith, "Sectoral Free Trade with Canada," *International Perspectives* May/June 1984.

8. J. Kelleher, "Notes for a Speech to the 55th Annual Meeting of the Canadian Chamber of Commerce," Toronto, September 25, 1984.

9. Government of Canada, *A New Direction for Canada: An Agenda for Economic Renewal* (Ottawa: Department of Finance, 1984, p. 33).

10. J. Kelleher, "Notes for an Address to the Centre for International Business Studies Trade Conference," Halifax, Dalhousie University, November 1, 1984.

11. *Globe and Mail*, November 19, 1984.

12. Government of Canada, *How to Secure and Enhance Access to Export Markets* (Ottawa: Department of External Affairs, 1985).

13. D. Leyton-Brown, "Canada-U.S. Relations: Towards a Closer Relationship," in M. Molot and B. Tomlin (eds.), *Canada Among Nations 1985: The Conservative Agenda* (Toronto: James Lorimer and Company, 1986), p. 182.

14. Leyton-Brown, "Canada-U.S. Relations: Towards a Closer Relationship."

15. R. Lipsey and M. Smith, *Canada's Trade Policy Options* (Toronto: C.D. Howe Institute, 1985).

16. Government of Canada, *Competitiveness and Security: Directions for Canada's International Relations* (Ottawa: Department of External Affairs, 1985).

17. M. Molot and B. Tomlin, "The Conservative Agenda," in M. Molot and B. Tomlin (eds.), *Canada Among Nations 1985: The Conservative Agenda* (Toronto: James Lorimer and Company, 1986), p. 18.

18. *Minutes of Proceedings and Evidence of the Special Joint Committee of the Senate and of the House of Commons on Canada's International Relations* (Ottawa: Queen's Printer, 1985).

19. W. Watson, "Canada-U.S. Free Trade: Why Now?" *Canadian Public Policy* 13, 3 (1987), p. 346.

20. Quoted in the *Toronto Star*, September 27, 1985, p. A21. Italics added.

21. See J. Bernstein and L. Schembri, "Industrial Adjustment in Canada: Causes and Effects," in B. Tomlin and M. Molot (eds.), *Canada Among Nations 1986: Talking Trade* (Toronto: James Lorimer and Company, 1987), p. 100; and R. Harris, *Trade, Industrial Policy and International Competition* (Toronto: University of Toronto Press, 1985).

22. See G. Tobin, *U.S.-Canada Free Trade Negotiations: Getting Approval to Proceed (A)* (Cambridge, Mass.: Kennedy School of Government), Case C16-87-785.0, p. 10.

23. Quoted in Tobin, *U.S.-Canada Free Trade Negotiations (A)*, p. 12.

24. For a more detailed description of the process of changing votes, see G. Tobin, *U.S.-Canada Free Trade Negotiations: Getting Approval to Proceed (B)* (Cambridge, Mass.: Kennedy School of Government), Case C16-87-786.0.

25. G. Tobin, *U.S.-Canada Free Trade Negotiations: Getting Approval to Proceed: Sequel* (Cambridge, Mass.: Kennedy School of Government), Case C16-87-786.1, p. 3.

3: A LONG AND WINDING ROAD

1. See W. Coleman, *Business and Politics* (Montreal: McGill-Queen's University Press, 1988), Chapter 5.

2. See. J. Richards and L. Pratt, *Prairie Capitalism* (Toronto: McClelland and Stewart, 1979), Chapters 7 and 9; and A. Tupper and G.B. Doern, "Alberta Budgeting in the Lougheed Era," in A. Maslove (ed.), *Budgeting in the Provinces* (Toronto: Institute of Public Administration of Canada, 1989), pp. 121-141.

3. See. G.B. Doern and G. Toner, *The Politics of Energy* (Toronto: Methuen, 1985), Chapter 7.

4. For an interesting set of reflections on the dynamics of the Macdonald Commission's deliberations and work see R. McQueen, "The Macdonald Commission Then and Now," *Financial Post*, December 13, 1989, p. 12; D. Cameron and D. Drache, "The Macdonald Commission Revisited," *Studies in Political Economy*, No. 26 (Summer 1988); and R. Simeon, "Inside the Macdonald Commission," *Studies in Political Economy*, No. 22 (Spring 1987).

5. These policies are discussed further in Chapter. 11. It should be noted at this stage that Macdonald's use of the Swedish example was selective, rather than comprehensive. For example, his final report did not advocate corporatist decision-making, as it is practised in Sweden among business, labour unions, and government. Scholars see corporatism as being central to the construction of Sweden's social and labour market policies.

6. See Canada, Royal Commission on the Economic Union and Development

Prospects for Canada, *Report*, Volume I, pp. 302-367 (Ottawa: Department of Supply and Services, 1985).

7. Royal Commission, pp. 308-310.

8. See Donald Creighton, *John A. Macdonald: The Old Chieftain* (Toronto: Mac-Millan of Canada, 1955).

9. See J. L. Granatstein, "Free Trade Between Canada and the United States: The Issue That Will Not Go Away," in D. Stairs and G. Winham (eds.), *The Politics of Canada's Economic Relationship With the United States* (Toronto: University of Toronto Press, 1985).

10. See G. Winham, *Trading with Canada* (New York: Priority Press, 1988).

11. See F. Stone, *Canada, The GATT and the International Trade System* (Montreal: Institute for Research on Public Policy, 1984).

12. See M. Hart, "The Mercantilist's Lament: National Treatment and Modern Trade Negotiations," *Journal of World Trade Law* No. 6 (December, 1987).

13. See R. de C. Grey, *United States Trade Policy Legislation: A Canadian View* (Montreal: Institute for Research on Public Policy, 1982).

14. See H. von Riekhoff, "The Third Option in Canadian Foreign Policy," in B. Tomlin (ed.), *Canada's Foreign Policy: Analysis and Trends* (Toronto: Methuen, 1978); also G. Mace and G. Hervouet, "Canada's Third Option: A Complete Failure?" *Canadian Public Policy* XV, No. 4 (December 1989).

15. G. Winham, *Trading in Canada*, p. 16.

16. See I. Destler, *American Trade Politics: System Under Stress* (New York: Institute For International Economics, 1986).

17. See J. Findlayson, "Canada, Congress and U.S. Foreign Economic Policy," in D. Stairs and G. Winham (eds.), *The Politics of Canada's Economic Relationship With the United States* (Toronto: University of Toronto Press, 1985).

18. See A. Rugman and A. Anderson, *Administered Protection in America* (London: Croom Helm, 1987).

4: ADDING UP THE DEAL

1. See *The Canada-U.S. Free Trade Agreement* (Ottawa: Department of Supply and Services, 1988).

2. For a range of opinion regarding the FTA and its component parts, see R. Lipsey and R. York, *Evaluating the Free Trade Deal* (Toronto: C.D. Howe Institute, 1988); D. Cameron (ed.), *The Free Trade Deal* (Toronto: James Lorimer and Company, 1988); and M. Gold and D. Leyton-Brown (eds.), *Trade-Offs on Free Trade* (Toronto: Carswell, 1988).

3. See J. Gilson, *World Agricultural Changes: Implications for Canada* (Toronto: C.D. Howe Institute, 1989).

4. See J. McRae and M. Desbois (eds.), *Traded and Non-Traded Services: Problems of Theory, Measurement and Policy* (Halifax: Institute for Research on Public Policy, 1987).

5. For an account of the drug patent story, see R. Campbell and L. Pal, *The Real Worlds of Canadian Politics* (Peterborough: Broadview Press, 1989), Chapter 2.

6. See M. Percy and C. Yoder, *The Softwood Lumber Dispute and Canada-U.S. Trade in Natural Resources* (Halifax: Institute for Research on Public Policy, 1987).

5: THE UNITED FRONT

1. See L. Thibault, "Address on the Release of the Joint CMA-NAM Statement on Bilateral Trade Negotiations," Washington, April 13, 1987, p. 3.

2. In this chapter, we focus on BCNI and the CMA. But business pressure in support of free trade also came from the other two main business lobbies, the Canadian Chamber of Commerce and the Canadian Federation of Independent Business (CFIB). Because these organizations have far higher proportions of small businesses in their membership than the CMA and BCNI, their impact and lobbying is more local and regionally dispersed. But it was also frequently quite vocal. The CFIB, for example, published continuous results from the polling of its own members, which showed very strong support for free trade.

3. See W. Coleman, *Business and Politics* (Montreal: McGill-Queen's University Press, 1988).

4. We leave until Chapter 9 our discussion of the role played by the overarching business coalition group, the Canadian Alliance for Trade and Job Opportunities.

5. A classic compromise led to the formation of an Advisory Council on Adjustment, headed by Bell Canada Chairman Jean de Grandpré). Its report, tabled in March 1989, agreed with the basic ITAC position. See *Adjusting to Win* (Ottawa: Department of Supply and Services Canada, 1989).

6. This is a general impression we formed based on interviews conducted with over 20 SAGIT members and participants.

7. See A. Rugman and A. Anderson, *Administered Protection in America* (London: Croom Helm, 1987), Chapter 5.

8. See R. Litan, *What Should Banks Do?* (Washington: The Brookings Institution, 1987); W. Thomas, *The Big Bang* (Oxford: Phillip Allan, 1986); and T. Courchene, "Global Financial Developments: Implications for Canada," in J. McRae and M. Desbois (eds.), *Traded and Non-Traded Services* (Halifax: Institute for Research on Public Policy, 1988), pp. 243-254.

9. See G. Toner, "Stardust: The Tory Energy Program," in M. Prince (ed.), *How Ottawa Spends 1986-87* (Toronto: Methuen, 1986), pp. 119-148.

10. In the electricity sector, where provincially owned utilities are dominant, provincial governments and the utilities themselves communicated directly with TNO. Hydro-Québec was by far the most important and had a direct channel because of the close alliance between Bourassa and Mulroney. We do not deal with electricity here, but focus instead on oil and gas interests.

11. See G.B. Doern and G. Toner, *The Politics of Energy* (Toronto: Methuen, 1985).

6: NO SEAT AT THE TABLE

1. For a discussion of the role of the provinces in trade policy see D. Cameron, *The Free Trade Deal* (Toronto: James Lorimer and Company, 1988), Chapters 17 and 21; M. Gold and D. Leyton-Brown (eds.), *Trade-Offs on Free Trade* (Toronto: Carswell, 1988), Chapter 5; D. Protheroe, *Imports and Politics* (Montreal: Institute for Research on Public Policy, 1980); Royal Commission on the Economic

Union and Development Prospects for Canada, *Report,* Volume I (Ottawa: Supply and Services, 1985), pp. 350-373; and G. Winham, "Bureaucratic Politics and Canadian Trade Negotiation," *International Journal* Vol. 34 (Winter 1978–79), pp. 64-89.

7: PLAYING OUT THE STRING

1. Quoted in V.S. Jenkins, *The U.S.-Canada Free Trade Negotiations (II): The Canadian Dilemma* (Cambridge, Mass.: Kennedy School of Government), Case C16-89-862.0, p. 6.

2. See G. Winham, *Trading with Canada: The Canada-U.S. Free Trade Agreement* (New York: Priority Press Publications, 1988), p. 27.

3. For a discussion of these issues, see D. Leyton-Brown, "The Politicals Economy of Canada-U.S. Relations," in B. Tomlin and M. Molot (eds.), *Canada Among Nations 1986: Talking Trade* (Toronto: James Lorimer and Company, 1987); and M. Percy and C. Yoder, *The Softwood Lumber Dispute and Canada-U.S. Trade in Natural Resources* (Halifax: Institute for Research on Public Policy, 1987).

4. Quoted in V.S. Jenkins, *The U.S.-Canada Free Trade Negotiations (II): The Canadian Dilemma* (Cambridge, Mass.: Kennedy School of Government), Case C16-89-862.0, p. 12.

5. For a discussion of domestic preoccupations in international negotiations, see R. Fisher, "Negotiating Inside Out," *Negotiation Journal* 5, 1:33-42. For a conceptual discussion of the representation of organizational interests in negotiation, see D. Druckman, "Boundary Role Conflict: Negotiation as Dual Responsiveness," in I.W. Zartman (ed.), *The Negotiation Process: Theories and Applications* (Beverly Hills, Ca.: Sage, 1978).

8: A WEEKEND IN WASHINGTON

1. The fast-track deadlines were ambiguous, but the consensus among U.S. officials was that the president would have to sign letters to the Chairs of the Senate and House Committees announcing an agreement by midnight on October 4. Since this date would fall on a Sunday, and presidential letters were never sent to the Congress on a Sunday, the deadline became midnight Saturday.

2.   J. Richard and R. Dearden, *The Canada-U.S. Free Trade Agreement: Commentary and Related Documents* (Toronto: CCH Canadian Limited, 1987), p. 17.

9: TWO NATIONALIST VISIONS

1.   For an analysis of the union role in the free trade debate, see C. Gonick and J. Silver, "Fighting Free Trade," *Canadian Dimension*, Vol. 23, No. 3 (April 1989), pp. 6-14; and B. White, "From Defeat to Renewal," *This Magazine*, Vol. 23, No. 1 (May/June 1989), pp. 23-26.

2.   See D. Cameron (ed.), *The Other Macdonald Report* (Toronto: James Lorimer and Company, 1985); and *The Free Trade Papers* (Toronto: James Lorimer and Company, 1986), "Introduction."

3.   See S. Bashevkin, "Free Trade and Feminism: The Case of the National Action Committee on the Status of Women," *Canadian Public Policy*, Vol. XV, No. 4 (December 1989), pp. 363-375.

4.   See A. Frizzell and A. Westell, "The Media and the Campaign," in A. Frizzell, J. Pammett and A. Westell (eds.), *The Canadian General Election of 1988* (Ottawa: Carleton University Press, 1989), pp. 75-90.

5.   Frizzell and Westell, p. 89.

6.   See Compas Inc., *The Compas Forecast: Respondent's Report Spring/Summer, 1989* (Ottawa: Compas Inc., 1989).

7.   For a discussion of the role of narrative analysis for policies where quantitative evaluation criteria are unavailable see T. Kaplan, "The Narrative Structure of Policy Analysis," *Journal of Policy Analysis and Management* 5 (1986): 761-778.

8.   This statement can be found in Duncan Cameron (ed.), *The Free Trade Papers* (Toronto: James Lorimer and Company, 1986), pp. 3-10.

10: THE GREAT FREE TRADE ELECTION

1.   See D. King, *The New Right* (London: Macmillan, 1987); and G.B. Doern, A. Maslove and M. Prince, *Budgeting in Canada* (Ottawa: Carleton University Press, 1988), Chapter 1.

2. For a discussion of Turner's leadership problems during the election, see G. Fraser, *Playing for Keeps: The Making of the Prime Minister, 1988* (Toronto: McClelland and Stewart, 1989).

3. See S. Clarkson, "The Liberals: Disoriented in Defeat," in A. Frizzell, J. Pammett and A. Westell, *The Canadian General Election of 1988* (Ottawa: Carleton University Press, 1989), pp. 27-42.

4. The NDP's predecessor, the CCF, faced similar circumstances in 1945. See A. Whitehorn, "The NDP Election Campaign: Dashed Hopes," in A. Frizzell, J. Pammett and A. Westell (eds.), *The Canadian General Election of 1988* (Ottawa: Carleton University Press, 1989), pp. 43-54.

5. See Canadian Labour Congress, "Presentation of the Canadian Labour Congress to the House of Commons Standing Committee on External Affairs and International Trade" (Ottawa: Canadian Labour Congress, December 4, 1987).

6. See B. White, "From Defeat to Renewal," *This Magazine*, Vol. 23, No. 1 (May/June 1989), pp. 23-26; and C. Gonick and J. Silver, "Fighting Free Trade," *Canadian Dimension*, Vol. 23, No. 3 (April 1989), pp. 6-14.

7. See *Globe and Mail*, October 10, 1988, p. B10; and the speech by John Turner, House of Commons, *Debates*, August 30, 1988, pp. 19058-19068.

8. New Democratic Party of Canada, *A Time to Choose Canada: The New Democrats' Trade Option*, Ottawa, January 1988, p. 39.

9. J. Pammett, "The 1988 Vote," in A. Frizzell, J. Pammett and A. Westell, *The Canadian General Election of 1988* (Ottawa: Carleton University Press, 1989), p. 123.

10. In his book on the 1988 election, Graham Fraser expressed the widely shared view that in re-electing the Mulroney government 43 per cent of the electorate chose to endorse the FTA. According to Fraser, " . . . it was clear that, in casting their ballots, Canadians were making a clear policy choice on the Free Trade Agreement." See *Playing for Keeps: The Making of the Prime Minister, 1988* (Toronto: McClelland and Stewart, 1989), p. 14.

11. Pammett, p. 125.

12. A. Frizzell, R. Roth and A. Westell, "The Media, the Election and Free Trade" (unpublished paper, Carleton University, 1990).

13. See R. Johnson, A. Blais, H. Brady and J. Crete, "Free Trade and the Dynamics of the 1988 Canadian General Election" (paper presented to the Annual Meeting of the Canadian Political Science Association, Laval University, June 1989).

14. Quoted in a shorter version of the same paper in the *Globe and Mail*, December 19, 1989, p. 7.

15. See J. Brodie, "The Free Trade Election," *Studies in Political Economy* No. 28 (Spring 1989), pp. 175-182.

11: SOVEREIGNTY VERSUS POLICY CAPACITY

1. G. Williams, "Canadian Sovereignty and the Free Trade Debate," in A. Maslove and S. Winer (eds.), *Knocking on the Back Door* (Halifax: Institute for Research on Public Policy, 1987).

2. S. Gill and D. Law, *The Global Political Economy* (London: Wheatsheaf, 1988).

3. S.M. Lipset, *Continental Divide: The Values and Institutions of the United States and Canada* (New York: Routledge, 1990).

4. A. Blais (ed.), *Industrial Policy* (Toronto: University of Toronto Press, 1986), Chapter 1.

5. R. Lipsey and R. York, *Evaluating the Free Trade Deal* (Toronto: C.D. Howe Institute, 1988), pp. 13-18.

6. The handful of cases decided in 1989 and 1990, whatever their rhetorical value to both sides of the free trade debate, do not yet constitute a sufficient basis for judging the FTA.

7. See J-F. Bence and M. Smith, "Subsidies and the Trade Laws: The Canada-U.S. Dimension," *International Economic Issues* April/May 1989 (Ottawa: Institute for Research on Public Policy); and G.B. Doern and B. Tomlin, "The Free Trade Sequel: Canada-United States Subsidy Negotiations," in F. Abele (ed.), *How Ottawa Spends 1991–92* (Ottawa: Carleton University Press, 1991).

8.   C. Morton, *Subsidies Negotiations and the Politics of Trade* (Washington, D.C.: National Planning Association, 1989).

9.   See G.B. Doern, "The Department of Industry, Science and Technology: Is There Industrial Policy After Free Trade?" in K. Graham (ed.), *How Ottawa Spends 1990-91* (Ottawa: Carleton University Press, 1990); and R. Lipsey and W. Dobson (eds.), *Shaping Comparative Advantage* (Toronto: C.D. Howe Institute, 1987).

10. D. McFetridge (ed.), *Canadian Industrial Policy in Action* (Toronto: University of Toronto Press, 1986).

11. See McFetridge, Chapter 1, and Lipsey and Dobson, *Shaping Comparative Advantage.*

12. M. Atkinson and W. Coleman, *The State, Business and Industrial Change in Canada* (Toronto: University of Toronto Press, 1989).

13. On Japan, see D. Okimoti, *Between MITI and The Market* (Stanford: Stanford University Press, 1989).

14. R. Harris, *Trade, Industrial Policy and International Competition* (Toronto: University of Toronto Press, 1985).

15. For a range of views on the energy provisions, see J. Dillon, "Continental Energy Policy," in D. Cameron (ed.), *The Free Trade Deal* (Toronto: James Lorimer and Company, 1988); and A. Plourde and L. Waverman, "Canadian Energy Trade: The Past and the Future," in G.C. Watkins (ed.), *Petro Markets* (Vancouver: Fraser Institute, 1989).

16. G. Drover (ed.), *Free Trade and Social Policy* (Ottawa: Canadian Council on Social Development, 1988).

17. J. Rice, "Restitching the Safety Net: Altering the National Social Security System," in M. Prince (ed.), *How Ottawa Spends 1987–88* (Toronto: Methuen, 1988).

18. Drover, *Free Trade and Social Policy.*

19. T. Courchene, "Towards the Reintegration of Social and Economic Policy," in G.B. Doern and B. Purchase (eds.), *Canada at Risk? Canadian Public Policy in The 1990s* (Toronto: C.D. Howe Institute, 1990).

20. G.B. Doern and B. Purchase, "Whither Ottawa?" in Doern and Purchase.

21. K. Phillips, *The Politics of Rich and Poor* (New York: Random House, 1990).

12: FAITH, FEAR, AND CONSEQUENCES

1. For a perceptive analysis of the zone of agreement and attempts by parties to a negotiation to influence the bargaining range, see H. Raiffa, *The Art and Science of Negotiation* (Cambridge, Mass.: Harvard University Press, 1982).

2. *Debates*, House of Commons, 2nd Session, 33rd Parliament, Vol. IV, March 16, 1987, p. 41–46.

3. The effects of incentives to take risks on concession-making are well known to negotiation analysts, and are described in M. Neale and M. Bazerman, "Perspectives for Understanding Negotiation," *Journal of Conflict Resolution* 29, 1 (1985).

4. For a discussion of non-agreement alternatives and their effects on negotiation outcomes see D. Lax and J. Sebenius, "The Power of Alternatives and the Limits to Negotiation," *Negotiation Journal* 1 (1985).

5. For studies that, on balance, focus more on the economics of the FTA, see R. Lipsey and R. York, *Evaluating the Free Trade Deal* (Toronto: C.D. Howe Institute, 1988); and M. Gold and D. Leyton-Brown, *Tradeoffs on Free Trade* (Toronto: Carswell, 1988).

6. One advocate of this position is University of Alberta economist Bruce Wilkinson. See his "Canada-United States Free Trade: Setting the Dimensions," in A. Maslove and S. Winer (eds.), *Knocking on the Back Door* (Halifax: Institute for Research on Public Policy, 1987). See also R. Harris, *Trade, Industrial Policy and International Competition* (Toronto: University of Toronto Press, 1985).

7. For assessments of the FTA after two years of operation, see "Making It Work: Year Two of the Canada-U.S. Free Trade Agreement," Ottawa, Strategico Inc., 1991, and "On Track: Canada-U.S. Free Trade Agreement after Two Years," Calgary, Canada West Foundation, 1991.

8. For reviews of some of these complementary policy needs see the essays in G.B. Doern and B. Purchase (eds.), *Canada at Risk? Canadian Public Policy in the*

1990s (Toronto: C.D. Howe Institute, 1990); and K. Graham (ed.), *How Ottawa Spends 1990–91* (Ottawa: Carleton University Press, 1990).

9. For an analysis of why no middle-of-the-road view emerged in the free trade debate, including the role of the Liberal Party, see R. Young, "Why Did We Ignore the Middle Ground?" *Globe and Mail*, November 24, 1988, p. A7.

10. R. Gwyn, "Canada at Risk" in G.B. Doern and B. Purchase (eds.), *Canada at Risk?: Canadian Public Policy in the 1990s* (Toronto: C.D. Howe Institute, 1990).

11. H. Lithwick and A. Maslove, "The Sum of the Parts: Free Trade and Meech Lake," in K. Graham (ed.), *How Ottawa Spends 1989-90* (Ottawa: Carleton University Press, 1989).

12. See G.B. Doern and B. Tomlin, "The Free Trade Sequel: Canada-United States Subsidy Negotiations," in F. Abele (ed.), *How Ottawa Spends 1991-92* (Ottawa: Carleton University Press, 1991); and M. Hart, *A North American Free Trade Agreement* (Halifax: Institute for Research on Public Policy, 1990).

REFERENCES

Anderson, Andrew, and Alan Rugman, "Subsidies in the U.S. Steel Industry: A Conceptual Approach to the Literature," *Working Paper Series* No. 14 (Toronto: Ontario Centre for International Business, University of Toronto, April 1989).

Anderson, J.J. and R.D. Cairns, "The Softwood Lumber Agreement and Resource Politics," *Canadian Public Policy* Vol. XIV, No. 2 (June 1988), pp. 186-196.

Atkinson, Michael and William Coleman, *The State, Business and Industrial Change in Canada* (Toronto: University of Toronto Press, 1989).

Attorney General for Ontario, *The Impact of the Canada-U.S. Trade Agreement: A Legal Analysis* (Toronto, 1988).

Audley, Paul, *Canada's Cultural Industries* (Ottawa: Canadian Institute for Economic Policy, 1983).

Auer, L., *Canadian Prairie Farming, 1960-2000: An Economic Analysis* (Ottawa: Supply and Services Canada, 1989).

Barrows, David and Mark Boudreau, "The Evolving Role of the Provinces in International Trade Negotiations," in A. Maslove and S. Winer (eds.), *Knocking on the Back Door* (Halifax: Institute for Research on Public Policy, 1987), pp. 135-151.

Bashevkin, Sylvia, "Free Trade and Feminism: The Case of the National Action Committee on the Status of Women," *Canadian Public Policy* Volume XV, No. 4 (December 1989), pp. 363-375.

Bence, Jean-Francois and Murray G. Smith, "Subsidies and the Trade Laws: The Canada-U.S. Dimension," *International Economic Issues* (April-May 1989), Ottawa: Institute for Research on Public Policy, pp. 1-36.

Bienefeld, Manfred, "Canadian Industry and the Free Trade Agreement," Paper prepared for the Ontario Federation of Labour, October 1988.

Blais, André (ed.), *A Political Sociology of Public Aid to Industry*, The Royal Commission on the Economic Union and Development Prospects in Canada, No. 45, 1986, pp. 11-56.

Breton, Albert, "Endorsing an Unsuitable Model of Federalism: The Macdonald Commission, Then and Now," *Financial Post*, December 19, 1989, p. 14.

Brodie, Janine, "The Free Trade Election," *Studies in Political Economy*, No. 28 (Spring 1989), pp. 175-182.

Cameron, Duncan (ed.), *The Free Trade Deal* (Toronto: James Lorimer and Company, 1988).

Cameron, Duncan (ed.), *The Other Macdonald Report* (Toronto: James Lorimer and Company, 1985).

Cameron, Duncan and Daniel Drache, "The Macdonald Commission Revisited," *Studies in Political Economy*, No. 26, (Summer 1988), pp. 173-180.

Campbell, Robert M. and Leslie A. Pal, *The Real Worlds of Canadian Politics* (Peterborough: Broadview Press, 1989).

Canada, Department of Agriculture, *The Canada-U.S. Free Trade Agreement and Agriculture*, 1988.

Canada, Department of Energy, Mines and Resources, *The Canada-U.S. Free Trade Agreement and Energy*, 1988.

Canada, Department of External Affairs, *Competitiveness and Security: Directions for Canada's International Relations*, 1985.

Canada, Department of External Affairs, *How to Secure and Enhance Access to Export Markets*, 1985.

Canada, Department of External Affairs, *Canadian Trade Policy for the 1980s: A Discussion Paper*, 1983.

Canada, Department of Finance, *A New Direction for Canada: An Agenda for Economic Renewal*, 1984.

Canada, Department of Supply and Services, *Adjusting To Win*, 1989.

Canada, Department of Supply and Services, *The Canada-U.S. Free Trade Agreement*, 1988.

Canada, Department of Supply and Services, *Royal Commission on the Economic Union and Development Prospects for Canada*, Volume I, 1985.

Canada, Parliament, *Minutes of Proceedings and Evidence of the Special Joint Committee of the Senate and of the House of Commons on Canada's International Relations*, 1985.

Canada West Foundation, *Putting the Cards on the Table: Free Trade and Western Canadian Industries* (Calgary: Canada West Foundation, 1986).

Canada West Foundation, *On Track: Canada-U.S. Free Trade Agreement after Two Years* (Calgary: Canada West Foundation, 1991).

Canadian Labour Congress, "Presentation of the Canadian Labour Congress to the House of Commons Standing Committee on External Affairs and International Trade," Ottawa, December 4, 1987.

Carmichael, E. and K. Macmillan, *Focus on Follow-through* (Toronto: C.D. Howe Institute, 1988).

Clarkson, Stephen, *Canada and the Reagan Challenge: Crisis in the Canadian-American Relationship* (Toronto: James Lorimer and Company, 1982).

Clarkson, Stephen, *Canada and the Reagan Challenge: Crisis and Adjustment*, Second Edition (Toronto: James Lorimer and Company, 1985).

Clarkson, Stephen, "The Canada-United States Trade Commission and the Institutional Basis of the FTA," in Duncan Cameron (ed.), *The Free Trade Deal* (Toronto: James Lorimer and Company, 1988) pp. 26-43.

Clarkson, Stephen, "The Liberals: Disoriented in Defeat," in A. Frizzell, J. Pammett and A. Westell, *The Canadian General Election of 1988* (Ottawa: Carleton University Press, 1989), pp. 27-42.

Cohen, Marjorie, *Free Trade and the Future of Women's Work* (Ottawa: Government Press, 1987).

Coleman, William D., *Business and Politics* (Montreal: McGill-Queen's University Press, 1988).

Compas Inc., *The Compas Forecast: Respondent's Report Spring/Summer, 1989* (Ottawa: Compas Inc, 1989).

Cooper, S. Kerry and D.R. Fraser, *Banking Deregulation and the New Competition in the Financial Services Industry* (Cambridge: Ballinger, 1984).

Courchene, Thomas, "Global Financial Developments: Implications for Canada," in James McRae and M. Desbois (eds.), *Traded and Non-Traded Services* (Halifax: Institute for Research on Public Policy, 1988), pp. 243-254.

Courchene, Thomas, "International Finance: Evolution and Revolution." Ottawa, Senate of Canada, Standing Committee on Foreign Affairs, July 26, 1988.

Courchene, Thomas, "Social Policy and Regional Development," in John Crispo (ed.), *Free Trade: The Real Story* (Toronto: Gage Educational Publishing Company, 1988), pp. 135-147.

Courchene, Thomas, "Towards the Reintegration of Social and Economic Policy," in G. Bruce Doern and B. Purchase (eds.), *Canada at Risk? Canadian Public Policy in the 1990s* (Toronto: C.D. Howe Institute, 1990), pp. 125-148.

Creighton, Donald, *John A. Macdonald: The Old Chieftain* (Toronto: Macmillan of Canada, 1955).

Destler, I.M. *American Trade Politics: System under Stress* (New York: Institute for International Economics, 1986).

Dillon, John, "Continental Energy Policy," in Duncan Cameron (ed.), *The Free Trade Deal* (Toronto: James Lorimer and Company, 1988), pp. 104-116.

Doern, G. Bruce, "The Department of Industry, Science and Technology: Is There Industrial Policy After Free Trade?" in Katherine Graham (ed.), *How Ottawa Spends 1990-91* (Ottawa: Carleton University Press, 1990), pp.49-72.

Doern, G. Bruce, "Liberal Priorities 1982: The Limits of Scheming Virtuously," in G.B. Doern (ed.), *How Ottawa Spends Your Tax Dollars* (Toronto: James Lorimer and Company, 1982), pp. 1-36.

Doern, G. Bruce, "The Tories, Free Trade and Industrial Adjustment Policy: Expanding the State Now to Reduce the State Later?" in Michael Prince (ed.), *How Ottawa Spends 1986-87* (Ottawa: Methuen, 1986), pp. 61-94.

Doern, G. Bruce, A. Maslove and M. Prince, *Budgeting in Canada* (Ottawa: Carleton University Press, 1988).

Doern, G. Bruce, and Bryne Purchase (eds.), *Canada at Risk? Canadian Public Policy in the 1990s,* (Toronto: C.D. Howe Institute, 1990).

Doern, G. Bruce, and B. Purchase, "Whither Ottawa?" in G.B. Doern and B. Purchase (eds.), *Canada at Risk? Canadian Public Policy in the 1990s* (Toronto: C.D. Howe Institute, 1990), pp. 1-24.

Doern, G. Bruce and Brian W. Tomlin, "The Free Trade Sequel: Canada-United States Subsidy Negotiations," in Frances Abele (ed.), *How Ottawa Spends 1991-92* (Ottawa: Carleton University Press, 1991).

Doern, G. Bruce, and Glen Toner, *The Politics of Energy* (Toronto, Methuen, 1985).

Drover, Glen (ed.), *Free Trade and Social Policy* (Ottawa: Canadian Council on Social Development, 1988).

Druckman, Daniel, "Boundary Role Conflict: Negotiation as Dual Responsiveness," in I. William Zartman (ed.), *The Negotiation Process: Theories and Applications* (Beverly Hills, Ca.: Sage, 1978).

Economic Council of Canada, *A Framework for Financial Regulation*, Ottawa, 1987.

Economic Council of Canada, *Competition and Solvency: A Framework for Financial Regulation*, Ottawa, 1986.

Economic Council of Canada, *Managing Adjustment: Policies for Trade-Sensitive Industries*, Ottawa, 1988.

Economic Council of Canada, *Venturing Forth*, Ottawa, 1988.

Economist, "Europe's Internal Market after 1992," Special Edition, July 9, 1988, pp. 5-52.

Economist, "World Trade: Jousting for Advantage," September 22, 1990, pp. 5-39.

Farrow, Maureen and Alan Rugman, *Business Strategies and Free Trade* (C.D. Howe Institute, 1988).

Fillmore, N., "How Business Won the Free Trade Battle," *This Magazine* Vol. 22 (April 1989), pp. 13-20.

Findlayson, Jock A., "Canada, Congress and U.S. Foreign Economic Policy," in D. Stairs and G. Winham (eds.), *The Politics of Canada's Economic Relationship with the United States* (Toronto: University of Toronto Press, 1985), pp. 127-178.

Finger, Michael and Julio Nogues, "International Control of Subsidies and Countervailing Duties," *The World Bank Economic Review* I:4 (1987), pp. 707-725.

Fisher, Roger, "Negotiating Inside Out," *Negotiation Journal* 5, 1 (1989), pp. 33-42.

Frizzell, Alan, Robert Roth and Anthony Westell, "The Media, the Election and Free Trade" (unpublished paper, Carleton University, 1990).

Frizzell, Alan, and Anthony Westell, "The Media and the Campaign," in A. Frizzell, J. Pammett and A. Westell (eds.), *The Canadian General Election of 1988* (Ottawa: Carleton University Press, 1989), pp. 75-90.

Gill, Stephen, and David Law, *The Global Political Economy* (London: Wheatsheaf, 1988).

Gillespie, I. and A. Maslove, "Volatility and Visibility: The Federal Revenue and Expenditure Plan," in G.B. Doern (ed.), *How Ottawa Spends Your Tax Dollars* (Toronto: James Lorimer and Company, 1982), pp. 37-42.

J.C. Gilson, *World Agricultural Changes: Implications for Canada* (Toronto: C.D. Howe Institute, 1989).

Gold, Marc, and David Leyton-Brown, *Trade-Offs on Free Trade* (Toronto: Carswell, 1988).

Gonick, Cy, and Jim Silver, "Fighting Free Trade," *Canadian Dimension* Vol. 23, No. 3 (April 1989), pp. 6-14.

Gotlieb, A. and J. Kinsman, "Reviving the Third Option," *International Perspectives*, January/February 1981, pp. 2-5.

Graham, Katherine A. (ed.), *How Ottawa Spends 1990-91* (Ottawa: Carleton University Press, 1990).

Granatstein, J.L., "Free Trade Between Canada and the United States: The Issue That Will Not Go Away," in D. Stairs and G. Winham (eds.), *The Politics of Canada's Economic Relationship With the United States* (Toronto: University of Toronto Press, 1985), pp. 11-55.

Grey, Rodney de C., *United States Trade Policy Legislation: A Canadian View* (Montreal: Institute for Research on Public Policy, 1982).

Grieco, Joseph, *Cooperation Among Nations: Europe, America and Non-Tariff Barriers to Trade* (Ithaca: Cornell University Press, 1990).

Gwyn, Richard, "Canada at Risk," in G.B. Doern and B. Purchase (eds.), *Canada at Risk?: Canadian Public Policy in the 1990s* (Toronto: C.D. Howe Institute, 1990).

Harris, Richard, *Trade, Industrial Policy and International Competition* (Toronto: University of Toronto Press, 1985).

Hart, Michael, *A North American Free Trade Agreement* (Halifax: Institute for Research on Public Policy, 1990).

Hart, Michael, *Canadian Economic Development and the International Trading System* (Toronto: University of Toronto Press, 1986).

Hart, Michael, "GATT Article XXIV and Canada-United States Trade Negotiations," *Review of International Business Law*, Vol. I, No. 3 (1987).

Hart, Michael, "The Mercantalist's Lament: National Treatment and Modern Trade Negotiations," *Journal of World Trade Law* No. 6 (December 1987), pp. 37-61.

Hazeldine, T. "Canada-U.S. Free Trade? Not So Elementary, Watson," *Canadian Public Policy* Vol. XIV (June 1988), pp. 204-213.

Hufbauer, Gary, "A View of the Forest," in Bela Balassa (ed.), *Subsidies and Countervailing Measures* (Washington, D.C.: World Bank, 1989), pp. 11-27.

Hufbauer, Gary, and Joanna Shelton Erc, *Subsidies in International Trade* (Washington: Institute for International Economics, 1984).

Jenkins, V.S. *The US-Canada Free Trade Negotiations (II): The Canadian Dilemma* (Cambridge, Mass.: Kennedy School of Government).

Johnson, Jon, *The Free Trade Agreement: A Comprehensive Guide* (Aurora: Canada Law Book Inc., 1988).

Johnson, Richard, André Blais, H. Brady and J. Crete, "Free Trade and the Dynamics of the 1988 Canadian General Election," Paper presented at the Canadian Political Science Association Annual Meeting, Laval University, June 1-3, 1989.

Kaplan, T., "The Narrative Structure of Policy Analysis," *Journal of Policy Analysis and Management* Vol. 5 (1986), pp. 761-778.

Kelleher, J., "Notes for an Address to the Centre for International Business Studies Trade Conference," Halifax, Dalhousie University, November 1, 1984.

Kelleher, J., "Notes for a Speech to the 55th Annual Meeting of the Canadian Chamber of Commerce," Toronto, September 25, 1984.

King, Desmond S., *The New Right* (London: Macmillan, 1987).

Lax, D., and J. Sebenius, "The Power of Alternatives and the Limits to Negotiation," *Negotiation Journal* Vol. 1 (1985), pp. 163-179.

Laxer, James, *Leap of Faith: Free Trade and the Future of Canada* (Edmonton: Hurtig, 1986).

Leyton-Brown, David, "Canada-U.S. Relations: Towards a Closer Relationship," in M. Molot and B. Tomlin (eds.), *Canada Among Nations 1985: The Conservative Agenda* (Toronto: James Lorimer and Company, 1986), pp. 177-195.

Leyton-Brown, David, "The Political Economy of Canada-U.S. Relations," in Brian W. Tomlin and Maureen Appel Molot (eds.), *Canada Among Nations 1986: Talking Trade* (Toronto: James Lorimer and Company, 1987), pp. 149-168.

Lipset, Seymour M., *Continental Divide: The Values and Institutions of the United States and Canada* (New York: Routledge, 1990).

Lipsey, Richard, "The Economics of a Canadian-American Free Trade Association," in M.D. Henderson (ed.), *The Future at the Table* (Toronto: Masterpress, 1987), pp. 35-54.

Lipsey, Richard, "Canada at the U.S.-Mexico Free Trade Dance: Wallflower or Partner?" *Commentary*, No. 20 (Toronto: C.D. Howe Institute, August 1990).

Lipsey, Richard, and Wendy Dobson (eds.), *Shaping Comparative Advantage* (Toronto: C.D. Howe Institute, 1987).

Lipsey, Richard, and D. Drache, "The Costs and Benefits of the Free Trade Agreement," in M. Gold and D. Leyton-Brown (eds.), *Trade-Offs on Free Trade* (Toronto: Carswell, 1988) pp. 65-88.

Lipsey, Richard and Murray G. Smith, *Taking the Initiative: Canada's Trade Options in a Turbulent World* (Toronto: C.D. Howe Institute 1985).

Lipsey, Richard, and Robert York, *Evaluating the Free Trade Deal* (Toronto: C.D. Howe Institute, 1988).

Litan, Robert E., *What Should Banks Do?* (Washington: The Brookings Institution, 1987).

Lithwick, Harvey, and Allan Maslove, "The Sum of the Parts: Free Trade and Meech Lake," in Katherine Graham (ed.), *How Ottawa Spends 1989-90* (Ottawa: Carleton University Press, 1989), pp. 25-52.

Mace, G. and G. Hervouet, "Canada's Third Option: A Complete Failure?," *Canadian Public Policy*, Vol XV, No. 4 (December 1989), pp. 387-404.

Michel, Ann et al., *An Annotated Inventory of Federal Business Subsidy Programs in the United States* (Ottawa: Institute for Research on Public Policy, 1986).

McDougall, Ian, "Energy and the Constitution," unpublished paper, 1988.

McFetridge, Donald (ed.), *Canadian Industrial Policy in Action* (Toronto: University of Toronto Press, 1986).

McRae, James J. and M. Desbois (eds.), *Traded and Non-Traded Services: Problems of Theory, Measurement and Policy* (Halifax: Institute for Research on Public Policy, 1987).

Molot, Maureen Appel and Brian W. Tomlin, "The Conservative Agenda," in M. Molot and B. Tomlin (eds.), *Canada Among Nations 1985: The Conservative Agenda* (Toronto: James Lorimer and Company, 1986), pp. 3-24.

Morton, Colleen, *Subsidies Negotiations and the Politics of Trade* (Washinton, D.C.: National Planning Association, 1989).

Mutti, John, *Taxes, Subsidies and Competitiveness Internationally* (Washington, D.C.: National Planning Association, 1982).

Neale, M. and M. Bazerman, "Perspectives for Understanding Negotiation," *Journal of Conflict Resolution* Vol. 29, No. 1 (1985), pp. 33-55.

New Democratic Party, *A Time to Choose: The New Democrats' Trade Option*, Ottawa, January 1988.

Okimoto, Daniel, *Between MITI and the Market* (Stanford: Stanford University Press, 1989).

Organization for Economic Cooperation and Development, "Industrial Subsidies in the OECD Economies," *OECD Economic Studies*, No. 15, 1990.

Oxley, Alan, *The Challenge of Free Trade* (London: Harvester Wheatsheaf, 1990).

Pammett, Jon, "The 1988 Vote," in A. Frizzell, J. Pammett and A. Westell (eds.), *The Canadian General Election of 1988* (Ottawa: Carleton University Press, 1989).

Perry, Ross, *The Future of Canada's Auto Industry* (Toronto: Canadian Institute for Economic Policy, 1982).

Paquet, Gilles, "Elegant But Not Helpful to Navigation: Social Sciences Research and the Free Trade Debate," in A. Maslove and S. Winer (eds.), *Knocking on the Back Door* (Halifax: Institute for Research on Public Policy, 1987), pp. 165-199.

Percy, Michael B. and Christian Yoder, *The Softwood Lumber Dispute and Canada-U.S. Trade in Natural Resources* (Halifax: Institute For Research on Public Policy, 1987).

Phillips, Kevin, *The Politics of Rich and Poor* (New York: Random House, 1990).

Plourde, André, and Leonard Waverman, "Canadian Energy Trade: The Past and The Future," in G. Campbell Watkins (ed.), *Petro Markets* (Vancouver: Fraser Institute, 1989), pp. 141-172.

Prince, Michael, "Little Help on the Prairie: Canadian Farm Income Programs and the Western Grain Economy," in Katherine Graham (ed.), *How Ottawa Spends 1990-91* (Ottawa: Carleton University Press, 1990), pp. 137-171.

Protheroe, David, *Imports and Politics* (Montreal: Institute for Research on Public Policy, 1980).

Rice, James J., "Restitching the Safety Net: Altering the National Social Security System," in Michael J. Prince (ed.), *How Ottawa Spends 1987-88* (Toronto: Methuen, 1988), pp. 211-236.

Richard, John D., and Richard G. Dearden, *The Canada-U.S. Free Trade Agreement: Commentary and Related Documents* (Toronto: CCH Canadian Limited, 1987).

Richards, John, and Larry Pratt, *Prairie Capitalism* (Toronto: McClelland and Stewart, 1979).

Ritchie, Gordon, "The Negotiating Process," in John Crispo (ed.), *Free Trade: The Real Story* (Toronto: Gage Educational Publishing Company, 1988), pp. 16-22.

Robertson, Gordon, "The United States and Problems of Canadian Federalism," in Charles F. Doran and John H. Sigler (eds.), *Canada and the United States: Enduring Friendship, Persistent Stress* (Washington, D.C.: Council on Foreign Relations, 1985), pp. 9-45.

Rugman, Alan, "Living with Free Trade: How Multinationals Will Adjust to Trade Liberalism," *Business Quarterly* (Fall 1987), pp. 85-90.

Rugman, Alan, and Andrew Anderson, *Administered Protection in America* (London: Croom Helm, 1987).

Russell, Peter H., "The Constitutional Dimension," in John Crispo (ed.), *Free Trade: The Real Story* (Toronto: Gage Educational Publishing Company, 1988), pp. 161-169.

Safarian, A.E. "Government Control of Foreign Business Investment," in John Whalley (ed.), *Domestic Policies and the International Economic Environment* (Toronto: University of Toronto Press, 1985), pp. 7-56.

Schott, Jeffrey J., and M. Smith (eds.), *The Canada-U.S. Free Trade Agreement: The Global Impact* (Washington, D.C.: Institute for International Economics, 1988).

Simeon, Richard, "Federalism and Free Trade," in M.D. Henderson, (ed.), *The Future on the Table* (Toronto: Masterpress, 1987), pp. 79-100.

Simeon, Richard, "Inside the Macdonald Commission," *Studies in Political Economy* No. 22 (Spring 1987).

Skogstad, Grace, "Agriculture: Sharing the Responsibility," in M. Prince (ed.), *How Ottawa Spends, 1987-88* (Toronto: Methuen, 1988), pp. 268-293.

Skogstad, Grace, "The Application of Canadian and U.S. Trade Remedy Laws: Irreconcilable Expectations?" *Canadian Public Administration* Vol. 31, No. 4 (Winter 1988), pp. 539-565.

Skogstad, Grace, *The Politics of Agricultural Policy Making in Canada*, (Toronto: University of Toronto Press, 1987).

Smith, Murray, and Frank Stone, *Assessing the Canada-U.S. Free Trade Agreement* (Ottawa: Institute for Research on Public Policy, 1987).

Smith, M.R. "A Sociological Appraisal of the Free Trade Agreement," *Canadian Public Policy* Vol. XV (March 1989), pp. 57-71.

Smith, Michael, "Sectoral Free Trade with Canada," *International Perspectives* May/June 1984, pp. 17-19.

Stairs, Denis, "Non-Economic Implications of a Comprehensive Canada-U.S. Free

Trade Agreement," in A. Maslove and S. Winer (eds.), *Knocking on the Back Door* (Halifax: Institute for Research on Public Policy, 1987), pp. 79-101.

Stone, Frank, *Canada, The GATT and the International Trade System* (Montreal: Institute for Research on Public Policy, 1984).

Strategico Inc., *Making It Work: Year Two of the Canada-U.S. Free Trade Agreement* (Ottawa: Strategico, Inc., 1991).

Tarullo, Daniel, "Beyond Normalcy in the Regulation of International Trade," *Harvard Law Review* Vol. 100 (1987), pp. 547-626.

Thibault, L., "Address on the Release of the Joint CMA-NAM Statement on Bilateral Trade Negotiations," Washington, D.C., April 13, 1987.

Thomas, W.A. *The Big Bang* (Oxford: Phillip Allan, 1986).

Tobin, G. *U.S.-Canada Free Trade Negotiations: Getting Approval to Proceed* (Cambridge, Mass.: Kennedy School of Government).

Tomlin, Brian, "The Stages of Prenegotiation: The Decision to Negotiate North American Free Trade," *International Journal* Vol. 44 (Spring 1989), 254-279.

Toner, Glen, "Stardust: The Tory Energy Program," in Michael J. Prince (ed.), *How Ottawa Spends 1986-87* (Toronto: Methuen, 1986), pp. 119-148.

Trebilcock, Michael, *The Political Economy of Economic Adjustment* (Toronto: University of Toronto Press, 1986).

Trebilock, Michael, Marsha Chandler, and Robert Howese, *Trade and Transition: A Comparative Analysis of Adjustment Policies* (London: Routledge, 1990).

Tupper, Alan, and G. Bruce Doern, "Alberta Budgeting in the Lougheed Era," in Alan Maslove (ed.), *Budgeting in the Provinces* (Toronto: Institute of Public Administration of Canada, 1989), pp. 121-141.

Varley, Thorald K., "Issues in Canadian Agricultural Trade Policy," in John Whalley (ed.), *Canada-United States Free Trade* (Toronto: University of Toronto Press, 1985), pp. 267-294.

Von Riekhoff, Harald, "The Structure of Foreign Policy Decision Making and Management," in B. Tomlin and M. Molot (eds.), *Canada Among Nations 1986: Talking Trade* (Toronto: James Lorimer and Company, 1986), pp. 14-30.

Von Riekhoff, Harald, "The Third Option in Canadian Foreign Policy," in B. Tomlin (ed.), *Canada's Foreign Policy: Analysis and Trends* (Toronto: Methuen, 1978), pp. 87-110.

Warnock, John W., *Free Trade and the New Right Agenda* (Vancouver: New Star Books, 1988).

Watson, W., "Canada-U.S. Free Trade: Why Now?" *Canadian Public Policy* Vol. 13, No. 3 (1987), pp. 337-349.

Whalley, John, "Now That the Deal Is Over: Trade Policy Options in the 1990s," *Canadian Public Policy* Vol. XVI, No. 2 (June 1990), pp. 121-136.

White, Bob, "From Defeat to Renewal," *This Magazine* Vol. 23, No. 1 (May/June 1989), pp. 23-26.

Whitehorn, Alan, "The NDP Election Campaign: Dashed Hopes," in A. Frizzell, J. Pammett and A. Westell (eds.), *The Canadian General Election of 1988* (Ottawa: Carleton University Press, 1989), pp. 43-54.

Wilkinson, Bruce, " Canada-United States Free Trade: Setting the Dimensions," in A. Maslove and S. Winer (eds.), *Knocking on the Back Door* (Halifax: Institute For Research on Public Policy, 1987), pp. 7-32.

Williams, Glen, "Canadian Sovereignty and the Free Trade Debate," in A. Maslove and S. Winer (eds.), *Knocking on the Back Door* (Halifax: Institute for Research on Public Policy, 1987), pp. 101-121.

Winham, Gilbert, "Bureaucratic Politics and Canadian Trade Negotiation," *International Journal*, Vol. 34 (Winter 1978-79), pp. 64-89.

Winham, Gilbert R., *Trading with Canada: The Canada-U.S. Free Trade Agreement*. A Twentieth Century Fund Paper (New York: Priority Press Publications, 1988).

Wonnacott, Ronald, "Canada and the U.S.-Mexico Free Trade Negotiations," *Commentary* , No. 21 (Toronto: C.D. Howe Institute, September 1990).

Wonnacott, Paul, *U.S. and Canadian Auto Policies in a Changing World Environment* (Toronto: C.D. Howe Institute, 1987).

Wright, Gerald, "Bureaucratic Politics and Canada's Foreign Economic Policy," in D. Stairs and G. Winham (eds.), *Selected Problems in Formulating Foreign Economic Policy* (Toronto: University of Toronto Press, 1985), pp. 9-58.

Young, Robert, "Canada-United States Free Trade: Economic Realities and Political Choices," Department of Economics Papers, University of Western Ontario, 1987.

Young, Robert, "Political Scientists, Economists and The Canada-US Free Trade Agreement," *Canadian Public Policy* Vol. XV (March 1989), pp. 49-56.

Young, Robert, "Why Did We Ignore the Middle Ground?" *Globe and Mail*, November 24, 1988, p. A7.

INDEX